Corporate Information Factory

Second Edition

W. H. Inmon

Claudia Imhoff

Ryan Sousa

Wiley Computer Publishing

John Wiley & Sons, Inc.

NEW YORK · CHICHESTER · WEINHEIM · BRISBANE · SINGAPORE · TORONTO

Publisher: Robert Ipsen
Editor: Robert M. Elliott
Assistant Editor: Emilie Herman
Managing Editor: John Atkins
Text Design & Composition: D&G Limited, LLC

Library of Congress Cataloging-in-Publication Data:

ISBN: 0-471-39961-2

Printed in the United States of America.

10 9 8 7 6 5 4 3 2 1

CONTENTS

Some books describe *how* to do things; they're called how-to books or manuals. Other books describe *why* we do things; these include books on philosophy and psychology. Still other books describe *where* things are—for example, atlases. But other books simply describe *what* we should be doing. This is one of those kinds of books.

The usefulness of a *what* book is that it provides direction. There is an old saying among sailors, "When there is no destination, any route will do." This book describes a very substantial destination port for sailors navigating the sea of information. After the corporation understands that there is a port and where it is, it is easy to set the information organization's rudder on the right heading to the appropriate destination, even through stormy seas.

The Origins of Data Warehousing

The world of computers and information technology has grown quickly, sequentially, and in a surprisingly uniform manner. In the era of punch-card and paper-tape systems, we used the computer as a calculating beast of burden, running such systems as accounts payable and accounts receivable.

With the advent of disk storage, cheaper memory, more sophisticated operating systems, and direct end-user interface devices, a whole new style of computing became a reality—online processing. With online processing, the computer changed from a beast of burden to an Arabian stallion. Reservation systems, automated bank tellers, and a host of other new systems became a reality.

Next came the revolution of the end user. Personal computers, spreadsheet applications, and fourth-generation language (4GL) technology opened up computing to an audience that previously had been denied. As the costs of computing plummeted, a Pandora's box was opened; computing now fell outside the classical domain of the information systems organization. Anyone with a budget could begin to take charge of their information destiny.

End users were very happy having such complete control, but this autonomy was a mirage. It soon became apparent that even with unlimited computing power, turning over control to end users created new issues, such as a lack of integration and proper economies of scale. For all of the appeal of autonomous control of processing at the end-user level, the case for centralization was equally valid and appealing.

Simultaneously, people discovered that data derived from processing operational transactions was difficult to access and insufficient for effective decision-making. Historical and integrated data was needed at both a summary and detailed level.

Thus, the data warehouse was born. Shortly thereafter, data volumes and end-user demands and diversity exceeded the pace at which the data warehouse could be tailored and tuned. For all its strength in integrating and managing a common view of corporate data, the data warehouse was not keeping up with the business demands for information. In response, different departments found that a customized subset of the data warehouse—something called a data mart—provided them the needed autonomy to drive the interpretation and use of corporate information.

Companies also discovered that a need for operational data integration existed. The data warehouse—for all it provided—did nothing for the people who needed operational integration. Into the fray came an architectural entity known as the *operational data store*. Finally, with the advent of the Internet and low-cost commodity hardware, the data warehouse, data marts, and operational data stores are scaling to answer increasingly complex questions, using more data, in support of a broader user community. It is no longer uncommon for a user to access hundreds of gigabytes of data, integrated from a dozen sources, just to answer a single question. Additionally, it is becoming increasingly common for the user community to consist of groups outside the company such as business partners or even customers—the ultimate benefactors.

Seeing the Forest for the Trees

Those of us who have been witnesses to some or all of these developments have suffered from two disadvantages in understanding what has transpired. First, we have been too close to the technology and the maturation of the technology to truly grasp its significance. We have marveled at the details without understanding the larger form and function. As such, we, like the six blind men describing the elephant, simply have a limited understanding of that with which we are the most intimate.

The second disadvantage is that of watching this development unfold sequentially day by day. The speed of day-by-day developments has blinded us to the larger picture that is unfolding, and we can only guess what tomorrow will bring.

The objective of this book is to overcome these obstacles by taking a step back and examining the evolution of business information systems across the globe. In the pages that follow, we strive to make sense of this evolution and describe a proven architecture that embraces it. Additionally, we describe the key components of this architecture and how they fit together. This architecture defines the corporate information factory (CIF).

We are particularly interested in what happens when a company attempts to build its systems in a fashion other than what has been suggested by the architecture. The brief history of the corporate information factory has shown that:

- You certainly can build an architecture other than the one described here
- When you do build a variation of the described architecture, there is a price to pay, in terms of:
  - Infrastructure cost
  - Efficient performance
  - Lack of integration
  - Seamlessness of technology
  - End-user satisfaction
  - Responsiveness to change

The corporate information factory is hardly the only way to build systems. But, it is the best way to meet the long-term goals of the information processing company.

In many cases, it will be tempting to violate the architecture; however, systems designers must remember there is a price to pay.

Our purpose in writing this book is to alert readers of a proven way to organize information systems; that when this way is not chosen, they must be willing—and able—to live with the consequences. These consequences can range from the waste of large amounts of development resources to the failure to deliver an effective information resource.

A number of factors led to the evolution of the corporate information factory including:

- Evolving business demands
- Shrinking costs of technology

- Increasing sophistication and breath of the user community
- Growth of hardware, software, and network capabilities

In addition, corporate communities began to move toward very distinct styles of computing. For example, operational, legacy processing set the stage for the data warehouse, which then led to the data mart. Spreadsheets and their many derivatives opened up the desktop to many more analytical capabilities. These various benchmarks led to the evolution of a new mode of corporate computing, which we describe in the chapters to follow.

Why We Wrote the Second Edition

The first edition of this book addressed the larger picture of corporate information systems as they were evolving in the world of information technology. At the time of the first edition, the description found in the book was accurate, to the best of our knowledge. But almost immediately after the book came out, we began to notice that other important components of modern information systems architecture were left out.

The exploration warehouse, alternative storage, and decision-support systems (DSS) applications appeared as major components of information architecture. Many large, vertical multinational corporations began to build multiple data warehouses, and coping with more than one corporate information factory became an issue. In the ever-changing world of technology, the Internet, customer relationship management (CRM), and enterprise resource planning (ERP) applications made an appearance in a big way. Because of all of these changes to the landscape of information systems, it became necessary to publish a second edition of the book, that is at the center of the corporate information factory.

The second edition is predicated on the architecture described in the centerfold of the January 2000, issue of *Data Management Review* magazine and shown in Figure 2.1. That description is the current thinking on what constitutes the corporate information factory. If you want a copy of the centerfold, you can contact *DMR* magazine, or you can download it (for free) from the Web site—www.billinmon.com. Many thanks to Ron Powell and Jean Schauer for their sponsorship in the creation of the centerfold and to IBI Corp. for their financial sponsorship in the creation of the centerfold.

Who Should Read This Book

The corporate information factory can be used in many useful ways by a wide variety of people, such as:

- **The IT manager.** The information technology (IT) manager can use the corporate information factory to predict what the next steps ought to be for systems development and architecture. Instead of spending money unproductively on projects that do not move the organization to the paradigm suggested by the corporate information factory, the manager who understands its implications can use the corporate information factory as a benchmark that tells what the future directions ought to be.

- **The developer.** After a project has begun, the developer can determine whether the project is organized in concert with the corporate information factory. If a design is contrary to the corporate information factory, the designer can make corrections before the design is cast in concrete.

- **The investor.** An easy way to determine how fruitful a technology investment will be is to gauge it against the world described by the corporate information factory. If the architecture of the investment is not aligned with the corporate information factory, then the investor can be alerted to problems with marketplace acceptance.

- **The end user.** At the heart of the corporate information factory is the success of end users who can use it to form their expectations and to assess whether their expectations are out of line. When implemented properly, the corporate information factory makes life very easy and productive for the end user.

How This Book Is Organized

This book is organized to suit the needs of a wide range of readers from novice to experienced in implementing the corporate information factory. If you are new to the corporate information factory, you will want to read this book from beginning to end. Each chapter builds on the previous chapter, providing you a broad understanding of what the corporate information factory is and how to build and manage it. If you are a veteran, you will probably want to read the first two chapters and dive right into whatever chapter suits your needs. In particular, you will probably be interested in Chapter 9, 10, 13, and 17. These chapters introduce some new components and concepts.

The book is divided into four parts. The first part—Chapters 1 and 2—are introductory. They provide you with an overview of the corporate information factory and the drivers in its evolution. The second part—Chapters 3 through 14—reviews the corporate information factory architecture. These chapters review each component of the architecture, how they are combined to deliver decision support capabilities and the implications of varying the architecture. The third part—Chapters 15 through 17— discusses how to build and manage the corporate information factory. The fourth part—Appendix A—provides guidelines for assessing and examining your corporation information factory.

The Evolution of This Book

This book is part of a larger series of books by Bill Inmon. In the first of the books, *Data Architecture: The Information Paradigm*, the notion of a larger architecture was first introduced, and the data warehouse was first mentioned. The next book in the series, *Building the Data Warehouse*, fully explored the data warehouse. The book is now enjoying sales in the second edition. Next came *Using the Data Warehouse*, in which the techniques and considerations of the effective use of the data warehouse were discussed, and the operational data store was introduced. At about the same time, *Building the Operational Data Store* appeared (in the second edition as published in 1999). This book probed the design and technological implications of the ODS. The next book in the series was *Managing the Data Warehouse*. In this book, the assumption is that the data warehouse has already been built and that the issues of cost of data warehousing and complexity of data warehousing are starting to crop up. As people began building, using, and managing their data warehouse environment, they also began asking for more specifics on how to optimize and exploit it. In response, *Data Warehouse Performance* and *Exploration Warehousing* were published.

The second edition of *Corporate Information Factory* in many ways is a capstone book. It brings together the many aspects of the architected information systems environment—the *information ecosystem*—and presents those aspects in an integrated manner.

DEDICATION

It wasn't enough that we asked our families to endure the many days we were away from home working and the long hours we spent at home writing the first edition; we asked if we could do it again. Well, you know what, they said yes. Not only did they say yes, they encouraged our efforts knowing we had much more to say about the corporate information factory. They remain the wind beneath our wings and the joy in our hearts.

ACKNOWLEDGMENTS

We wish to express thanks to the many colleagues, clients, and friends who have enriched our understanding of the corporate information factory over the years. It is through their collective efforts that ideas become reality, and it is from this reality that we learn and write. We would like to extend a special thanks to:

John Zachman, Zachman International

John Bair, Independent consultant

Lowell Fryman, C/Net

Roger Geiwitz, Independent consultant

Sue Osterfelt, Bank of America

JD Welch, IBM

Dennis McCann, ambeo

Ken Richardson, ambeo

Dale Brocklehurst, ambeo

Joyce Norris-Montanari, Braun Consulting

Jon Geiger, Braun Consulting

Steve Miller, Braun Consulting

Jim Kalustian, Braun Consulting

Mike Evanisko, Braun Consulting

Dave Imhoff, Intelligent Solutions

Rob Geller, Quest

Robert Grim, Independent consultant

Pete Simcox, Genesis

Mark Mays, Arrowhead Consulting

warehouseMCI team

John Ladley, Knowledge Interspace

Doug Laney, Meta Group

Bob Lokken, Knosys

Brian Burnett, AppsCo

Steve Murchie, Microsoft

Bill Baker, Microsoft

Allen Perry, Coglin Mill

Ron Powell, DM Review

Bill Prentice, SAS

Mike Wipperfeld, Informix

Lisa Loftis, Braun Consulting

Steve Hill, Informix

Keven Gould, Sybase

Stephen Gardner, NCR

Ron Swift, NCR

Marc Demarest, Independent consultant

Jeanne Friedman, Independent consultant

Greg Battas, Tandem Computers

Ralph Kimball, Kimball and Associates

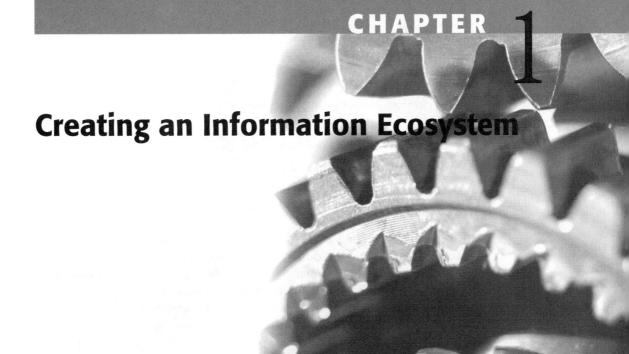

CHAPTER 1

Creating an Information Ecosystem

B usiness is quickly reshaping itself to compete in a global economy governed by the needs of the customer (e.g., individual, business, etc.). The economies gained over the past three decades by automating manual business processes are no longer enough to gain a competitive advantage in today's marketplace. To compete, businesses need to be able to build a new set of capabilities that deliver *best-of-breed* business intelligence and business management solutions that can leverage this legacy environment.

But wait! Perhaps the genesis is already upon us. Your IT department is being bombarded with a growing number of targeted information architectures, technologies, methodologies, terms, and acronyms. Each of these advances promises to deliver competitiveness in one easy step, such as:

- Data warehousing
- Data repository
- Operational data store
- Data marts
- Data mining
- Internet and intranet
- Multidimensional and relational databases

- Exploration processing
- Star schema, snowflake, and relational database design techniques
- High-performance computing (Massively Parallel Processing & Symmetrical Multiprocessing)
- Data acquisition and data delivery
- Online Analytical Processing (OLAP)
- Data warehouse administration
- Metadata management

Each of these advances in modern information technology has promise, but trying to make sense of these point solutions while still getting the job done in a short time frame can be confusing and intimidating. This is largely due to the fact that no model exists that combines these elements of the information primordial pool into a balanced ecosystem that aligns with the evolving needs of the business. An information ecosystem is needed to orchestrate the use of various information technologies and constructs and to foster communication and the cooperative exchange of work, data processing, and knowledge as part of a symbiotic relationship.

Information Ecosystem Briefly Defined

An information ecosystem is a system with different components, each serving a community directly while working in concert with other components to produce a cohesive, balanced information environment. Like nature's ecosystem, an information ecosystem must be adaptable, changing as the inhabitants and participants within its aegis change. Over time, the balance between different components and their relationship to each other changes as well, as the environment changes. Sometimes the effect will appear on seemingly unrelated parts (sometimes disastrously!). Adaptability, change, and balance are the hallmarks of the components of a healthy information ecosystem.

As an example of an information ecosystem, consider a data warehouse working with a data mart to deliver business intelligence capabilities or an operational data store working to deliver business management capabilities. This environment is found in many marketing groups. At first, there is the need for better business intelligence in the form of market segmentation, customer analysis and contact analysis. Then, at some point, marketing wants to take action on the "intelligence" gained. Although the data warehouse and data mart are well suited to support business intelligence, they lack the content and form to drive business-management activities associated with contacting the customer. What is needed is an operational data store to provide near *real-time* access to integrated, current customer information.

As will be discussed in this book, different business needs require that a different set of ecosystem components work in tandem. Ultimately, the information ecosystem will be business-driven, as capabilities delivered (business intelligence and business management) are aligned with the needs of the business (marketing, customer service, product management, etc.). The result is an information environment that allows companies to capitalize on a constantly changing business landscape characterized by customer relationships and customized product delivery.

Shifting Business Landscape

Three fundamental business pressures are fueling the evolution of the information ecosystem: growing consumer demand, increased competition and complexity, and continued demands for improvements in operating efficiencies as seen in Figure 1.1.

Consumer Demand

The first fundamental pressure is growing consumer demand. Consumers expect companies to understand and respect their needs and desires. Because the customer drives the business relationship, business people must hear what the customer has to say and respond by delivering relevant, competitive, and

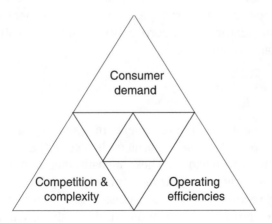

Figure 1.1   The business drivers in today's world.

timely products and services. Companies can no longer expect to sell just a few general products and services to the masses but must tailor many products and services (i.e., mass customize) to the individual consumer. This proposition is called customer relationship management and/or mass customization. The fundamental challenge to many businesses is that their systems, people, and processes are designed around the product. Furthermore, most of these companies have begun to extend these environments with a series of unarchitected point solutions to address their immediate needs for customer management. A healthy information ecosystem will be embodied by an architecture that:

- Leverages this legacy environment
- Delivers new information capabilities that allow companies to thrive in an environment characterized by customer relationships and customized product delivery
- Supports a migration strategy that is evolutionary in nature and delivers incremental value to the business

Competition and Complexity

The second business pressure is that of increased competition and complexity. The ability to refocus and enhance a product mix in response to evolving competition is a critical success factor for any business. The key is to be able to anticipate the needs of the marketplace before your competitors do. Many companies find this difficult or impossible to do, given today's mishmash of technologies, architectures, and systems.

Why is this important? Corporations today are facing more and more deregulation, mergers, and acquisitions, which blur the relationships with their customers. Additionally, globalization of the marketplace and the consumer is opening up businesses to new avenues for expansion and, subsequently, competition. Therefore, it is mandatory for a corporation to quickly restructure itself without losing the ability to compete.

Operating Efficiencies

The third pressure is that of continued improvements in operating efficiencies. The ability to rapidly measure and predict returns on investment is something that corporations find difficult to perform. These measurements indicate the health of the corporation, and the ability to determine them rapidly allows a corporation to change its direction with a minimal loss in time or money. Other examples of improved efficiency include the ability to determine the most efficient channels for contacting customers, to target the best product mix to the best customers, and to identify new product opportunities before the competition does.

Responding to Change

In response to these very real business challenges, companies must be able to support more than just classical business operations (legacy systems that automate manual business processes such as billing, order processing, etc.). Competitive corporations need capabilities to support business intelligence and business management. In this way, they can respond to the dynamics of a quickly changing business landscape, as seen in Figure 1.2.

The information ecosystem provides a context for understanding the needs of your business and taking actions based on those needs while still running the day-to-day business. Additionally, the information ecosystem provides businesses with a comprehensive model for leveraging the growing number of distinctive information constructs and technologies that are required to deliver diverse and pressing business capabilities to support these needs. Figure 1.3 illustrates the central role of the corporate information factory in supporting

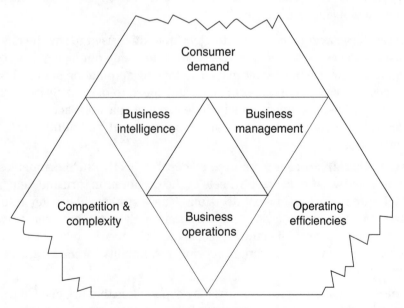

Figure 1.2 The need for business capabilities to compete in a quickly changing business landscape.

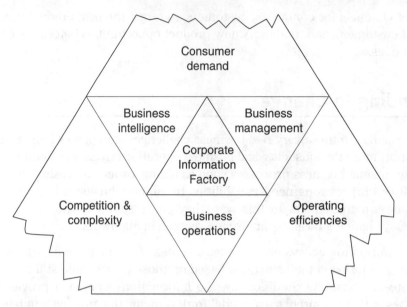

Figure 1.3 The corporate information factory is central to a business and its needed capabilities.

the evolving areas of business proficiency: business operations, business intelligence, and business management.

Business operations are supported by capabilities used to run the day-to-day business. These systems have traditionally made up our legacy environment and have provided a competitive advantage by automating manual business processes to gain economies of scale and speed-to-market. Systems that exemplify business operations include accounts payable, accounts receivable, billing, order processing, compensation, and fulfillment/distribution.

Business intelligence is supported by capabilities that help companies understand what makes the wheels of the corporation turn and help predict the future impact on current decisions. These systems play a key role in the strategic planning process of the corporation. Systems that exemplify business intelligence include medical research, market analysis, customer contact analysis, segmentation, scoring, profitability forecasting, and inventory forecasting.

Business management is supported by capabilities that are needed to effectively manage actions resulting from the business intelligence gained. If business intelligence helps companies understand *what* makes the wheels of the corporation turn, business management helps *direct* the wheels as the business landscape changes. These systems are characterized by robust real-time reporting and tight integration with business intelligence and business operations systems. Systems that exemplify business management include fulfillment management, channel management, inventory management, resource management, and customer information management. These systems generally augment and/or evolve from business operations.

In summary, the information ecosystem provides companies with a complete information solution by complementing traditional business operations with capabilities to deliver business intelligence and business management. In addition, the information ecosystem provides a comprehensive model for making sense and exploiting the growing and diverse information constructs and technologies that are transforming our information paradigm. The physical embodiment of the information ecosystem is the corporate information factory.

Corporate Information Factory

First introduced by W. H. Inmon in the early 1980s, the corporate information factory (CIF) is the physical embodiment of the notion of an information ecosystem. The CIF is at the same time generic in its structure (to the point that it is easily recognizable across different corporations) and is unique to each company as it is shaped by business, culture, politics, economics, and technology. The corporate information factory is made up of the following components:

External world. It is the businesses and people who generate the transactions that fuel the CIF and who produce and benefit from the information produced.

Applications. Applications are the family of systems from which the corporate information factory gathers raw detail data. There are two types of applications: integrated and unintegrated. Integrated applications represent those systems that have been developed according to the guidelines set forth by the corporate information factory. Unintegrated applications are traditionally represented by those core operational systems that have been used to drive day-to-day business activities like order processing, accounts payable, etc. Over time, these unintegrated applications will become integrated as their role transcends beyond traditional business operations to support business management.

Operational data store. It is a subject-oriented, integrated, current-valued, volatile collection of detailed data used to support the up-to-the-second collective tactical decision-making process for the enterprise.

Integration and transformation layer. This is where the data gathered by the applications is refined into a corporate structure.

Data warehouse. It is a subject-oriented, integrated, time-variant (temporal), and nonvolatile collection of summary and detailed data used to support the strategic decision-making process for the enterprise.

Data mart(s). It is a customized subset of data from the data warehouse tailored to support the specified analytical requirements of a given business unit.

Internet/intranet. These are the lines of communication along with data flows and different components that interact with each other.

Metadata. It is the information catalog infrastructure to the CIF. This catalog provides the necessary details to promote data legibility, use, and administration.

Exploration and data mining warehouse. This is where the explorer can go to do analysis and does not have to think about the impact on the resources.

Alternative storage. It is where "overflow" and "bulk" storage can be used, extending the warehouse to infinity. The costs of warehousing are greatly mitigated by moving masses of data to alternative storage.

Decision support systems. These systems are a whole body of applications whose center of existence is the data warehouse. These applications are large and distinctive enough that they form their own component of the corporate information factory.

The different components of the CIF create a foundation for information delivery and decision-making activities that can occur anywhere in the CIF. Many of these activities are in the form of decision-support systems (DSS) that provide the end user with easy-to-use, intuitively simple tools to distill information from data.

People and Processes

The people and processes that work within the structure of the information ecosystem represent the roles, workflow, methods, and tools used in constructing, managing, and using the corporate information factory. Activities that occur here include:

- Customer communications (newsletters, surveys, etc.)
- Request management (logging, prioritizing, and managing)
- Delivery of information (data mart enhancements, corrections)
- Configuration management (versioning of metadata, database design, extraction, programs, transformation programs, etc.)

- Data quality management (performing audits, integrity checks, alerts)
- Systems administration (determining capacity, conducting performance tuning, etc.)

The people and processes of the CIF are perhaps one of the more difficult issues for a corporation because, in planning this function, the corporation must take into consideration its culture, politics, economics, geography, change, and other concerns. For example, companies that have traditionally managed their information systems from a central organization may have challenges supporting data marts that are owned and managed by line-of-business information systems personnel. Alternatively, organizations that have managed information systems at the line-of-business level may have problems giving up the control necessary to form an information systems group to build and manage a corporate data warehouse.

The nature of these variables makes this function a much more customized one for the enterprise and, therefore, harder to implement. There is less uniformity across different corporations in how this aspect of the information ecosystem is implemented than perhaps anywhere else.

Summary

The information ecosystem is a model that supports all of a corporation's information processing. The physical embodiment of the information ecosystem is the corporate information factory. The different components of the corporate information factory have been introduced and defined briefly to give the information systems (IS) architect an idea of how they fit into the overall architecture. Each component must be in balance with the others to avoid a malfunctioning environment, much like nature's ecosystem.

The forces of business coupled with the advances in technology and the symbiotic relationship of technology to the business process cause the world of technology to constantly evolve. In years past when technology was slow and expensive, there was no opportunity for the sophistication that is possible today. But with the decreasing cost of technology, the increasing speed, and new capacities, there are possibilities for the exploitation of technology in the business equation as never before. At the heart of these possibilities is an evolving architecture that has become increasingly apparent, the *corporate information factory*. It has evolved from many systems and technologies now found in the world of corporate information processing.

In the next chapter, we will take a closer look at the corporate information factory, its use, and its evolution.

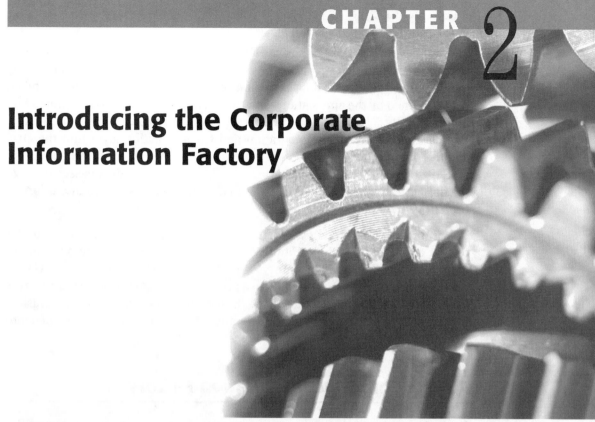

CHAPTER 2

Introducing the Corporate Information Factory

A s discussed in Chapter 1, the corporate information factory (CIF) is an architecture—an infrastructure—for the information ecosystem, consisting of the following components:

- External world
- Applications
- Integration and transformation layer (I & T layer)
- Operational data store (ODS)
- Data warehouse
- Data mart(s)
- Internet and intranet
- Metadata repository
- Exploration and data mining data warehouse
- Alternative storage
- Decision Support Systems (DSS)

The simplest way to understand the CIF is in terms of the data that flows in and the information that flows out of the corporate information factory. Data enters the CIF as detailed, raw data collected by the applications. The raw detailed data is refined by the applications and then passes into a layer of programs that fundamentally integrates and transforms functional data into corporate data. The data passes from the integration and transformation layer into the ODS and the data warehouse. The data warehouse can be fed data from either the ODS or the integration and transformation layer. After the data passes through the data warehouse, data is accessed, analyzed, and transformed into information for various purposes.

The architecture and the flow of data that have been described are very similar to that of an actual factory. Raw and assembly goods enter a factory and are immediately collected by inventory and store management processors. Assembly lines then turn the raw goods into a product. Throughout the manufacturing process, different products are made. Some products are completely finished products; others represent a partial assembly that can be further assembled into many finished products.

Data in the Corporate Information Factory

Key components of the corporate information factory are shown in Figure 2.1. Let's begin with external data. External data enters the corporate information factory from the world outside of the corporation. It is not generated internally, nor is it captured and manipulated at a detailed level internally. Instead, external data represents events and objects outside of the corporation in which the corporation is interested. External data can be used throughout the corporate information factory—at the data mart, data warehouse, ODS, and/or application levels.

Reference data is data that is stored in a shorthand fashion that serves to tie together multiple and diverse users. It is used to speed and standardize processing across many different departments and is typically found at the application level. As reference data passes into the architectural components of the corporate information factory, it takes on a slightly different form, that of historical reference data. The difference between reference data and historical reference data is that reference data represents information that is current and accurate as of the moment of usage. Historical reference data is the historical record of that same reference data, except that it is collected and managed over time. As current reference data changes over time, those changes are collected along with the effective change date in order to create historical reference data. Historical reference data is of great use to the data mart and the data warehouse analyst in that it provides details that help describe data in the data warehouse and data marts.

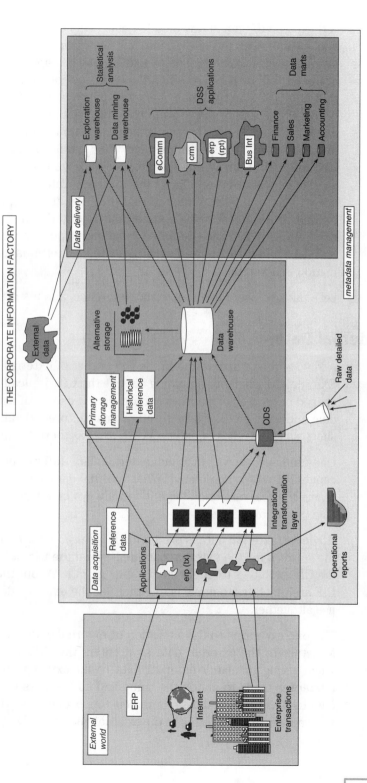

Figure 2.1 The basic structure of the corporate information factory.

A third type of data is raw detailed data. This data is generally captured at the application level and loaded into the data warehouse and ODS via the I & T layer. However, some raw detailed data may be captured and managed directly in the ODS. This happens when the end-user community needs access to data that is not currently being managed by an application. In effect, the ODS becomes the authoritative source of this data and source system to the data warehouse. Some may try to manage this data directly in the data warehouse; however, this is not recommended. This would be like trying to bulldoze a large mound of dirt with a Ferrari. The data warehouse is designed for strategic decision support and lacks the form and function to effectively store and access transaction-level data in real time. Additionally, if the data warehouse became the *authoritative* source of this raw detail data, it is likely that it would quickly become pressured to support operational activities for which it was designed to augment. This is likely to be a terminal condition for the information ecosystem.

Let's take a closer look at external, reference, and historical data.

External Data

A key source of data found in the CIF is that of external data (see Figure 2.2). External data is data originating outside the CIF. Typically, external data is purchased or created by another corporation. It can be of almost any type and volume and can be either structured or unstructured, detailed or summarized. In short, as many types of external data exist as there are internal data.

One fundamental way in which external data differs from internal data is in its capability to be manipulated. When internal data needs to be changed, the programs that capture and shape it can always be altered. In that sense internal data is very malleable.

However, external data is pretty much *what you see is what you get*. Because the sources for the external data lie beyond the CIF, it is beyond the scope of the CIF architect to effect such a change in it. About the only real choice the CIF architect has to make is to either use the external data as is or to reject its use altogether.

The one exception to the alteration of external data is that of modifying a key structure to the external data as it enters the CIF. This happens quite often when trying to match external data to an existing customer. Generally, an attempt is made to match the name and address associated with the external data to a name and address in the customer database. If a match is made, the external key is replaced with the internal customer ID, and the external data is stored.

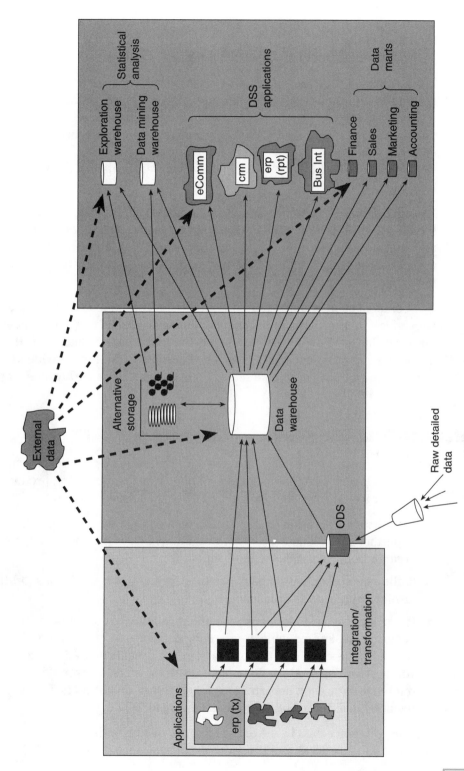

Figure 2.2 External data is an integral part of the CIF environment.

In many cases, the external data will have a key structure that is quite different from the key structure used within the CIF. The external data needs to have its keys modified in order to be used meaningfully within the confines of the CIF.

The modification of the external key can be a simple or a difficult thing to accomplish. In some cases, the external key goes through a simple algorithm to convert it to the CIF key. In other cases, reference tables are used in conjunction with an algorithm. And in the worst case, the conversion is made manually, on a record-by-record basis. The manual approach to key resolution is not viable for massive amounts of data and/or where the manual conversion must be done repeatedly.

External data can be made available to any and all components of the CIF. If the external data is to be used in multiple data marts, it is a good policy to place the external data first in the data warehouse and then transport it individually to the data mart. By placing it first inside the data warehouse, reconcilability of the data is maintained.

The component in which external data is most prominent is the exploration warehouse. In this environment, analysts endeavor to gain new insight about the business that cannot be distilled using internal transactional data. It is not uncommon for these analysts to use the exploration warehouse to identify new market opportunities or to characterize customers so that the business can better respond to their needs.

Reference Data

Some of the most important data any corporation has is reference data. One very popular type of reference data describes valid products and product hierarchies for a company. Reference data fulfills the following roles:

- It allows a corporation to standardize on a commonly used name for important and frequently used information, such as product, state, country, organization, customer segment, and so forth.

- It allows commonly used names to be stored and accessed in a short-hand fashion, which saves disk space.

- It provides the basis for consistent interpretation of corporate data across departments. For example, if reference data existed, we could be reasonably assured that three separate departments analyzing sales volumes for dog food would come up with the same answer. Without this reference data, each department is likely to roll-up products differently, resulting in different sales volumes for dog food.

In short, reference data is one of the most important kinds of data that a corporation has. Figure 2.3 shows the presence of reference data in the CIF.

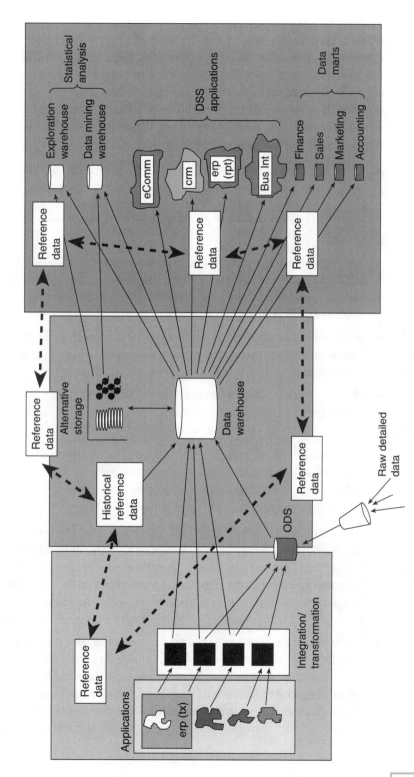

Figure 2.3 Reference data makes up an important part of the CIF. Note that reference data contained in the data warehouse is historical.

Reference data is notoriously unstructured and is, at best, a hit-and-miss proposition. This is in contrast to other forms of data, which are core to running the day-to-day businesses that require and receive great care in systematization. For example, data is needed to invoice a customer correctly. Programs and procedures are written for the update, creation, and deletion of nonreference data. But because reference data is so commonly used, programs and procedures needed for the systematization of reference data are not formalized. Several reasons exist for the lack of formalization:

- The volume of data that constitutes reference data is usually very small compared to other types of data found in the corporation. Reference data consumes only a fraction of a fraction of the space required for regular data. Because of its small size, reference data is often treated as an afterthought.

- Reference data is usually very slow to change. Unlike other types of data, which are constantly being created, deleted, and updated, reference data is very stable. Because of this stability, no one pays attention to the need for systematization of reference data.

- Reference data is often dictated by external sources. There are standard abbreviations for states, countries, and so on. There is no need for systematization of these types of reference data.

- Reference data often belongs to the entire corporation, not just a single department. Because reference data is a common corporate property, no one steps forward to *own* and manage the reference data.

For these reasons and more, reference data is often not managed with the same discipline that other data in the CIF is managed, yet it still requires as careful attention as any other type of data. For at least three reasons, reference data plays a very important role in the world of the CIF:

1. Reference data can simplify I & T layer processing. If reference data in an application is the same as reference data in the data warehouse, then the task of I & T is made much simpler. However, if the I & T layer must completely discard one approach to reference data and create an entirely brand new reference system (which can be done in extreme cases), then the logic of I & T processing becomes very complex and cumbersome.

2. Reference data is one of the primary ways that the different components of the CIF communicate and maintain continuity with each other. Whether you have implemented a data mart, exploration warehouse, ODS, or any other component of the CIF, well-formed and maintained reference data will help to ensure that such measures as revenue by *product group* and households by *customer segment* are consistent across the CIF.

3. Reference data ages over time. In the data warehouse, as reference data ages, a historical record must be kept so that the historical data that resides in the warehouse can have references made to the data that are accurate as of the moment of the creation of the data warehouse record. In other words, because historical data is stored in the data warehouse, an historical reference needs to be kept. If the DSS analyst is going back to 1995 to look at data in the data warehouse, he needs to know what the reference data was for 1995. It will not do to have the DSS analyst looking at 1995 data from the data warehouse where the DSS is trying to use reference tables from 1997. The need for historical referencability is one of the important and peculiar needs of the data warehouse within the context of the CIF.

Historical Data

Even when data has been entered onto a computer system and it is ten seconds old, it is historical in the sense that it represents events now passed. Of course, the event that has passed is much more current than events that may have occurred a week ago or a month ago. Nevertheless, all data entered into a computer system can be thought of as historical data (with the exception of forecast data). The issue is not whether data is historical, but just how historical the data is. The implications of historical data are many, including:

Volume of data. The longer the history is kept, the greater the amount of data.

Business usefulness. The more current a unit of information, the greater the likelihood that it is relevant to current business.

Aggregation of data. The more current the data, the greater the chance that the data will be used at the detailed level. The older the data, the greater the chance that the data will be used at the summary level.

Many other implications of history exist. These are merely the obvious ones. Figure 2.4 shows that the components of the CIF contain different phases of corporate information history.

The applications environment contains very current information, up to 30 days. Of course, the actual time parameters vary across industries and businesses. Some industries may have more than 30 days worth of information; other industries may have less.

The ODS environment has a time period identical to that of the applications. The difference between the ODS and the applications is that the ODS contains integrated corporate data, and the applications do not.

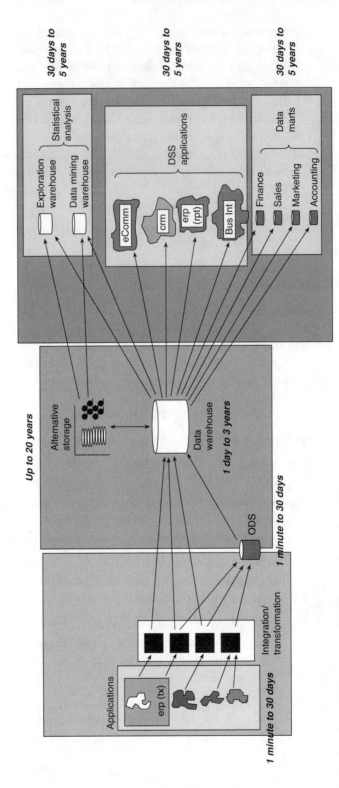

Figure 2.4 The amount of historical data that is found in the CIF differs from component to component.

The data warehouse contains data that is at least 24 hours old, up to 5 to 10 years worth of history. The actual length of time found here is highly dependent on the industry that is being represented by the data warehouse.

The data mart contains the widest variety of data found in the environment. The amount of history contained by a data mart is dependent on:

- The industry the corporation is in
- The company within the industry
- The department within the company

By far the greatest volume of historical data is found in alternative storage. This is where much of the historical transaction data from the data warehouse is archived. Historical data is even found in the exploration and data mining warehouses. Fortunately, use of historical data in these environments is project oriented so history is fairly pruned and temporary. As a result, the exploration and data mining warehouses don't require the large amounts of long-term storage or I & T layer processing to maintain history as do many of the other components of the CIF (data warehouses, alternative storage, data mart, etc.)

Of special interest is where different components overlap. The first overlap is between the applications arena and the ODS. As previously stated, the ODS contains corporate collective data, and the applications contain application-detailed (generally unintegrated or at best functionally integrated) data. There is overlap in the time frame, but no overlap in terms of the integration of the data.

The second overlap is between the data warehouse and the applications. An application may have data stored within it, up to 30 days or so. The data warehouse may have that same data stored. There are a few differences, however. The data warehouse contains data that has been passed through the I & T layer. As such, the data warehouse data may or may not be physically the same as the applications data. The second difference is that the data warehouse historical data is stored along with other historical data of the same ilk. The applications data is stored in an isolated manner.

The Decision-Support System to Operational Feedback Loop

The standard flow of data throughout the CIF is from left to right, that is, from the consumer to the application, from the application to the I & T layer, from the I & T layer to the ODS or the data warehouse, from the ODS to the data warehouse, and from the data warehouse to the data marts. The flow occurs as described in a regular and normal manner. However, another feedback loop is at work, as depicted in Figure 2.5.

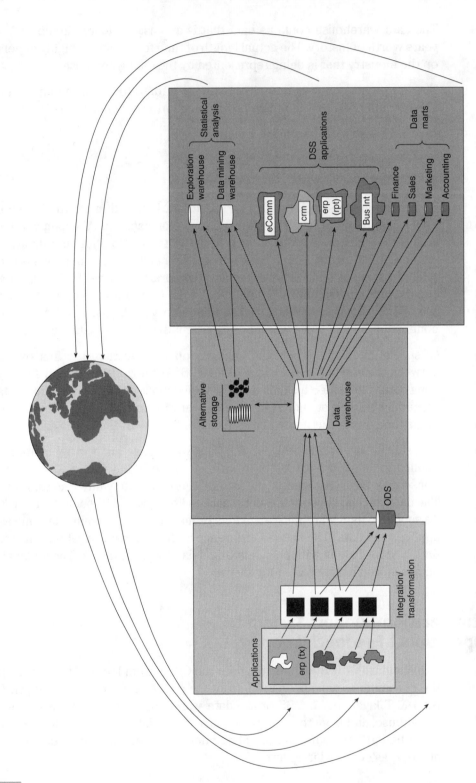

Figure 2.5 The feedback loop from the DSS/informational environment to the applications environment.

Figure 2.5 shows that as data is used in the DSS (or information) environment, decisions are made. As an example, a manager in the insurance environment decides to raise rates on a certain kind of policy based on the information derived from the DSS environment. Perhaps a bank manager decides to raise rates on car loans. Another example is a retailer deciding to produce more of product ABC based on strong demand detected in the DSS environment. In short, the DSS environment provides a basis for making business decisions.

However, after those business decisions have been made, they have an impact, which is first detected by the applications environment. For example, when the retailer decides to produce more of product ABC, sales are boosted across the United States, and the increase in sales is measured by the applications systems having a direct interaction with the consumer. Likewise, when an insurance executive decides to lower rates for a policy type, more policies are sold, which in turn is measured by the applications environment. In any case, the CIF operates as part of a holistic system. This ecosystem is regulated by the feedback loop shown in Figure 2.5. It is through this feedback loop that the different components of the CIF find a balance and constantly adjust to each other.

The Flow of Data

A predictable or normal-flow of data moves throughout the corporate information factory. The normal flow is indicated by the solid lines with arrows that connect the different components of the corporate information factory in Figure 2.6.

In general the flow of data is from left to right. Usually, 95 to 99 percent of the data in the corporate information factory flows as indicated in Figure 2.6. For example, a large amount of data flows from the legacy environment into the integration and transformation component, or a large amount of data flows from the data warehouse to the data mart environment.

Another very important flow of data in the corporate information factory is not along the lines of the normal flow. Data **back flow** exists in the corporate information factory. In Figure 2.6, dotted lines indicate the back flow of data, which is normally not voluminous. In fact, the back flow of data is minuscule to the point that in some cases it is so small as to be unmeasurable. But, just because it is small in volume does not mean that it is not important to the business.

Examples of back flow include:

- The marketing department deciding to raise the rates for certain lines of insurance. The raise itself is a small amount of data that has a large consequence for the business.

- The exploration statistician notes that there appears to be a growing market for goods for consumers from the ages of 15 to 20. The decision is

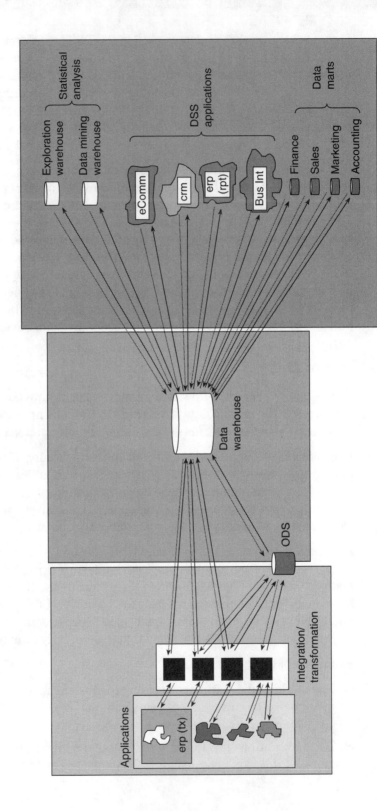

Figure 2.6 The normal flow of data in the CIF is shown with solid lines. Back flow is represented by dotted lines.

made to price certain articles aimed at that marketplace even lower in order to attract market share.

- The enterprise resource planning (ERP) application produces information that indicates certain assembly lines are more productive than other lines. The decision is made to monitor the less productive lines carefully.

- The banking sales and product department notes that loans for homes are slowing down. The decision is made to reduce home loan rates by $1/2$ percent. The movement of data characterizing the lowering of rates is minuscule, but the business impact is enormous.

- Analysis is done in the data warehouse to select certain customers for preferred treatment. The list of preferred customers is sent to the ODS so that when those customers call in, they are immediately identified. The list of preferred customers is a short list that flows from the data warehouse to the ODS, but the business impact is large.

The one place where there is a regular back and forth flow of data in the corporate information factory is from the data warehouse to and from alternative storage. The flow here depends on query activity and the nature of the queries. The more detail history required to supports a query, the more likely the alternative storage will need to be accessed.

Variations to the Corporate Information Factory

One of the common and valid variations to the corporate information factory occurs when there is no ODS. The ODS is peculiar in that many organizations find that they do not need an ODS to run their business. An ODS can be:

- Expensive and difficult to build
- Expensive to operate
- Challenging to maintain

There must be a very sound business case for an ODS. Of course, when an ODS is needed, there is nothing to replace it. Typically, large, decentralized businesses that require product integration and businesses that do a lot of high-performance transaction processing are candidates for an ODS.

Because many corporations operate successfully without an ODS, one valid variation of the classical corporate information factory architecture, as shown in Figure 2.1, is an architecture without an ODS. When there is no ODS, the flow of all data is from the I & T layer directly to the data warehouse.

Other variations exist to the corporate information factory. One variation is having no data in alternative storage. Data warehouses do not start out as large databases. Even the largest data warehouse started small at some point in time and as long as a data warehouse is of a small to modest size, no need exists for alternative storage. But as a data warehouse grows large, the need for alternative storage becomes apparent.

Another variation on the classic architecture of a corporate information factory is a no exploration warehouse. Only when a corporation starts to do a significant amount of exploration does the exploration warehouse become a standard part of the CIF. In addition, the exploration warehouse services both data mining and exploration needs until the company starts to do a really large amount of exploration.

Yet another variation to the CIF is multiple exploration warehouses. Exploration warehouses are typically project driven, with definite beginnings and endings. Having two or three exploration warehouses up and running is normal for a large corporation.

These are only a few variations of the corporate information factory. The classic CIF is never fully built. Instead, parts of the CIF are constantly being constructed, modified, reconstructed, and so forth.

Operational Processing and DSS Processing

Where operational processing ends and DSS/informational processing begins is clearly delineated. Figure 2.7 depicts that demarcation. The figure shows that the applications environment is entirely in the world of operational processing. Data marts and the data warehouse are completely in the world of DSS/informational processing. The ODS sits squarely in the middle of the world of informational and operational processing. With an ODS, both operational and informational processing are in the same structure. This is one of the reasons why the ODS is the most complex part of the information ecosystem. Every other part of the infrastructure can be optimized to suit one style of processing or the other, but the ODS must be optimal (or at least acceptable!) for more than one style of processing. This factor greatly complicates the life of the builder and the manager of the ODS environment.

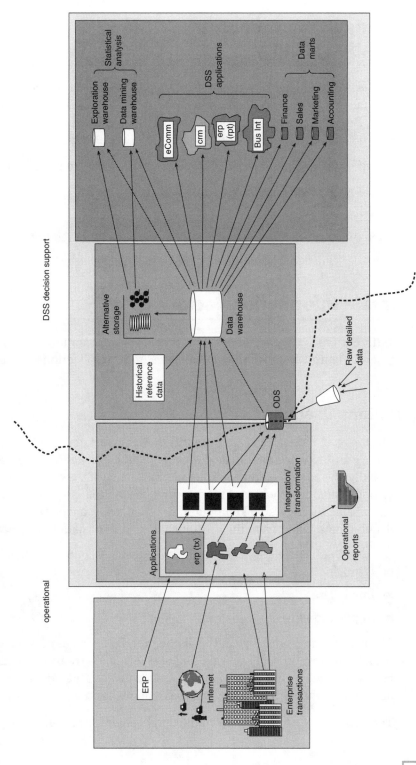

Figure 2.7 A very clearcut dividing line exists between operational processing and DSS informational processing in the CIF.

Reporting in the Corporate Information Factory

Analysis of data and reporting can be done throughout the corporate information factory. There is no point at which data is locked up and becomes unavailable. But at each different component of the architecture, the reporting that is done is quite different. The different kinds of reporting are:

- Operational reporting—ODS reporting for collective integrated data
- Data warehouse reporting
- Data mart departmental reporting

Each of the types of reporting has its own unique characteristics.

Corporate Information Factory Users

Different types of users access the corporate information factory at different places. Figure 2.8 shows the typical users of the applications of the CIF.

Applications Users

The users of applications are primarily clerical workers or sales/service professionals and, in some cases, the customers of the corporation themselves. Occasionally, the customers have direct interaction with the corporate applications through facilities such as ATMs, kiosks, Web sites, and even through direct entry using their personal computer. In other cases, a clerk is required to enter detailed data taken from the customer. The kind of data that is handled at the application level is:

- Detailed
- Immediate
- Application-oriented

The user of the technology at the application level can expect immediate feedback in the form of transactions. High-performance transactions are the order here with one second response time as the norm. A high degree of availability across the network supports that type of application.

The nature of the applications in the corporate information factory includes:

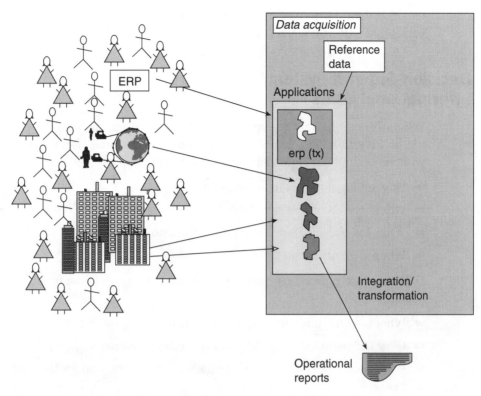

Figure 2.8 The users of the applications expect detailed information that is accurate up to the second and down to the last penny.

- Interacting with the end user
- Collecting data
- Editing data
- Auditing data
- Allowing adjustments and corrections to be made
- Verifying transactions
- Keeping an accurate record of events
- Keeping online data accurate with a high degree of integrity
- Allowing small units of data to be accessed very rapidly
- Securing data and transactions, etc.

The interaction with the end users at the application level is through reports and terminals (usually preprogrammed and tightly controlled). The applications have their own store of data, which is augmented by reference data and external data. As a rule, the applications environment is unintegrated, where each application serves a particular need and a unique set of requirements.

Decision-Support System/ Informational Users

DSS/information users are very different from operational users. They are solving or investigating longer-term questions. Operational users are concerned with very immediate and very direct decisions, such as:

- How much money is in an account right now?
- Where is a shipment right now?
- What coverage is there for a policy right now?
- When is an order due?

DSS users are concerned with decisions that are much broader and long term, such as:

- What type of customer is the most profitable for our business?
- Over the years, how has transaction activity changed?
- Where has sales activity been highest in the springtime for the past three years?
- When we change prices, how much elasticity is there in the marketplace?

The DSS analysts have a whole different perspective on the use and value of information. They look at:

- Information that has been integrated across the corporation
- Broad vistas of information, instead of small divisions of information
- Information over a lengthy period of time, rather than very current data

Some very different characteristics are found between the use of information by DSS analysts and operational analysts, such as:

- The DSS analyst often looks at very large amounts of information as opposed to the operational analyst who looks at tiny bits of information.
- The DSS analyst does not need to have information returned immediately. Five minutes, 30 minutes, or even overnight in many cases is just fine for the DSS analyst, as opposed to the operational analyst who needs two to three seconds response time.

In addition, the very way that information is sought is different between the DSS analyst and the operational analyst. The DSS analyst looks for information

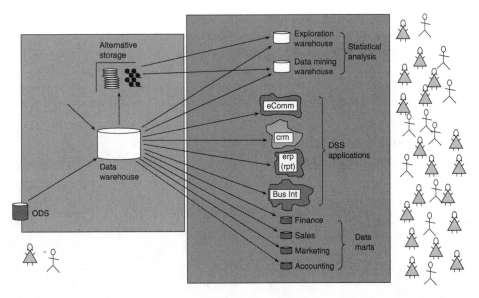

Figure 2.9   DSS/informational users' needs are very broad as compared to operational users.

heuristically, where the next step of analysis is profoundly shaped by the results obtained in the previous step of analysis and where the exact shape or even the extent of an analysis cannot be determined at the outset.

The operational analyst operates in a mode where queries and questions are preformatted into a very structured format. The same activity is repeated over and over again, where all that changes is the data that is being operated on in the world of the operational user.

Figure 2.9 shows that many different kinds of DSS analysts exist. At the departmental level are data mart analysts who do decision support through the eyes of their department. Typical departments are finance, marketing, and sales. The customized summary/subset data that is found in the data mart is exactly what the data mart analyst needs to satisfy their unique needs of data mart DSS processing.

Exploratory analysis is done at the data warehouse. The integrated, detailed data and the robust amount of history found at the data warehouse are ideal for this type of analysis.

Collective integrated operational analysis can be done at the ODS. Admittedly, much true operational processing is done at the ODS. But, occasionally, a need presents itself to do operational DSS processing. When that need arises, the ODS is the ideal place for processing.

Different types of DSS users are scattered throughout the corporate information factory. The four most common types of DSS users are tourists, farmers, explorers, and miners.

Tourists

Tourists are those DSS analysts who specialize in being able to find a breadth of information, as illustrated in Figure 2.10.

In the figure, a tourist is seen as an individual who uses the Internet/intranet and knows where to find many things. A tourist understands the structure of the corporate information factory and knows where in the structure of things to find almost anything. However, the tourist is an unpredictable analyst, sort of a walking directory of information.

- Look over lots of data on a random basis
- Often never look over the same data twice
- Do not know what the requirements are
- Make heavy use of metadata
- Occasionally stumble on something that proves to be useful
- Use Internet regularly
- Monitor beds of data regularly
- Look over huge amounts of data on a regular basis
- Sporadically use data
- Heavily rely on tools for profiling
- Sometimes find arenas for further exploration

Figure 2.10   One type of DSS user is the tourist.

Farmers

A farmer is a very different kind of DSS analyst than a tourist, as shown in Figure 2.11.

- Regularly access data
- Know what they are looking for
- Access small amounts of data
- Have predictable access to data
- Conduct predictable processing after data is accessed
- Know requirements before searching for data starts
- Access data marts regularly
- Rarely access current level of detail
- Find small flakes of gold regularly
- Make use of tools of presentation

Figure 2.11   A second type of DSS user is a farmer.

A farmer is someone who is predictable and knows what he or she wants before setting out to do a query. A farmer looks at small amounts of data because the farmer knows where to find the data. The farmer is somewhat repetitive in the search for information and seldom wanders far from data that is familiar. The farmer operates as comfortably on detailed data as on summary data. In many regards, because summary data is compact and concise, summary data suits the needs of the farmer quite nicely. In addition, the data the farmer is looking for is almost always here.

Explorers

A third type of DSS analyst is someone known as an explorer, as shown in Figure 2.12.

Explorers have some traits similar to both the tourist and the farmer but are unique unto themselves. The explorer is someone who operates with a great degree of unpredictability and irregularity and looks over massive amounts of detail. The explorer seldom has much use for summary data and frequently makes requests that seem to be farfetched. Often times the explorer finds nothing, but occasionally the explorer finds huge nuggets in the most unexpected places. The explorer becomes an expert in one arena within the corporate information factory.

- Have irregular access to data
- Do not know what they are looking for
- Look over masses of data
- Have an unpredictable pattern of access
- Sometimes find huge nuggets
- Often find nothing
- Have totally unknown requirements
- Access current level detail regularly
- Look at relationships of data rather than occurrences of data
- Make use of tools of discovery and statistical analysis and exploration

Figure 2.12   A third type of DSS user is an explorer.

- Are statisticians
- Work from hypotheses, assertions
- Prove or disprove validity of hypotheses
- Work on large amounts of data
- Work on "flat" data, where the same occurrence of data appears repeatedly
- Work closely with explorers in a symbiotic manner
- Often discover new hypotheses and assertions
- Submit very, very large queries
- Use tools that are peculiar to the trade

Figure 2.13   A fourth type of DSS user is the data miner.

Miners

The fourth type of DSS analyst is an individual known as a miner, shown in Figure 2.13.

Miners have a great affinity to the explorer, and they form a symbiotic relationship. The explorer creates assertions and hypotheses. The miner proves the validity or invalidity of those assertions and hypotheses. The miner is a statistician. The miner begins by testing one or more hypotheses against a large body of data, usually transaction data. The miner then comes up with a statistically based opinion about the strength of the hypotheses. In many cases, examining one hypothesis leads the miner to discover other hypotheses. These newly discovered hypotheses are then reported back to the explorer for further examination.

Queries submitted by the miner are the largest found in the corporate information factory. A miner will typically look over many, many rows of data to discern the truth about a hypothesis.

Types of DSS Usage in the Corporate Information Factory Environment

Understanding that there are different kinds of DSS users with very different goals and techniques is the first step in resolving many seemingly complex and contradictory facets of the corporate information factory. Without this perspective, many DSS components of the corporate information factory do not make sense.

As an example of the perspective provided, consider that different parts of the DSS environment within the corporate information factory attract and apply to different types of users, as seen in Figure 2.14.

The figure shows that data mart and departmental analysis apply to farmers and the occasional tourist. Explorers are attracted to the data warehouse and, once in a while, the tourist finds his or her way into it. The ODS environment is almost exclusively the domain of farmers. It is worthwhile noting that the farmers found at the ODS environment are quite different from the farmers found at the data mart. The data mart farmers are those people who are analyzing a problem for possible future action. The farmers at the ODS environment are those who are interested in an immediate short-term tactical corporate decision, not some long-term consideration. For example, is this customer a good credit risk?

One of the reasons why the separation of the DSS analyst community into different audiences is important is that it explains why there are such diverse design and development practices throughout the DSS portion of the corporate information factory.

Centralized or Distributed?

One of the most important issues of the corporate information factory is whether the underlying component of the architecture is (under normal circumstances)

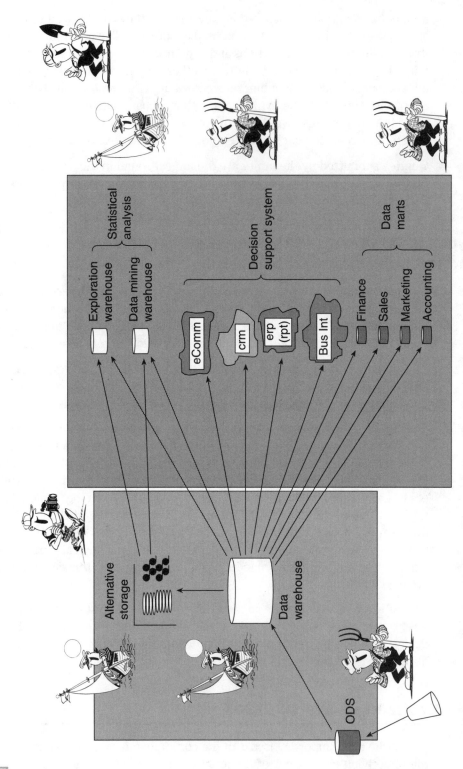

Figure 2.14 Different types of users fit in different places in the DSS/informational component of the CIF.

centralized or distributed. This issue is salient to the implementation, functionality, and economics of the ultimate deployment of the corporate information factory. It needs to be considered on a case-by-case basis for each of the different components of the architecture. Figure 2.15 addresses centralization of the applications environment.

Because the applications environment can be either centralized or distributed, the decision is usually made by history: The hardware, and the past development and deployment of the application environment determine whether the applications are centralized or distributed.

As a rule, large transaction-processing applications are centralized, and smaller offline, sequential applications tend to be distributed. The ODS is almost always centralized, as seen in Figure 2.16.

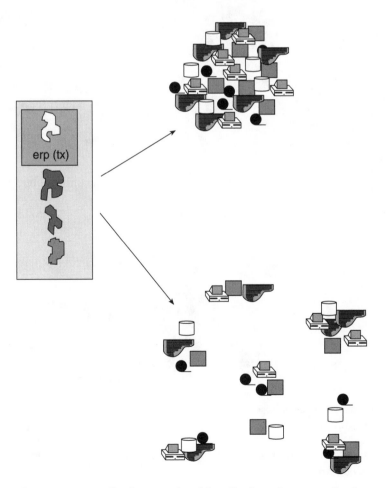

Figure 2.15 Applications can be either distributed or centralized.

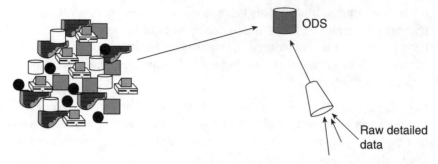

Figure 2.16 The ODS is almost always centralized.

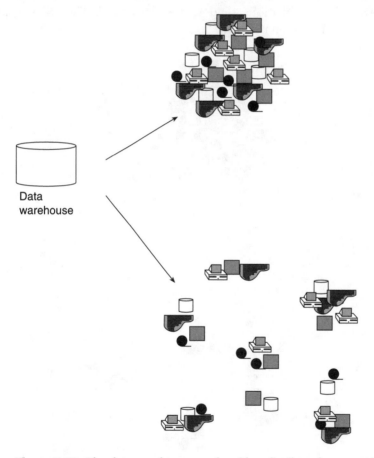

Figure 2.17 The data warehouse can be either distributed or centralized.

While in theory it may be possible to have a distributed ODS environment, in practice all ODS are centralized.

The data warehouse is another matter. The data warehouse can be either centralized or distributed, as shown in Figure 2.17.

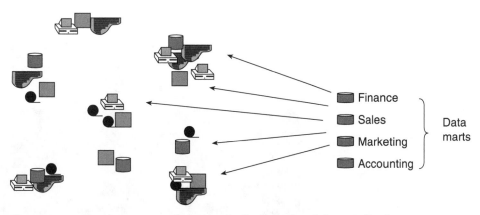

Figure 2.18   The data mart environment is distributed and decentralized.

In general, most data warehouses are centralized. But some very notable and successful examples of distributed data warehouses do exist. These have a slightly different form from a classic centralized data warehouse. When a data warehouse is distributed, the detail of the system is left at the local level. The architectural construct known as the distributed data warehouse is really centered around a lightly summarized level of data. This level of data becomes the corporate data warehouse. In this regard, the distributed data warehouse is a mutant form of a more standard data warehouse.

Data marts are exclusively distributed, as seen in Figure 2.18.

The very nature of data marts is that they be unique to the environment that owns or controls them. As such, data marts are distributed around the different departments of the corporation in many shapes and forms.

Data Modeling and the Corporate Information Factory

The CIF has many disparate parts. Although an overall dynamic pervades the corporate information factory, each component has its own parts and internal interactions. Therefore, some mechanism or technique must allow the CIF to function in a coordinated, cohesive manner. The structure of the different components is unified by means of a data model. The data model allows each of the architectural components of the corporate information factory to have as much autonomy as it needs, and at the same time allows the CIF to operate in a unified manner. The data model is the data blueprint and intellectually unifies the data warehouse. Figure 2.19 shows the role of the data model to the corporate information factory.

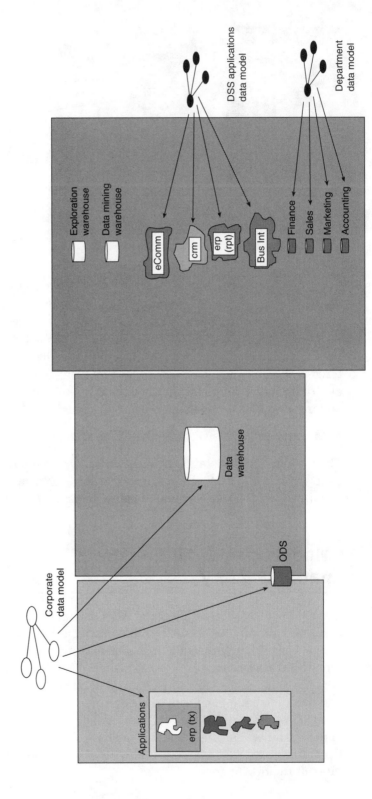

Figure 2.19 Different data models form the structural basis of the different components found in the CIF.

The data model exists for the entire organization and plays a different role for each of the architectural components in the corporate information factory:

- Serves as a guide for the ongoing reconstruction of the applications environment. Because the applications environment is notoriously unintegrated, the data model serves as a basis for bringing together the different applications as they are rewritten or as they are modified.

- Is the basis for subject-area design for both the ODS and the data warehouse. The general structuring of the ODS and the data warehouse begins with an orientation towards the major subject areas of the corporation. The orientation corresponds precisely to the entities that are defined in the high-level logical data model.

But the corporate data model does not directly serve the needs of the departments that have data marts. The departmental data marts are patterned after the requirements that apply and are unique to a particular department. As such, their data models are shaped by their processing requirements. Finance will have its data model; accounting will have its data model; sales will have its data model; and so forth. The data models at the department level typically represent data that is denormalized and summarized. With that said, the departmental data model is a subset of or is profoundly shaped by the corporate data model.

Because all departments are a smaller part of a larger whole, an indirect relationship exists between the corporate data model and the individual departmental data models that shapes the design of the various data marts.

Migrating to the Corporate Information Factory

The size and complexity of the corporate information factory dictates that the fully matured architecture be achieved a step at a time. For all practical purposes, it is impossible to build the corporate information factory all at once. In fact, many good reasons support a step-at-a-time approach to the building of the corporate information factory, such as:

Cost. The cost of the infrastructure and the cost of development are simply prohibitive to consider the building of the corporate information factory at anything but a step at a time.

Complexity. The corporate information factory entails the usage of many different kinds of technologies. An organization can absorb only so many technologies at once.

Nature of the environment. The DSS portion of the environment is built iteratively in any case. It does not make sense to build the DSS environment in a "big bang" approach.

Value. Above all else, the implementation of the corporate information factory must demonstrate incremental value to the business. This is best accomplished through a series of three- to six-month iterations.

For these reasons the corporate information factory emerges from the information systems of a corporation over time, not all at once.

There is a typical progression to the building of the corporate information factory, as shown in Figures 2.20 and 2.21.

Figure 2.20 shows that on Day 1 is a chaotic information systems environment without shape and form. On Day 2, the data warehouse begins to emerge and grows incrementally. With each advance in the data warehouse, data is removed and integrated from the amorphous information systems environment. On Day 3, data marts start to grow from the data warehouse. Indirectly, more processing and data is removed from the information systems environment as different departments begin to rely on their data marts for DSS processing.

Figure 2.21 shows that on Day 4, integrated applications start to appear. The integrated applications require an integration and transformation layer in order to feed the data to the data warehouse. The emergence of the integrated applications comes slowly and, in many cases, imperceptibly.

On Day 5, the ODS is built. The ODS is fed from the integration and transformation layer and, in turn, feeds its data to the data warehouse. By this time, the systems that were once known as the production systems environment have almost disappeared. The legacy environment is only a very small vestige of its former invincible self.

The path to the building of the corporate information factory is seldom linear. Different parts of the corporate information factory are being built simultaneously and independently. For example, a finance data mart is being built while an exploration warehouse is being built, or an ODS is being built while the alternative storage component is being constructed.

Plenty of other migration paths are possible other than the one that has been shown. However, the path that has been suggested is one that is:

- Proven
- Least risky
- Fastest
- Avoids many pitfalls
- Least expensive with the greatest probability of success

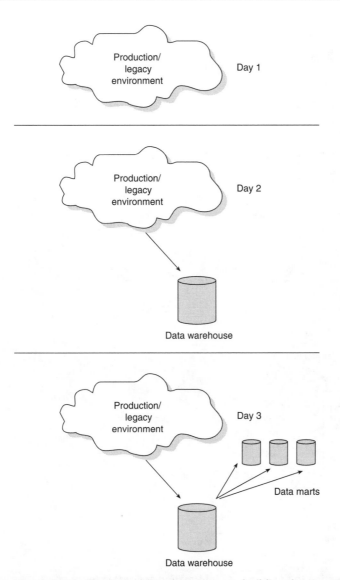

Figure 2.20 The typical first three steps to building the corporate information factory from the production/legacy environment.

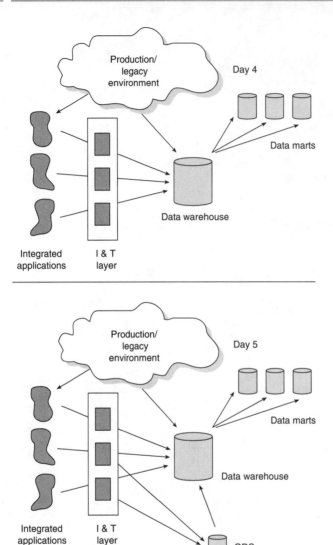

Figure 2.21 Migrating to the corporate information factory—latter phases.

Structuring Data in the Corporate Information Factory

One of the interesting features of the corporate information factory is the diversity of data structures that are found there. Figure 2.22 shows the different types of data structures found in the CIF.

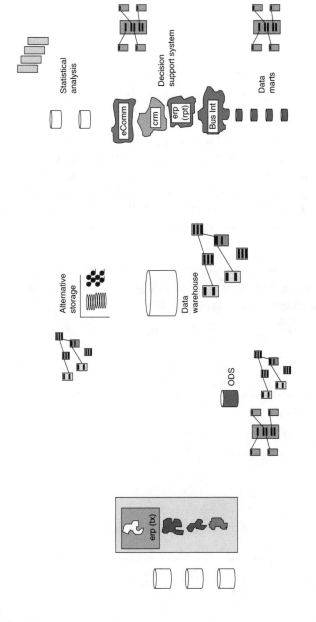

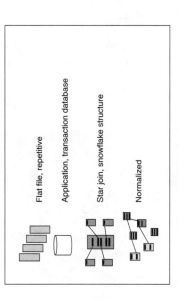

Flat file, repetitive

Application, transaction database

Star join, snowflake structure

Normalized

Figure 2.22 Different design approaches can be seen throughout the CIF.

45

Common types of structural design techniques are:

- Flat, repetitive files, where the same structure type is represented again and again for different occurrences of data

- Application transaction databases, where online transactions are supported in the face of application requirements

- Star joins/snowflake structures, where data is denormalized and aggregated for the purpose of optimizing application requirements

- Normalized structures, where data is separated according to its natural data relationships

The world of applications naturally sees a lot of application database design. The world of the ODS contains a mixture of star joins and normalized structures. The data warehouse is essentially a normalized structure. The alternative storage environment is one in which data is best stored in a normalized manner. When doing statistical analysis, a flat file with a repetitive structure is optimal. And star join/snowflake structures are optimal for DSS applications and data marts.

The diversity of design approaches is one of the hallmarks of the corporate information factory. No one design approach is optimal everywhere, primarily because very different requirements exist across the CIF when it comes to:

- Volumes of data found in the component of the corporate information factory

- Performance

- The ability or inability to understand the requirements for processing prior to the creation of the structure

- The volume of data needed for transaction processing

- The nature of the workload being processed

- The age of the data

Summary

The corporate information factory has several recognizable and predictable components:

- External world

- Applications

- Integration and transformation layer (I & T layer)
- Operational data store (ODS)
- Data warehouse
- Data mart(s)
- Internet/intranet
- Metadata repository
- Exploration/data mining warehouses
- Alternative storage
- Decision Support Systems (DSS)

The applications play the role of gathering raw data from interactions with customers. The applications level is a transaction-processing environment.

The data warehouse is where historical integrated information for the corporation is stored. The data warehouse typically contains huge amounts of data and represents the essence of corporate data.

Data marts exist for the many different departments that need to do DSS processing. Data marts are a customized, summarized subset of the data that resides in the data warehouse.

The ODS environment is the place where collective, corporate online operational integration occurs. The ODS is the most challenging environment to build and operate because it sometimes needs to support both informational and operational processing.

The world of the CIF is split along the lines of operational processing and DSS/informational processing. Applications belong in the domain of operational processing. Data marts and data warehouses are clearly in the DSS/informational world. The ODS is split into information and operational aspects.

The community of DSS users can be divided into four classifications: tourists, explorers, farmers, and miners. Each of the different classifications of DSS users has its own distinct set of characteristics.

There is a standard progression from the classical production, legacy environment to the corporate information factory. First, the data warehouse is built; next the data marts are built; and finally, the ODS is built, if the ODS is built at all. Many corporations do not need an ODS.

So far, we have talked about the *heart* of the information ecosystem, the corporate information factory. In the next chapter, we will talk about the force that justifies and shapes the CIF, the *external world*.

CHAPTER 3

The External World Component

The alpha and the omega of the corporate information factory is the external world in which business is transacted. Without an external world of commerce, there would be no corporate information factory. So, let's take a quick look at this component that feeds the fuel and consumes the information produced by the CIF.

It is easy to focus on the technology and other aspects of the corporate information factory and forget the external world because the external world is full of normal occurrences and normal events. The very ordinary nature of the external world makes us take it for granted.

But the external world is where business and commerce takes place. In a sense, the corporate information factory is merely an adjunct to the external world. Stated differently, the external world would exist and commerce would go on without the corporate information factory. However, the corporate information factory could not exist without the external world's transaction producers and information consumers.

Transaction Producers

One of the focuses of the external world, at least insofar as the CIF is concerned, is to generate business transactions. A brief taxonomy of the important characteristics of the transactions that occur in the external world follows.

A Taxonomy of Transactions

- Is the transaction direct or indirect?
  - A direct transaction might be typified by the use of an ATM machine.
  - An indirect transaction might be typified by the use of a bank teller in order to cash a check.
- Is the transaction at the detailed or the summary level?
  - An example of a detailed transaction is the purchase of an airplane ticket.
  - An example of a summary level transaction is the raising of interest rates by the bank.
- Is the transaction immediate or delayed?
  - An immediate transaction might be the placing of a coin in a soda machine.
  - A delayed transaction might be the making of a loan application.
- Is the transaction large or small?
  - A large transaction might be the purchase of a company.
  - A small transaction might be the purchase of a pack of gum.
- Is the transaction wholesale or retail?
  - A wholesale transaction might be the acquisition of a ream of paper.
  - A retail transaction might be the purchase of a pencil.
- Is the transaction personal or machine assisted?
  - A personal transaction might be a massage.
  - A machine-assisted transaction might be the display of wares on the Internet.
- Is the transaction structured or unstructured?
  - A structured transaction might be an activity executed in SAP.

- An unstructured transaction might be the examination of food at a farmers market.

■ Is the transaction integrated or unintegrated?

- An integrated transaction might be the purchases made at Disney World.

- An unintegrated transaction might be an interaction with the telephone company in which you have two phones, and the telephone company does not realize it.

■ Is the transaction commercial or retail?

- A commercial transaction might be the exchange of goods between manufacturers.

- A retail transaction might be the placement of funds in an individual checking account.

In short, there are *many* facets to the way business is conducted. The corporate information factory must take into account *all* of these facets and more.

Consumers of Information

The relationship of the participants in the real world to the corporate information factory is both as a creator of transactions and as a consumer of the information. The transactions executed by the participants creates data that is captured by the corporate information factory. The information generated and manipulated is, in turn, used by the participants in the external world in order to make decisions.

Who Are the Participants?

The list of participants in the external world is a rather long one because, in one way or another, everyone is on the list. Furthermore, most people are on the list more than once because at different points in time the participants play different roles.

In general, the participants in the external world with whom the corporate information factory must interact include:

- Consumers
- Partners

- Vendors
- Clerical workers
- Managers
- Statisticians

The interface with the participant in the external world is germane to the success of the corporate information factory. To be successful, the interface needs to be:

- Fast
- Efficient
- Convenient
- Cheap
- Capable of performing a useful function
- Simple to use
- Scalable

The interface needs to accommodate *all* of these features. If any one feature is not present, then the interface may be deemed to be a failure despite the existence of attractive features.

Some "nice to have" features of the interface to the corporate information factory include:

- An elegant interface
- Flexibility to accomplish many functions in the same place
- Availability of the interface in many places and in many forms

The interface to the external participant can take many forms—some high tech and some decidedly low tech. Ultimately, the form will be driven by the capabilities of the application (e.g., ERP, CRM, etc.) and technology (e.g., Internet, Client/Server) used.

Summary

An important component of the corporate information factory is the external world, which consists of transaction producers and information consumers. These participants (individuals, employees, partners, and vendors) fuel the CIF. They provide the raw material (transactions), direct the machinery, and consume the final product (information). Without their participation, there would be no need for the corporate information factory to exist. Creating an effective interface is key to gaining and maintaining their participation.

Now that we have talked a bit about the external world and its value to the corporate information factory, let's focus our attention on the component of the CIF that collects transaction data from this external world, the *Applications* component.

CHAPTER 4

The Applications Component

Applications have been in existence since the earliest systems were built. The development lifecycle for applications, the day-to-day operation of the applications, and the ongoing maintenance that applications require is well documented. For all of these reasons, applications are well known to almost anyone looking at the corporate information factory.

Another way to think of the applications in the CIF is as a collection vehicle that is responsible for:

- Gathering detailed transaction data
- Interacting directly with the end user
- Auditing and adjusting data
- Editing data

Undoubtedly, the applications in the corporate information factory accomplish more than the simple functions listed here. For example, applications collect this data as part of their core function to automate key business processes within the corporation, such as accounts payable, accounts receivable, order processing, and transaction processing. The simple functions, however, are found in one form or another throughout the applications environment.

Dated Applications

The applications specified 20 years ago to address business problems are no longer sufficient alone to address the evolving needs of business. The corporation's business climate has changed dramatically over time, but the application infrastructure representing the business of the corporation has not. Therefore, applications are not without their own unique challenges.

If applications were easy to change once built, there would be no problem. However, applications are notoriously difficult to change once implemented, because over time, they have become a collective millstone around the neck of the corporation; each new application merely adds weight to it. In this sense, applications are anything but easy to understand and manage.

The inability to be responsive to change is not the only challenge associated with applications. Another challenge is their unintegrated nature.

Unintegrated Applications

The applications are unintegrated for a variety of reasons:

- The applications were built to suit the needs of one group, then another.
- Applications were required as part of a corporate merger.
- Applications were first built in-house and then augmented by third-party software packages.
- The cost justification process applied to the development of applications did not allow for anything other than an immediate and obvious set of requirements to be addressed, thereby limiting the extensibility and reuse of the application solution.

This lack of integration of applications surfaces in many ways, such as:

- Inconsistent key structures
- Inconsistent encoding structures
- Inconsistent structuring of data
- Inconsistent reference structures of data
- Inconsistent definitions of data
- Inconsistent code and calculations
- Inconsistent reporting

The lack of integration across the application environment severely affects its credibility and agility.

Applications' Response Times

One of the features of the applications environment is the level (i.e., the speed) of responsiveness to the users of its systems. Users of applications often expect very good response times for the transactions that are being executed by the application. Good response time usually means a response in one to two seconds from the moment the request was issued.

It is reasonable that the end user expects very good transaction response time because:

- Very little data is involved in any given transaction.
- Transactions are run on technology capable of giving good response time.
- The transactions operation details data that are directly and personally relevant to the consumer.

In some cases, the consumer interacts directly with the system, such as through an ATM or Web site. In other cases, the consumer interacts with the systems through an intermediary, such as an airline service professional or a bank teller.

Migrating from an Unintegrated State

Because the lack of integration of applications is a very large problem, it is normal for a company to migrate from an unintegrated state to an integrated state.

The problem with the migration suggested in Figure 4.1 is that it is expensive, painful, and slow to accomplish. Older unintegrated applications, for all of their faults, are very difficult to fundamentally alter largely because they run the day-to-day business. One of the burning issues of applications is how to achieve this migration. Five key steps are fairly common to the reengineering of these applications:

1. Define the strategic business vision. This includes a conceptual description of the evolving business landscape and the imperatives and competencies needed to compete on this landscape.

2. Define the information architecture needed to support the strategic business vision.

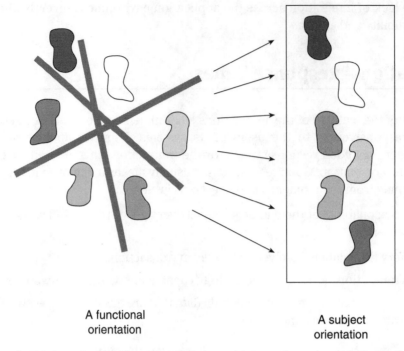

A functional
orientation

A subject
orientation

Figure 4.1 The transformation from an unintegrated state to an integrated state is slow, expensive, and still at a detailed level.

3. Assess the current application inventory and how this inventory aligns to the competencies defined in the strategic business vision.

4. Develop a migration plan that defines and prioritizes a series of three-to-four-month projects that will evolve, retire, or develop new applications to support the business vision. Each of these strategic projects should deliver immediate and incremental value to the business.

5. Execute the migration plan. To expedite the migration plan, companies may elect to purchase third-party application solutions from such companies as SAP, PeopleSoft, Baan, Epiphany, and Oracle.

External Data, Metadata, and Applications

Like other parts of the CIF, applications make use of external data and metadata. Figure 4.2 shows this relationship.

External data plays an important role in supporting detailed requests, at the most granular level. Applications also make use of metadata. Metadata keeps

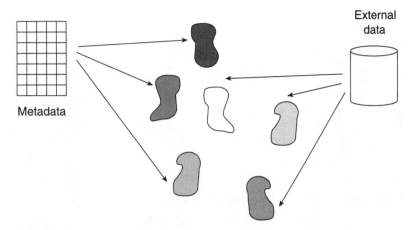

External
data

Metadata

Figure 4.2   External data and metadata are made available to the applications.

track of where data is coming from (end user, external companies, etc.), how data is being used (billing, order processing, etc.), and where data is going (data warehouse, ODS, etc.). Probably the most interesting distinction between metadata for the applications versus metadata for the data warehouse or ODS is that it is more important to the systems developer than it is to the end user. The systems developer is responsible for changes to the applications that interpret the data and, therefore, needs the knowledge of the applications provided by the metadata. Generally speaking, the end user deals with the applications environment through the system developer. In some respects, the systems developer becomes the "living" metadata repository for the end-user community. This is in contrast to the data warehouse where the end user is directly involved in evolving the DSS capabilities that interpret the data and, thus, needs access to the metadata that describes it.

Feeds into and out of the Applications Environment

The flow of data into and out of the applications is simple. Figure 4.3 shows that raw detailed data is collected directly from the end user. This data represents the input feed of data into the CIF. The raw detailed data then flows out of the applications to the I & T layer.

An important architectural component of the applications environment is the system of record. This resulting source of data is captured by the I & T layer,

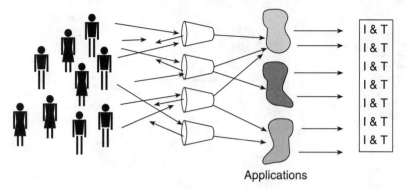

Applications

Figure 4.3 Applications feed data into the I & T layer.

transformed, and loaded into the data warehouse and/or ODS. The system of record represents the best source of data because it is:

- The most complete source
- The most accurate source
- The most current source
- The source that most closely conforms to the corporate data model

Note that the data in the system of record does not have to be perfect and may occasionally contain imperfections. Also, note that the system of record may contain multiple sources for the same unit of data. Under one set of conditions, the system of record may reside in Application A. Under a different set of conditions, the system of record may reside in Application B, and so forth.

A good way to understand the relationship of data and processing in applications versus data and processing in the ODS and the data warehouse is to think of data as operating on a continuum of time. This continuum is suggested by the measurement of seismic activity. In Figure 4.4, a stylus is constantly measuring seismic activity, and tape is constantly moving beneath the stylus. Applications represent the recording of the seismic activity and the first few seconds after the recording has been made. The ODS captures the next few seconds in the life of the data. Then the data warehouse captures the data historically.

The continuous spectrum of the flow of data and how the data resides in different components of the CIF explains the relationship of the data in the corporate information factory to the architectural component.

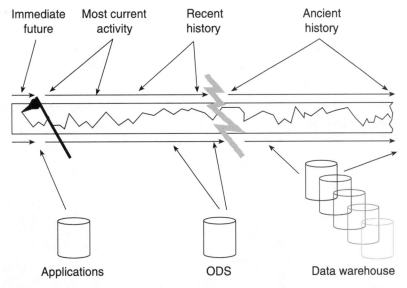

Figure 4.4 One way of viewing the relationship of the age of data within the corporate information factory: Imagine a seismograph tracking the shaking of the earth. The data that is gathered has a different age. Based on the age of the data, there is a different use of the data and different implications to the organization.

Summary

Applications are the component of the data warehouse where transaction data is gathered directly, either from the end user or directly from the consumer. The history of applications is such that they are unintegrated. This lack of integration shows up in many places, such as:

- Key structure of data
- Definition of the data
- Data layout
- Encoding structure of the data
- The use of reference tables

Transaction response time is an important issue for the applications component of the CIF. Another important issue is the integration of the applications. Unfortunately, applications are difficult and slow to integrate after they have been built and installed.

Data leaves the application layer and is fed into the I & T layer. An important decision to be made by the I & T layer is in selecting the system of record, the source of data that will flow into the I & T layer. The system of record represents the best data, not necessarily perfect data, that the corporation has collected in the applications.

Now that we understand where the detail/transaction data comes from, let's take a closer look at how the *I & T layer* brings it all together.

CHAPTER 5

The Integration and Transformation Layer Component

The source of data for the ODS and the data warehouse is an architectural component known as the integration and transformation layer (the I & T layer), discussed briefly in Chapter 4. Unlike the ODS, data warehouse, and data marts, which are made up primarily of data, the I & T layer is made up primarily of programs. In the spirit of the metaphor of an actual factory, the I & T layer is where most of the factory work takes place. Figure 5.1 shows the I & T layer (or interface).

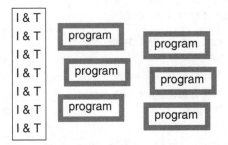

Figure 5.1 The I & T layer: a group of programs dedicated to the capture, transformation, and movement of data from the applications environment to the ODS and the data warehouse environment.

What Is the Integration and Transformation Layer?

The I & T interface is the place where unintegrated data from the applications is combined—or integrated—and transformed into corporate data. As we will see later in this chapter, significant transformations take place as data moves through the I & T layer. After this data has been molded into a corporate asset, the I & T layer loads it into the data warehouse and/or ODS for access by the user community.

An Unstable Interface

The I & T interface is a very unstable set of programs, because they constantly change over time for the following reasons (see Figure 5.2):

The applications are constantly changing. Every time an application changes, one or more programs in the I & T interface must also change.

The data warehouse is built incrementally. Pieces of the data warehouse are added over time; with each new increment comes changes to the I & T layer.

The data warehouse is built iteratively. In many cases, after the DSS analyst has seen what arrives in the data warehouse, the DSS analyst calls for a reshaping and retooling of the environment.

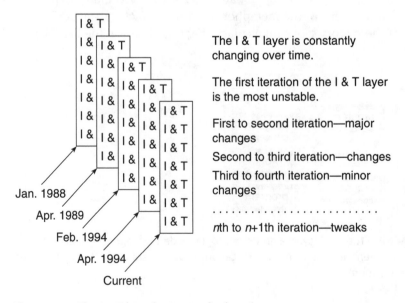

Figure 5.2   The I & T layer is constantly changing.

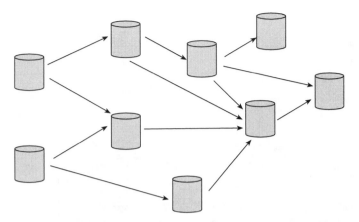

Figure 5.3 The speed of movement throughout the I & T layer is normally not an issue, with the exception of movement to Class I ODS.

Complexity of processing is not the only factor shaping the I & T layer. On occasion, the speed with which data can be moved through the I & T layer is a consideration as well, as illustrated in Figure 5.3.

As an example of a case in which speed of data movement through the I & T layer becomes a factor, consider the processing of data for a Class I ODS. In the case of a Class I ODS, the amount of time that data spends in the I & T layer is less than a second. When data is moved through the I & T layer at that speed, very little complex or significant processing can be done. In essence, transaction information passes through the I & T layer untouched in order to optimize on the processing speed.

Complexity and speed of processing, however, are not the only things that can be an issue. Another issue is that of the volume of data that needs to pass through the I & T layer. Figure 5.4 shows that large volumes of data can frequently back up at the application awaiting processing in the I & T layer.

Feeds into and out of the Interface

The primary feed into the I & T layer is from the many applications in which raw detailed data is captured and audited (see Figure 5.5). The feed of data into the I & T interface is complex from two perspectives:

1. A massive amount of data moves through the interface.
2. The amount of work that is done to the data is nontrivial.

The feeds out of the I & T layer go to two places:

- Into the ODS
- Into the data warehouse

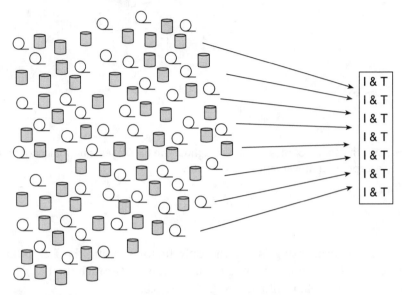

Figure 5.4 The primary issue of I & T processing is that of processing huge volumes of data.

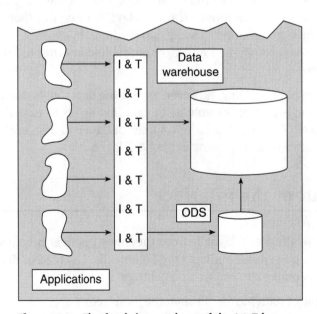

Figure 5.5 The feeds into and out of the I & T layer.

Complex Integration and Transformation Interface

The I & T interface is comprised of many different programs that accomplish many different functions. Figure 5.6 shows how complex the I & T interface can be.

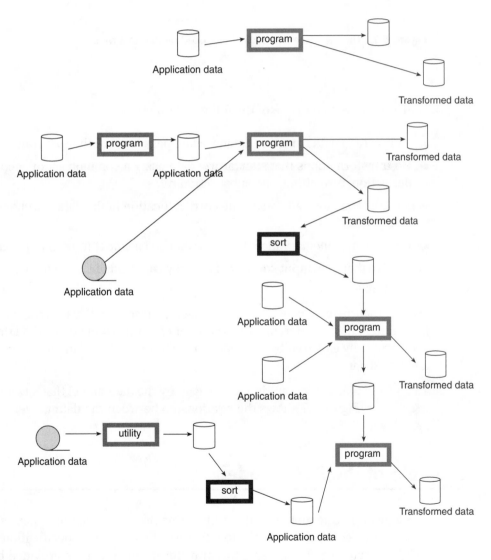

Figure 5.6 What the I & T environment looks like from a visceral perspective.

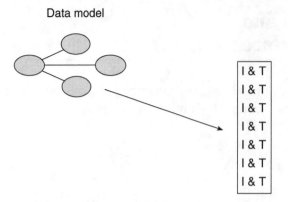

Data model

Figure 5.7 The I & T layer is heavily influenced by the data model.

I & T programs can do one of the following functions:

- Merely read data from one database and pass it to another program.
- Do transformations that standardize data using a common set of encoding, derivation, formatting, and substitution rules.
- Map the transformed data to the correct location in the data warehouse and/or ODS.
- Produce intermediary files that are then used as input into other programs.
- If more than one input source exists, they can produce more than one file as output.

Data is then resequenced, as input comes from external data and reference files as well. In short, a tremendous amount of work is done to the data that has been originally gathered by the applications to recast that data into the form of integrated data.

The overall plan for integration is provided by the data model that sits atop the I & T layer. Figure 5.7 shows the relationship between the data model and the I & T layer.

The Role of the Data Model

The logical data model acts like a blueprint that describes how data should look in the corporate information factory. From these specifications, the *builder* creates I & T programs that transform raw materials provided by the applications environment into the foundation, frame, roof, siding, and interior

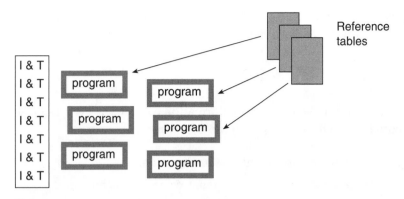

Figure 5.8 Reference tables are a standard part of the I & T layer.

that make up the CIF. The logical data model intellectually unifies the work that is done by the many programs that go into the I & T layer.

More than just raw detailed input goes into the I & T layer. Reference data and external data can both be input into the I & T layer, as seen by Figure 5.8.

Creating Metadata

One of the important outputs of the I & T activities is that of metadata that describes the process of transformation, as illustrated by Figure 5.9.

The metadata that is output in Figure 5.9 is descriptive of the logic of transformation. At the end of the day, the DSS analyst using the corporate information factory needs to know exactly what transpired in the logic that was executed in the I & T layer. The logic of processing is captured in the metadata that

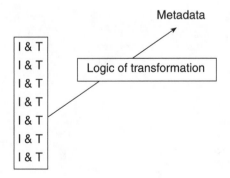

Figure 5.9 The logic of transformation is put into the metadata environment. It is one of the most important products of the I & T layer.

describes what is occurring in the I & T layer. The information that is captured is technically not *metadata* but *metaprocess* information.

Automatic Creation of I & T Code

In the early days of the corporate information factory, the I & T interface had to be created manually, which posed the following problems:

- The operational environment was always changing.
- The DSS data warehouse environment was always changing.
- The code was repetitive and boring. After the third I & T program was written, no intellectual challenge remained.
- The I & T code was complex.

Fortunately, as the corporate information factory environment matured, software became available for the code production necessary for the creation of the I & T interface. After a corporation had passed along the learning curve associated with one of the tools of automation, great productivity became the norm.

Processing in the Integration and Transformation Interface

The kinds of processing that occurs in the I & T interface is varied and complex. They include:

- Performing key transformations
- Creating profile/aggregrate records
- Encoding structures
- Simple reformatting
- Mathematical conversion
- Resequencing data
- Assigning default values

Performing Key Transformations

Perhaps the most basic kind of processing is that of key transformation. Figure 5.10 depicts some of the considerations of key transformation.

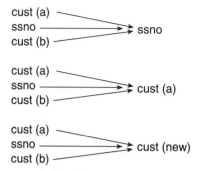

Figure 5.10 Three possibilities for resolving inconsistent key structures.

Three applications have different key structures for a customer. Application A has its unique key structure; application B has its own key structure; and application C uses a social security number for its key. In order to achieve uniformity of key structure, the DWA has several choices:

- Convert the key for all applications to the social security number.
- Convert applications B and C to the key structure suggested by A.
- Convert all applications to a new key structure.

Exactly which strategy for key conversion is proper is a function of several factors including:

- What does the data model specify?
- Is there a dominant application?
- Is most of the data already in a standard key format?

Adding an element of time to an operational key structure is a common thing to do as data passes through the I & T layer (see Figure 5.11).

An element of time consists of some form or measurement of time, such as a day, a week, or a month.

In many cases, data in the applications environment will not include time as part of the key structure. In order to fit in the data warehouse, an element of time needs to be added, usually to the tail end of the key structure. Some key structures naturally have time included, such as transaction data. Other key structures do not have time as part of the key. The creation of profile records is a very common activity as data passes from the applications environment to the data warehouse or the ODS.

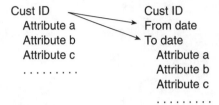

Figure 5.11 The addition of an element of time.

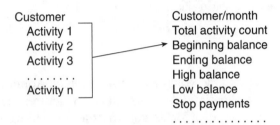

Figure 5.12 Creating profile or aggregate records from the many occurrences in the applications environment.

Creating Profile/Aggregate Records

The profile records are very useful for changing the granularity of data and managing the volume of data that ends up in the data warehouse (see Figure 5.12). Tremendous condensation of data is possible with their creation. Profile records are created from many small units of detail residing in the application environment, which are combined into a single aggregate record.

Encoding Structures

Standardization of encoding structures is a very common activity in the I & T interface, as seen by Figure 5.13. In this figure, different applications have represented gender in different manners. Logic in the I & T interface is required to create a standard representation of encoded data in the data warehouse and the ODS environment.

Simple Reformatting

Simple reformatting of dates and other fields is a common activity in the I & T interface. Figure 5.14 shows a simple reformatting of dates, in which a data field has been restructured to accommodate the year 2000.

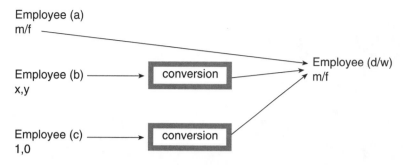

Figure 5.13 Conversion of encoded values to achieve consistency is another transformation activity.

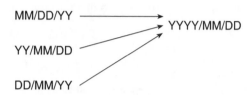

Figure 5.14 Reformatting data to achieve consistency.

Figure 5.15 Mathematical conversion.

Mathematical Conversion

Mathematical conversion is another common I & T activity. Figure 5.15 illustrates an example of a simple mathematical conversion.

Many reasons exist for a mathematical conversion, such as:

- A change in accounting periods
- A conversion of monetary rates
- Account adjustments

Resequencing Data

Resequencing data as it passes through the I & T interface is another activity, as seen in Figure 5.16. Resequencing data is a simple thing to do. The only complicating factor is that of managing the volumes of data that must be resequenced.

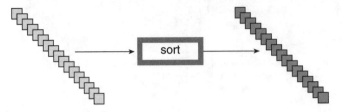

Figure 5.16   Resequencing data.

Figure 5.17   Specifying default values is another consideration of transformation.

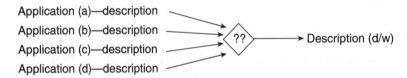

Figure 5.18   Choosing the best data from multiple sources.

Assigning Default Values

Sometimes data elements will be processed by the I & T layer that are not populated. On these occasions the DWA needs to have specified default values, as seen in Figure 5.17.

Handling Multiple Data Sources

On occasions data as it passes through the I & T interface is another activity, as seen in Figure 5.18. Resequencing data is a simple thing to do. The only complicating factor is that of managing the volumes of data that must be resequenced.

Log Tapes as a Source

Occasionally it make sense to use log and journal tapes that have been created as a by-product of application transaction processing as input into the I & T interface. Log and journal tapes can be a very efficient way of gathering data that needs to be transacted into the data warehouse. Figure 5.19 shows this option.

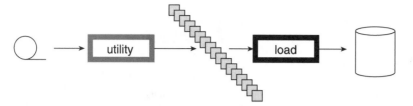

Figure 5.19 Using log tapes as a source for refreshment.

When log and journal tapes are used, the data is read by means of a utility in order to capture it off the log tape. When captured, the data is ready to be entered into the standard processing that occurs in the I & T interface.

Changing Platforms

In many cases, data resides on one architectural platform in the applications environment and on another platform in the data warehouse or the ODS environment. Figure 5.20 shows this change to data.

Many changes must occur when the underlying hardware platform changes, which must be effected in the I & T interface. However, changes in the hardware platform are not the only fundamental changes that must occur. Software changes in platforms are an important consideration as well, as seen in Figure 5.21.

Who Is in Charge?

I & T processing is in the domain of the data warehouse administrator (DWA) who understands the technical and business ramifications of running it. to let any other organizational function build and manage the I & T interface is a mistake. They generally do not understand these ramifications and are focused and measured on their ability to keep the applications, thus the wheels of the corporation, running. This leaves little time to understand or support the I & T layer.

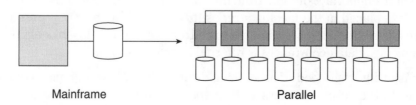

Mainframe   Parallel

Figure 5.20 Switching hardware architectures is a common transformation.

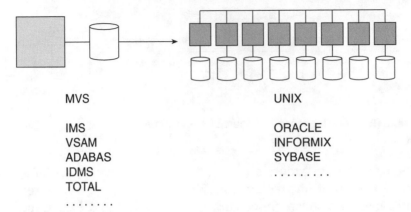

MVS   UNIX

IMS   ORACLE
VSAM   INFORMIX
ADABAS   SYBASE
IDMS   . . . .
TOTAL
. . . .

Figure 5.21   Software changes are important to consider.

Summary

The I & T layer is made up of programs that pass data from the applications environment to the ODS or the data warehouse environment. As the data is passed, it is integrated through a complex process. The integration process includes activities, such as:

- Key resolution
- Resequencing of data
- Restructuring of data layouts
- Merging of data
- Aggregation of data
- Summarization of data

The I & T layer's structure is heavily influenced by the data model, which serves as the intellectual road map for the work that is accomplished by the I & T programs. Reference tables are a standard part of the I & T interface.

One of the important outputs from the I & T layer is the logic of transformation, which is placed in the metadata repository. The metadata that represents the logic of transformation is captured and stored over time; this process of maintaining metadata occurrences is referred to as *versioning*.

Occasionally, the speed of processing through the I & T programs becomes an issue. In the case of a Class I ODS, speed of processing becomes an issue, because the I & T interface processes huge volumes of data.

So far, we have talked about the source of detail data in the corporate information factory, the external world via applications. We have also talked about how the I & T layer transforms this detail into a corporate asset. Now let's talk about the component of the CIF that takes this corporate asset and makes it available for tactical decision making, the *operational data store*.

CHAPTER 6

The Operational Data Store Component

For all of the benefits of a data warehouse and its associated data marts, there is still a need for collective, integrated operational, DSS/informational processing. When this need arises, an operational data store (ODS) is in order. An ODS is a hybrid structure that has equally strong elements of operational processing and DSS processing. This dual nature of the ODS easily makes it the most complex architectural structure in the corporate information factory (Figure 6.1).

What Is an Operational Data Store?

An ODS is a collection of detailed data that satisfies the collective, integrated, operational needs of the corporation. Generally, these needs arise in the following situations: as strategic decisions are made using the data warehouse and/or data mart and action is required; as integrated operational reporting is needed across multiple but related operational systems (e.g., distribution systems, customer service systems, etc.) The ODS is:

- Subject-oriented
- Integrated
- Volatile

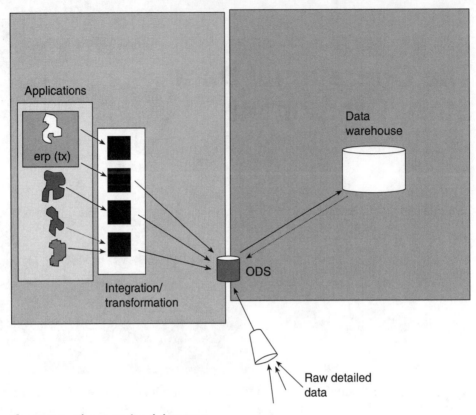

Figure 6.1 The operational data store.

- Current-valued
- Detailed

The ODS looks very much like a data warehouse when it comes to its first two characteristics, subject orientation and integration. However, the remaining characteristics of an ODS are quite different from a data warehouse. Because of the very nature of these fundamental differences in types of data and processing, it is never acceptable to combine an ODS and a data warehouse into the same physical environment.

Volatility

An ODS is volatile. That means that an ODS can be updated as a normal part of processing. A data warehouse is nonvolatile and is not updated under normal circumstances. Instead, a data warehouse contains snapshots; a new snapshot is created whenever a change needs to be reflected in the data warehouse.

Current-Valued

The second major difference is the timeliness of the data found in the ODS. An ODS typically contains daily, weekly, or maybe even monthly data, but the data ages very quickly in the ODS. The data warehouse, on the other hand, contains robust amounts of historical data. In fact, it may contain 5 or even 10 years worth of data.

Detailed Data

The third difference between an ODS and a data warehouse is that the ODS contains detailed data only, but a data warehouse contains both detailed and summary data. This characteristic is perhaps the most defining difference between a data warehouse and an ODS.

Feeds into and out of the Operational Data Store

The ODS is simple; it has two primary feeds into and one primary feed out of it (Figure 6.2).

The Integration and Transformation Layer Feed

The first primary feed into the ODS is from the I & T layer. The feed out of the ODS is to the data warehouse. This ODS-to-data-warehouse feed is activated as data ages.

The second primary feed is from the data warehouse itself. This is one of the more important feeds because it is through this feed that online response time can be achieved for DSS data warehouse data. This feed is typically known as the Class IV feed.

In a Class IV ODS feed, data is analyzed and synthesized at the data warehouse; then it is aggregated or summarized and passed back to the ODS. When in the ODS, the data is immediately available for decision making. There is no need to go back to the data warehouse and gather and analyze a lot of data in order to make a decision.

Class IV ODS are found in many places:

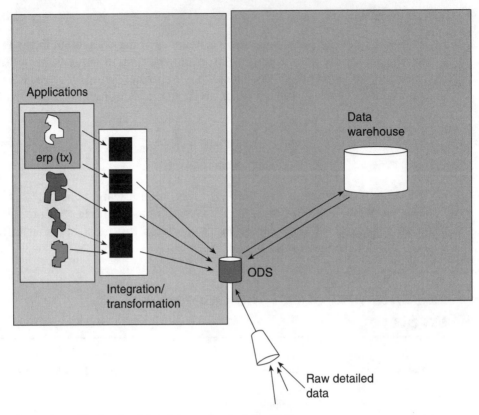

Figure 6.2 The feeds of data into and out of the ODS.

- In the telecommunications environment where the operator has direct contact with the customer
- In the banking environment where the teller has immediate loan authorization for a customer
- In the retail environment where the salesperson has up-to-the-second information about the sales status of an item
- In the insurance environment where the agent has prerated the customer/prospect

Another rather small feed of data into the ODS is a feed directly from the external environment. Although it is true that specialized applications can be written that will allow data to go directly into the ODS, bypassing the I & T layer, these applications are fairly rare. Under normal circumstances, data enters the ODS by passing through the I & T layer.

Different Classes of the Operational Data Store

The I & T interface is of special interest because it governs the different types (or classes) of ODS. Consider the four different I & T interfaces shown in Figure 6.3:

- Class I: Asynchronous—one-to-two-second delay
- Class II: Store and forward—two-to-four-hour delay
- Class III: Batch processing—overnight
- Class IV: Data from the warehouse

A single ODS will contain one, two, three, or perhaps all four classes of data.

Class I Operational Data Store

There is a synchronous interface in which a very, very small amount of time lapses between an application's transaction and the reflection of the transaction in the ODS. The amount of time is typically one second or less. This type of interface is called a Class I ODS. In this class, very little serious work can be done to the data as it passes through the I & T layer because there simply isn't time to do very much. The transaction passes through to the ODS in a fairly complete manner. For all practical purposes, the end user never sees a time lag between an operational transaction execution and the reflection of that transaction in the ODS when the ODS is Class I.

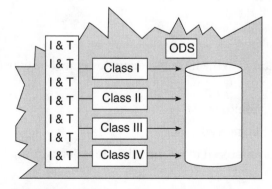

Figure 6.3 The four different classes of ODS can be classified by the speed of the feed of data into the ODS.

Class II Operational Data Store

If an hour or two passes from the time a transaction is created and interacted in the application environment until that transaction is reflected in the ODS, the ODS type is a Class II ODS. The I & T layer holds the data in abeyance in a store-and-forward mode. Because of the time lag, a serious amount of work can be done to the transaction data as it passes through the I & T layer. The data shows up as truly integrated data in the ODS. The end user may notice a difference between the data in the operational applications and the ODS while the data is held in a store-and-forward mode.

Class III Operational Data Store

In a Class III ODS, there may be a time lag between 12 hours and a day as transaction data is collected in the I & T interface. This is an overnight batch process and as much integration of data as desired can occur during processing in the I & T layer. The data that arrives at the ODS can be very integrated in this mode. The end user can definitely notice a difference between the values of data in the operational application environment and the ODS as the data sits in the I & T layer awaiting processing.

Class IV Operational Data Store

In a Class IV ODS, the data is fed into the ODS directly from the data warehouse. In this case, the data is read and analyzed in the data warehouse and derivations are passed to the ODS. Typical derivations passed to the ODS include customer segments and customer scores.

A Class IV ODS is important because it is here that online response time can be achieved when trying to access data derived in the data warehouse.

Determining the Class

Many technological implications to the intranet technology must be considered here, such as:

- Speed of movement of data into the ODS
- Volume of data that must be moved
- Volume of data that must be stored in intermediate locations during I & T processing
- Update of data and integrity of transaction processing
- The time of day the movement needs to occur

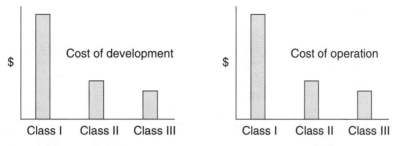

Figure 6.4 The cost of development and operation for a Class I ODS is significantly higher than the corresponding costs for a Class II and a Class III ODS.

The choice of whether a Class I, II, III, or IV ODS will be created is the first and one of the most important decisions the system's architect must make. Figure 6.4 outlines some of the considerations involved in the choice of a Class I, II, II, or IV ODS.

Furthermore, if integration is a primary consideration, then a Class I ODS is not a very good choice because not very much integration can be achieved with it. For these reasons then, there must be a very serious business justification for a Class I ODS. As a rule, a Class II or a Class III ODS serves most companies' needs for most processing.

Dynamic Summary Data

One of the distinguishing characteristics of an ODS is the fact that it stores only detailed data. Certainly, summary data can be created from detailed data, but storing that summary data after it is created is an entirely different matter. The summary data that is created in the ODS can be called dynamic summary data. This is data whose accuracy of summarization depends upon the moment of calculation.

Figure 6.5 shows a calculation that is made for a bank's current collective balance for IBM Corporation. At 10:37 A.M., IBM has a collective balance of $1,998,417.29. Later in the day, at 4:13 P.M., another calculation is made of the collective balance of IBM, showing $2,867,665.19. The accuracy of the summary data found in the ODS is a function of the moment in time when the calculation is made. It would be a mistake to store the 10:37 A.M. value in the ODS because it would be tempting to use that value for a business decision at 4:13 P.M. The business decision at 4:13 P.M. may well be a very different business

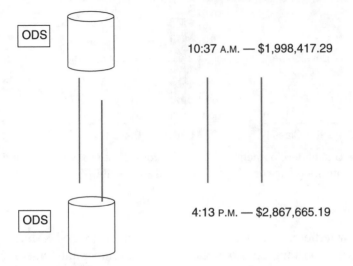

Figure 6.5 Dynamic summary data: The accuracy of the calculation depends on the moment in time that the calculation is made.

decision than the one made at the earlier time. For this reason, dynamic summary data is not normally stored in an ODS.

Static Summary Data

Now consider the summary data found in a data warehouse. Suppose that on Monday, a manager asks an analyst to determine what the expenses were for the last quarter in a department. The analyst calculates that quarterly expenses were $101,768.19 for the department.

Now suppose that another manager asks an analyst to make the same calculation on Friday. The analyst should calculate exactly the same amount— $101,768.19. There should be no variation in the amount calculated, even though the calculation is made at a different moment in time.

This type of summary data is called static summary data and is perfectly safe to place in a data warehouse. In fact, it is wasteful not to place this type of data in a warehouse. In the data warehouse, the DSS analyst is less interested in what expenses look like this instant and more interested in how expenses trend over time, compared to forecast, and compared to last year. In addition, the DSS analyst expects these complex questions to be answered in a very short time (2–3 minutes). This can be accomplished only through liberal use of static summaries in the data warehousing environment. Because of the differences between dynamic summary data and static summary data, summary data should not be stored in an ODS but in a data warehouse and/or data mart.

The Operational Data Store Workload

The ODS environment is the most technologically challenging environment because elements of very different kinds of processing must constructively cohabitate in the same technological infrastructure (Figure 6.6).

Load Processing

One kind of processing that must be done in the ODS is that of loading data. In the case of a Class I ODS, the loading is done in an online manner. The challenges faced in this environment are generally associated with the sophistication of technology or the lack of key technologies in the application and/or legacy environments.

In the case of a Class II or III ODS, loading is done asynchronously. The challenges surface when loading large volumes of data. This generally results in load processes that are complex to develop, certify, and maintain.

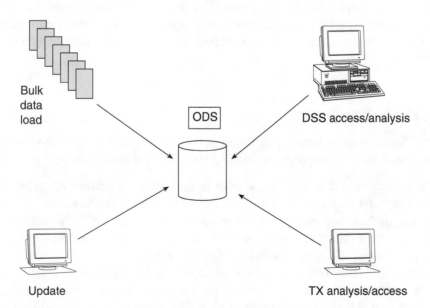

Figure 6.6 The kinds of processing that occur in the ODS environment.

In the case of a Class IV ODS, loads are done in batches and can be scheduled to run when the workload on the ODS is low. Additionally, data being loaded is less time sensitive given the degree that historical and external data are used. These characteristics make this class of ODS the easiest to implement.

Update Processing

The second kind of processing that can be done in the ODS environment is that of update processing. Even though direct updating is not frequently done, it still must be accommodated. When direct updating must be accomplished, there is a technological implication of update integrity. This is achieved within the confines of the DBMS structure by means of facilities that COMMIT work to be applied to the database, ROLLBACK work that has not been COMMITed, and RECOVER work that has been COMMITed and lost. Even though an update many be done for only a small number of transactions, *all* active transactions in the system pay the price of overhead for the update.

Access Processing

The third type of processing that occurs in the ODS is that of access processing. Many people may be using the ODS who expect consistent two-to-three-second response time. In fact, this type of processing is the dominant one in the ODS environment and entails the access of a few rows of data, not the update of data.

DSS Analysis Processing

The fourth type of processing found in the ODS environment is the occasional DSS analysis of data, where sweeping analysis is made across many records.

The complicating aspect of the ODS is that *all* of the different styles of processing must be accommodated within the ODS infrastructure. The problem is that optimizing any one style of processing compromises all other styles of processing. Said differently, when the designer of the ODS optimizes any one style of processing, the designer does so at the expense of all other styles of processing. The best the designer can do is achieve a comfortable level of performance for all styles of processing in the ODS. It is because of this compromise that the ODS is the most complicated of all the architectural constructs within the corporate information factory.

Different Processing Windows

In order to achieve the compromise between the types of processing, the ODS designer must carefully divide the ODS day into different processing windows, as shown in Figure 6.7. One of the most important reasons why the ODS processing window must be divided into a series of *mini* processing windows is that in order to achieve consistent processing time, that workload must be *homogeneous*.

What Is a Homogeneous Workload?

A homogeneous workload is one in which the different types of processing that reside in the workload are not mixed. Figure 6.8 shows the difference between a homogeneous workload and a heterogeneous workload in terms of system throughput.

On the left side of Figure 6.8 is a homogeneous workload in which only transactions of a given type—small, fast-running transactions—are found. In the

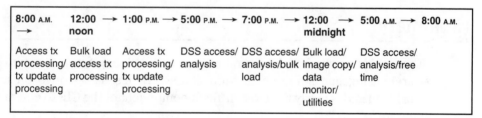

8:00 A.M. →	12:00 noon	→ 1:00 P.M. →	5:00 P.M. →	7:00 P.M. →	12:00 midnight	→ 5:00 A.M. →	8:00 A.M.
Access tx processing/ tx update processing	Bulk load access tx processing	Access tx processing/ tx update processing	DSS access/ analysis	DSS access/ analysis/bulk load	Bulk load/ image copy/ data monitor/ utilities	DSS access/ analysis/free time	

Figure 6.7 The cycle of daily processing for the ODS environment.

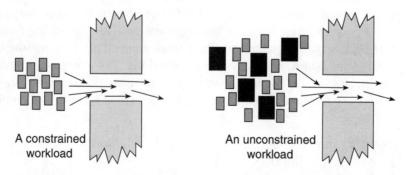

A constrained workload

An unconstrained workload

Figure 6.8 In order to achieve consistent and good response time, the workload flowing through the system needs to be constrained.

environment on the left, flow through the system is unimpeded, and an efficient and quick flow exists. Such a system exhibits good response time.

Now consider the workload represented on the right side of Figure 6.8. In this workload is a mixture of different kinds of transactions—very small, fast-running transactions and large slow-running transactions. The practice of keeping workloads homogeneous is called adherence to the *standard work unit* and has been known and practiced by online system designers for years. The concepts of the standard work unit apply to the ODS every bit as much as they have applied to OLTP.

External Data in the Operational Data Store

External data can be placed in the ODS just as it is placed in other parts of the corporate information factory. Metadata is likewise a part of the ODS environment. Although metadata is useful in the ODS environment, it is not nearly as important as it is in the data warehouse or the data mart environment.

Summary

The ODS is a hybrid architectural construct containing some elements of data warehousing and some application characteristics. It operates on a mixed workload and is easily the most difficult component of the CIF to construct and operate.

An ODS is not an essential part of the CIF. Some companies operate quite nicely without an ODS. Other companies find an ODS to be indispensable when their existing applications environments do not provide the necessary integration to support evolving business management activities resulting from business intelligence gained using the data warehouse. This is commonplace in many marketing, sales, and service organizations. These areas generally use the data warehouse to formulate strategies on how to best treat their customers and use the ODS to support contact activities related to execution of these strategies.

The feed into the ODS is the I & T layer. In addition, occasionally data is entered directly into the ODS.

Four types of ODS exist: Class I, Class II, Class III, and Class IV. The class of an ODS depends on the speed with which data is passed from the I & T layer. As a single ODS matures, it is possible that it may contain all classes of data.

The ODS contains dynamic summary data, data whose accuracy depends on the moment of calculation. Because of the ever-changing nature of dynamic summary data, it is normally not stored in the ODS.

The ODS operates on a severely mixed workload. Because of the dramatic differences in the nature of the workload, the ODS day is divided into slices. There is the OLTP time slice, the batch time slice, and the DSS time slice.

We have talked about the components of the corporate information factory responsible for providing, capturing, transforming, and integrating detail data. In addition, we have talked about how the ODS provides a platform for integrating this data for operational reporting. We also talked about how the ODS is used as a mechanism for inserting information derived in the data warehouse back into the applications—in a sense, making knowledge gained from analyzing data actionable. Now let's take a look at the best-known component of the CIF, the *data warehouse*. It is here that detail historical data is stored and made available for strategic analysis.

CHAPTER 7

The Data Warehouse Component

T he most prominent architectural component of the corporate information factory is that of the data warehouse. It is the basis for all strategic DSS processing. In many cases, the data warehouse is the first place integration of data is achieved anywhere in the environment. It is also where much historical processing is done.

What Is the Data Warehouse?

The data warehouse is an architectural structure that supports the management of data that is:

- Subject-oriented
- Integrated
- Time-variant
- Nonvolatile
- Comprised of both summary and detailed data

The data warehouse exists to support management's decisions which, in turn, support the strategic planning processes of the corporation. Data flows into the

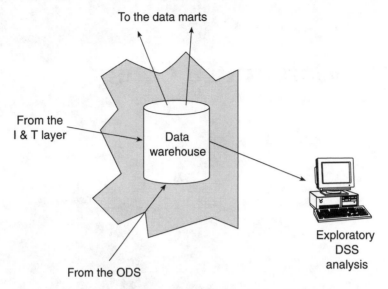

Figure 7.1   A data warehouse in the context of the CIF.

data warehouse from the ODS and the I & T layer. The flow of data out of the data warehouse goes to the data marts. Finally, DSS analysts use the data found in the data mart to support such activities as customer segmentation and scoring, product analysis, and projecting customer lifetime value. Figure 7.1 illustrates the data warehouse in the context of the corporate information factory.

Subject Orientation

The subject orientation of the data warehouse implies that it is organized along the lines of the major entities of the corporation, such as:

- Customers
- Products
- Vendors
- Transactions
- Orders
- Policies
- Accounts
- Shipments

In other words, the data warehouse is not functional or application oriented. This allows for the data use to change over time without fundamentally affecting its organization or structure. This is crucial given the large volumes of historical data that are managed within the data warehouse.

Integration

Integration of data warehouse data refers to the physical unification and cohesiveness of the data as it is stored in the warehouse. Integration covers many aspects of the warehouse, including common:

- Key structures
- Encoding and decoding structures
- Definitions of data
- Data layouts
- Data relationships
- Naming conventions

Data integration in the data warehouse is not achieved by merely copying data from the operational environment. Instead, as raw data passes through the I & T layer, a fundamental alteration is done to the data to achieve an integrated foundation that resides in the data warehouse.

Time Variancy

Another characteristic of a data warehouse is that of time variancy. Simply stated, any record in the data warehouse environment is accurate relative to some moment in time. One way time variancy is accomplished is through the creation of snapshot records. A data warehouse is often said to contain nothing but a massive series of snapshot records. Each snapshot has one moment in time when the record is accurate. Any implication about the record before or beyond the moment in time that the snapshot was made is misleading and may be inaccurate.

Because the data warehouse is made up of a massive series of snapshots, it can contain data over a lengthy period of time. It is common for a data warehouse to hold detail data (active or archival) that is 5 to 10 years old.

The time variancy of a data warehouse shows up as an element of time in the key structure. An element of time might be a day, a year, a month, or a quarter. The element of time is appended to the key of the record in the data warehouse. Two popular models are used in recording history, State and Event. A record using a State model has a "from" and "to" date that denotes the time period when the data in the record was accurate. An example of this is:

- Customer ID
- From date
- To date

A record using the Event model has an "event" date that reflects the moment in time when the data in the record was accurate. Two examples of this are:

- Order ID
- Part number
- Order date
- Account withdrawal ID
- Withdrawal date

Historical Data

The gathering and storage of historical data in the data warehouse gives it some unique properties not found elsewhere in the information-processing environment.

Often the question is asked, what if the operational transaction processing world changes? Doesn't that change the data warehouse? Indeed, the data warehouse is affected, but only at the particular moment in time the changes are made in the operational environment. Data entered into the data warehouse prior to the changes made in the operational environment is not impacted by the changes.

For example, suppose that a data warehouse starts collecting data in 1995. Data is collected up to 1999, at which point changes are made to the operational system. The data in the warehouse is changed for the year 2000 and beyond. But, the data collected from 1995 to 1999 is not impacted by the changes. No real justification exists for going back and altering historical data.

Nonvolatility

Yet another characteristic of a data warehouse is that of nonvolatility. This refers to the fact that update (in its purest sense—that of finding a record and making changes to the record) does not normally occur in a data warehouse. If update occurs at all, it occurs on an exception basis.

When changes occur that need to be recorded in a data warehouse, the changes are captured in the form of a time-variant snapshot. A new snapshot is added to the data warehouse to reflect the change instead of an update occurring. In capturing change by means of a series of snapshots, a historical record is formed.

Containment of Summary and Detailed Data

Finally, a data warehouse contains both detailed and summary data. Detailed data reflects the atomic-level transactions that turn the wheels of the corporation. This includes data that describes product usage, account activity, inventory movement, sales, and so forth. Two kinds of summary data are found in a data warehouse: the profile record and public summary.

Profile Record

One kind of summary data is created as raw detailed data in the I & T layer and combined to create a *profile record*. As an example of a profile record, consider the following example from the telecommunications industry.

In the operational environment there is a customer record and a record for each use of the telephone during the statement cycle. Throughout the statement cycle many usage records are created. When it comes time to create a data warehouse record at the end of the statement cycle, the usage transaction records are combined to create a single record, which is then placed in the data warehouse. The resultant record is an aggregate or profile record that contains summary data representing the lowest level of granularity of data warehouse data. This form of summary data—a transaction summary record—in the data warehouse is common for organizations dealing with very large amounts of data in their data warehouse. Typically, those organizations include:

- Telecommunications providers
- Retailers
- Insurance companies
- Financial institutions

Public Summary

The second type of summary data found in the data warehouse is a type of data that can be termed *public summary*. It reflects data that is calculated departmentally but has wide corporate outreach. An example of a public summary is the calculation made each quarter by the public accounting firm stating the financial status of the corporation. The quarterly statement includes such things as expenses, revenues, and profitability. The financial status reflects benchmark information that is used across the corporation by many departments and many managers. Although the quarterly statement is prepared departmentally, it is used throughout the corporation and as such is an example of public summary data. As a proportion of data, public summary data occupies a minuscule amount of space in the data warehouse compared to detail or profile summary data.

Data Warehouse Administration

As a rule, the data warehouse is managed by an organizational unit called a data warehouse administrator (DWA). The DWA organization has many charters, such as:

- Building the data warehouse
- Ongoing monitoring and maintenance for the data warehouse
- Coordinating usage of the data warehouse
- Management feedback as to successes and failures
- Competition for resources for making the data warehouse a reality
- Selection of hardware and software platforms

The Data Warehouse Drawn to Scale

One interesting way to look at the data warehouse as it sits in the corporate information factory is to look at it drawn to scale, as shown in Figure 7.2.

As the figure indicates, the data warehouse, in terms of data and processing, is much larger than any other component of the corporate information factory. As a rule (and this depends entirely on the company and its experience with the data warehouse), the data warehouse is one to one and a half orders of magnitude larger than any other architectural component. Of course, if a company is just embarking on the data warehouse and has very little experience in this environment, then the data warehouse will be proportionately smaller than that shown in Figure 7.2. The ratios depicted in Figure 7.2 are for a mature data warehouse environment.

Feeds into and out of the Data Warehouse

The data warehouse has data moved into it from the ODS and the I & T layer. In addition, the data warehouse feeds the data mart environment; each of the feeds has its own characteristics. Data also flows to and from the data ware-

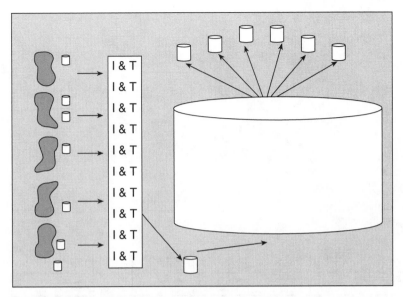

Figure 7.2 The data warehouse drawn to scale in comparison with some of the other components of the corporate information factory.

house to alternative storage, as well as the exploration warehouse. Figure 7.3 shows the feeds of data into and out of the data warehouse.

The Operational Data Store Feed

The ODS feed is one in which very little data is passed to the data warehouse; it is triggered by data aging in the ODS. The ODS feed is usually made daily and typically brings data into the data warehouse where that data is appended to other data in the warehouse. Because a small amount of data is moved from the ODS to the data warehouse, an intranet connection is very effective.

Oftentimes data is aggregated as it is moved out of the ODS and into the data warehouse. The programs that comprise the ODS to data warehouse interface are the domain of the DWA. Any other organizational unit having influence over this interface does not make sense.

The Integration and Transformation Layer Feed

The movement of data into the data warehouse from the I & T layer is one in which a massive amount of data crosses the line. The intranet connection must be capable of handling very large amounts of data transfer.

The I & T connection is one that is executed on an as-needed basis. Sometimes transfer is made daily; sometimes transfer is made weekly; and occasionally

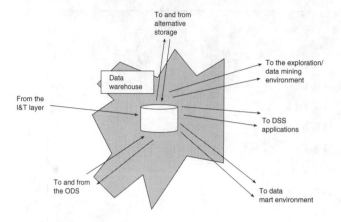

To/from the ODS	Very light	Daily	Mass load	Append to existing data
To/from the I&T layer	Very heavy	At night; as needed	Mass load	Replace; incremental update; append to existing data
To data marts	moderate	Varies by department	Selective or mass load	Customization and summarization
To/from alternative storage	Very heavy	As needed	Mass load or Selective load	Move then delete then load
To DSS applications	As needed; fluctuating	As needed	Mass load	Load on request
To exploration warehouse	As needed; often heavy	As needed	Selected mass load	Load selected tables

Figure 7.3 Some characteristics of the different feeds to and from the data warehouse to other components of the CIF.

transfer is made monthly or even quarterly. In any case, huge amounts of data regularly cross from the I & T layer into the data warehouse. The transfer is made on a casual basis in that there is no implication that a high-speed online update will be done after the data arrives at the data warehouse. The nature of update into the data warehouse is one of replace or addition.

Data can be passed in either an aggregated or detailed form into the data warehouse from the I & T layer. Note that the data that arrives in the data warehouse is often very changed from the original form and structure it had when leaving the application. The data that arrives in the data warehouse through the I & T layer is data that has undergone transformation. Because of this, the data usually has been altered: In some cases, the alteration has been severe; in other cases, the alteration has been superficial, depending on just how integrated the data was at the beginning.

Entering the Data Warehouse

The movement of data into the data warehouse is the last part of the I & T layer. As such, the programs are written and controlled by the DWA organization. It is very unusual for any other organizational entity to be involved with the specification and creation of the programs that comprise the I & T feed into the data warehouse other than the DWA.

Feeds into the Data Mart

Data moves into the data mart environment because it has been selected by the department for its own unique DSS processing. The data mart interface can be characterized by customization, denormalization, and summarization.

The department selects data from the data warehouse on an as-needed basis. In almost all cases, the department will not want the lengthy amount of detail history that is found in the data warehouse, and it will want to customize the data. The ultimate degree of customization will be heavily influenced by the business use and the DSS tool selected. Customization often includes:

- Restructuring the keys
- Resequencing the data
- Merging files together
- Aggregating data (creating corporate *profiles*)
- Denormalizing data

The volume of data that flows across this portion of the intranet is actually very slight, compared to other interfaces.

There are, of course, different ports for different data marts. There is no need for the sales department to share the same port into the data warehouse with marketing, for example. Likewise, the frequency of the data movement across the feed is strictly based on the needs of the department.

As a rule, the department builds and administers the programs that control the data warehouse to data mart interface. Only if extenuating circumstances exist is it necessary or advisable to bring a DWA programmer in to create and manage the programs for the interface. However, the department may want to look to the DWA for advice on how to best extract data from the data warehouse.

Alternative Storage Feeds

Data passes to and from the data warehouse to the alternative storage component of the corporate information factory on a regular basis. When a query is made against the data warehouse for data that resides in alternative storage, data is fetched and passed back to the data warehouse. When data becomes dormant in the data warehouse, it is moved back to the alternative storage component of the CIF.

The amount of data that is moved across the boundary from alternative storage to the data warehouse and back can be considerable. Data that moves into the data warehouse is always "in a hurry," because a query is waiting for it. Data that is moved to near line storage is always "lazy," because it has been dormant for quite a while.

The more predictable the query against the data warehouse, the less data that needs to pass between the data warehouse and alternative storage. Less predictable queries require that more data pass to and from the data warehouse to alternative storage. For this reason alone, an exploration warehouse makes sense. An exploration warehouse has the tendency to move unpredictable queries off to the exploration warehouse away from the data warehouse.

Exploration Warehouse Feeds

The data warehouse feeds data into the exploration warehouse on an as-needed basis. In some cases, only one feed is made. In other cases, depending on the nature of the exploration process, feeds of data are made regularly.

The amount of data that flows from the data warehouse to the exploration warehouse is considerable. The data that flows is detailed and historical, and, therefore, has considerable heft.

Data in the Data Warehouse

A large volume of detailed data is in the data warehouse (Figure 7.4). For the most part, any summary data that finds its way into the warehouse does not entail significant amounts of data. Data in the warehouse is integrated, so that it is distinctively corporate data. A rich amount of data history is in the data warehouse, from 5 to 10 years worth. As previously mentioned, the data is structured in terms of snapshots. The snapshots may be for an instant in time or for a period of time.

The design for the data found in the data warehouse is dominated by normalized design. This technique, introduced by E. F. Codd, consists of a series of normalization rules that define the enterprise data in terms of:

- **Entities.** Things of interest (e.g., customer, product, etc.)
- **Attributes.** Elements that describe the things of interest (e.g., customer name, product type, etc.)
- **Relationships.** Methods to describe the relationship among entities (e.g., a customer could have one or more products)

This design technique strived to eliminate data redundancy and produce a stable database design that would be largely unaffected as the processes of the

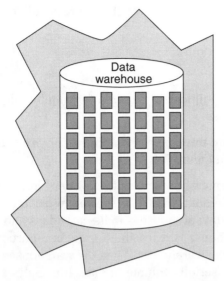

• Detailed
• Integrated
• Voluminous
• Historical
• Not updated (snapshots)
• Single snapshots and
  profile records
• Dominated by normalization

Figure 7.4   Data in the data warehouse.

business changed. Although some denormalization does take place to address the performance demands of the business, the design is essentially one that is normalized. Any redundancy of data found in the data warehouse design is planned and minimal.

Processing Data in the Warehouse

The processing in the data warehouse comes in five distinct flavors:

1. Loads from the ODS and the I & T layer into the data warehouse

2. Processes to perform post-load aggregations and derivations (e.g., scoring & segmentation)

3. Utilities required to maintain and operate the data warehouse

4. Unload and restructure processes to create data marts and other architectural entities

5. Some query processing from the DSS analyst community

Maintenance and operational utilities occasionally must be run that:

■ Monitor the amount of data being added to the data warehouse

■ Monitor the quality of data that has been entered into the data warehouse

■ Create a data content card catalog that tells what the content of the data warehouse is and projects future growth

- Prepare the data for recovery in the eventuality that there should be a problem with the data

- Remove data from the data warehouse

- Create indexes

In short, a number of background utilities are required for running the day-to-day operation of any data warehouse.

The more interesting programs that must be run are those that are submitted by the DSS analyst, as illustrated in Figure 7.5.

Using the analogy of tourists, farmers, miners, and explorers introduced in Chapter 2, the DSS analyst who operates directly on the data warehouse is usually an explorer. Only when the data warehouse is in its early days and a modest amount of data is in the warehouse is it feasible for general-purpose DSS analysis to be done directly from the warehouse. When the warehouse reaches a state of maturity and contains a serious volume of data, the analysis that is

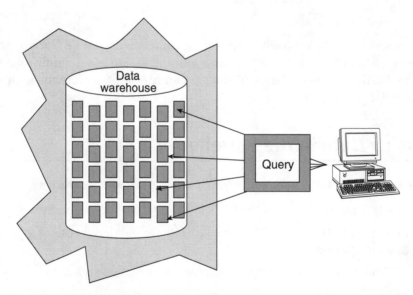

- Exploratory processing
- Looking at massive amounts of data
- Nonrepetitive
- Unpredictable
- Nonmission-critical
- Response time insensitive
- Browsing is common
- Unknown relationships are sometimes of interest
- Obscure data elements sometimes play an important role

Figure 7.5   DSS processing in the data warehouse.

done is almost exclusively done by the explorer. Farmers and tourists simply have little or no use for the warehouse once it matures. Miners, of course, look at data in the exploration warehouses or the data warehouse if no exploration warehouse exists.

The explorer typically looks for massive amounts of detailed data in a very non-repetitive manner, and the searches conducted are not mission-critical. The processing that occurs is response-time insensitive; that is, response time may be measured in minutes, hours, or even days. Browsing is a common activity, looking at relationships of data and units of data that may be obscure.

Managing Technological Challenges

The major technological challenges facing the DWA are depicted by the information in Figure 7.6.

The first and most important technological challenge facing the DWA is that of managing growth. Hand in hand is the issue of managing the volumes of data. Finally, there is the challenge of managing unpredictable and random access and the analysis of massive amounts of data.

Archiving Data out of the Data Warehouse

One way of addressing the challenges posed by large volumes of data is to properly archive the data that flows out of the data warehouse. The data warehouse has a large volume of data flowing into it, but there is no such thing as a database that constantly grows larger. At some point in time, it is necessary to purge or condense data out of the data warehouse. Figure 7.7 shows data being moved out of the data warehouse into siloed sequential storage, a typical approach.

Many things must be considered when moving data out of the data warehouse, such as:

- Should the data be actually discarded, or should the data be removed to lower-cost, bulk storage (i.e. alternative storage)?
- What criteria should be applied to data to determine whether it is a candidate for removal?
- Should the data be condensed (profile records, rolling summarization, etc.)? If so, what condensation technique should be used?
- How should the data be indexed after it is removed (if there is ever to be any attempt to retrieve the data)?

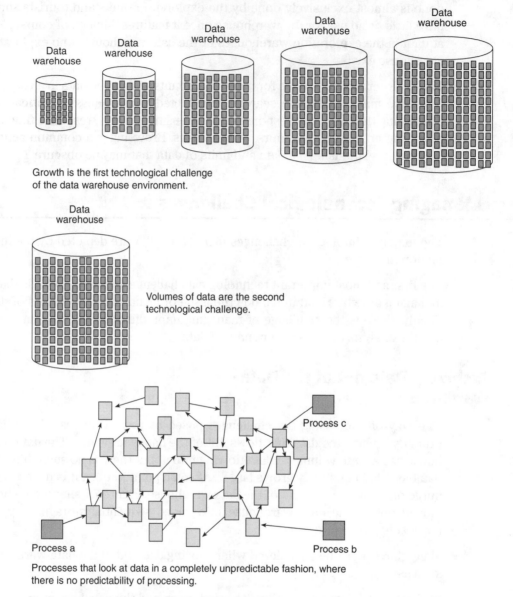

Growth is the first technological challenge
of the data warehouse environment.

Volumes of data are the second
technological challenge.

Processes that look at data in a completely unpredictable fashion, where
there is no predictability of processing.

Figure 7.6 Some of the more important technological challenges of the data warehouse
environment.

- Where and how should metadata be stored when the data is removed?
- Should metadata be allowed to be stored in the data warehouse for data
  that is not actively stored in the warehouse?

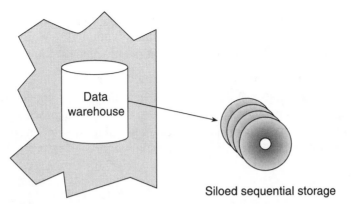

Siloed sequential storage

Figure 7.7 An integral part of the data warehouse environment is the occasional archiving of data out of active storage.

- What release information should be stored for the base technology (i.e., the DBMS) so that the data as stored will not become stale and unreadable?
- How reliable (physically) is the media on which the data will be stored?
- What seek time to first record is there for the data upon retrieval?

These are but a few of the questions that must be answered when deciding upon an exit strategy for the data that resides on the data warehouse. Most organizations do not spend much time thinking about these strategies until the data warehouse has become robust and mature.

Summary

The data warehouse is at the heart of corporate data and DSS processing. It is fed by the ODS and the I & T layer and, in turn, feeds the data marts. In addition, some direct analysis—primarily by explorers—is done at the data warehouse itself.

Drawn to scale, the data warehouse is significantly larger than other components of the CIF. The size of the warehouse is determined by how much historical data is to be contained within it and at what level of detail the data is to be stored.

There are very different characteristics of the data feeds into and out of the data warehouse. The differences center around the volume of data that passes over the feed, the timing of the feed, the mode the feed operates in, and the processing that occurs as a result of the feed.

Some of the more important technological challenges of the data warehouse center around the management of the data volume found in the warehouse and the unpredictable nature of the processing that occurs against the data.

Eventually, the demands for information and analytics exceed what can be provided by the data warehouse. A new information construct is needed that can turn the integrated data provided by the data warehouse into information. This component of the corporate information factory is called the data mart and will be discussed in the next chapter.

CHAPTER 8

The Data Mart Component

The data warehouse is at the heart of DSS/informational processing for the corporation. A data warehouse is often the first place integrated data is found in the corporation and is the appropriate place for historical data.

The data warehouse, however, is not the answer to all the problems of DSS processing for the following reasons:

- As the data warehouse evolves, it becomes increasingly difficult to access because its design evolves to efficiently integrate and manage large volumes of quality data. This resulting design generally does not present the data in a legible format or in a fashion that optimizes query performance.

- The data warehouse is a truly corporate utility, so its data is not stored in an optimal fashion for any given department.

- The data warehouse is used by many people, so considerable competition exists to get to the resources required to get inside the data warehouse.

- The large volumes and organization of data in the data warehouse require so much storage and processing power that the cost of DSS computing facilities is very expensive.

For these reasons, individual DSS analysts are finding that as a data warehouse grows in size and maturity, they are attracted to another sort of DSS structure. This structure is the data mart.

What Is a Data Mart?

A data mart is a collection of data tailored to the DSS processing needs of a particular department. It is a subset of a data warehouse that has been customized to fit the needs of a department. Alternatively, a data mart can become a resource shared by multiple departments in which common analytical needs exist (e.g., profitability analysis). Typically, data is denormalized, pruned, and summarized as it passes from the data warehouse to the data mart. Usually, many data marts attach to a data warehouse. Departments in which data marts are often found include marketing, finance, accounting, engineering, and actuarial. Figure 8.1 depicts a data mart.

Data marts have some degree of kinship with a data warehouse, but they have their own distinctive characteristics as well. Figure 8.2 details some of the salient characteristics of a data mart.

A data mart is a subset of a data warehouse, containing a small amount of detailed data and a generous portion of summarized data. It contains a limited amount of history, significantly less history than might be found in the data warehouse. The data in the data mart is customized to address the needs of the department to which it belongs and the DSS tool(s) selected for use.

Only one legitimate feed exists into the data mart; that feed comes from the data warehouse. Unless some unusual circumstance transpires, little or no data exchange occurs from one data mart to another. If there needs to be an exchange of data, the data to be exchanged is first passed to and stored at the data warehouse. When housed at the data warehouse, the data then is passed to the data mart that would like to share the data. By following this discipline of exchange, reconcilability of data is maintained across the architecture.

The Appeal of the Data Mart

There are many reasons why the data mart becomes so attractive as the data warehouse matures:

- **Control.** A department can completely control the data and processing that occurs inside a data mart. When a department does its own processing from the data warehouse, the department must share resources and facilities with other departments that are also using the data warehouse. In some cases, the sharing of facilities can be very restrictive and uncomfortable.

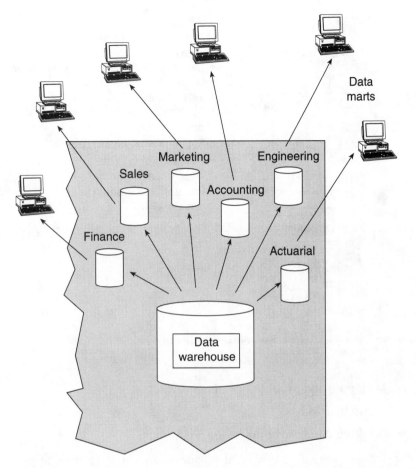

Figure 8.1   Data marts emanate from the data warehouse and feed the DSS needs of different departments.

- **Cost.** Because the department wants to analyze only a subset of data found in the data warehouse, the cost of storage and processing is substantially less when the department moves the desired data off to a departmental machine. Because the departmental machine is significantly smaller than the machine that houses the data warehouse, it is less expensive—in terms of total cost and unit cost as well.

- **Customization.** As data passes into the data mart from the data warehouse, the data is customized to suit the peculiar needs of the department. The data that comes from the warehouse can:

  - Have its keys restructured
  - Be resequenced

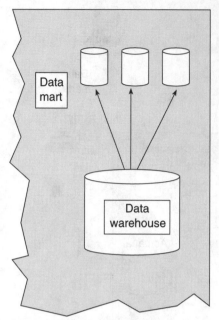

Data Marts
- A subset of data warehouse data
- Denormalized, pruned, and summarized
- Limited amount of history
- Very flexible
- Customized for departmental reporting and analysis
- Supports a variety of DSS tools
- Built according to the departmental data model
- Processors dedicated to department

Figure 8.2 The data mart in the context of the CIF.

- Be merged and pruned
- Be summarized
- Be edited and converted

In short, there are some powerful reasons why the data mart appears as an attractive augmentation to the data warehouse.

The appeal of data marts grows as the volume of the data in the data warehouse increases. As long as the data warehouse is small, the attraction of the data mart is not manifested. But as time passes, and the volume of the data and number of users grows, data marts become increasingly alluring.

The essence of a data mart is its flexibility and accessibility. Because much less data is in a data mart than a data warehouse, the data mart can accommodate queries and requests of many sizes and varieties, at almost any time of day.

The Data Warehouse to the Data Mart Interface

One of the important components of the corporate information factory is the intranet connection between the data mart and the data warehouse.

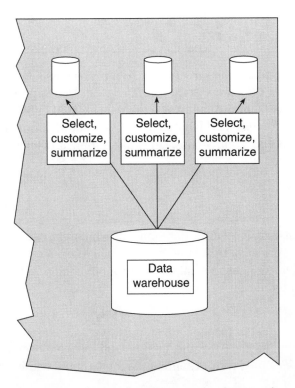

Figure 8.3 The interface between the data warehouse and the data marts is one in which data warehouse data is selected, summarized, and customized. There is one interface for each department.

Figure 8.3 shows that as data is collected into the data mart from the data warehouse, it is selected, customized, and summarized. The flow of data is one that is unidirectional, from the data warehouse to the data mart. The flow occurs on an as-needed, requested basis, as demands are made to the data warehouse to flow data to the data mart. As a rule, the volume of data that flows over the interface is minimal, at least in comparison to the volumes of data that flow elsewhere in the CIF. That is, after the initial load. Initial loads for the data mart can be very large as compared to ongoing incremental loads.

There is a separate flow and demand schedule for each department. There is almost never a consolidation of requirements for multiple departments for the coordination of the flow across the data warehouse to the data mart interface.

The programs that control the activity for the flow are normally created and maintained by the individual departments. It is only under very unusual circumstances that a DWA or a systems programmer would write the code that controls the flow of data into the data mart. The exception would be when a data mart was being created as a shared cross-departmental resource.

Different Kinds of Data Marts

There are three popular kinds of data marts. The first represents a simple sample, subset, or summary of the data warehouse. The other two support a style of analysis referred to as Online Analytical Processing (OLAP): Multidimensional Online Analytical Processing (MOLAP) data marts and Relational Online Analytical Processing (ROLAP) data marts. Let's take a look at these two types of data marts in more detail.

MOLAP Data Marts

The first type of data mart is a MOLAP data mart in which the data is loaded into the data mart in a very structured manner and where *dimensions* of the data are created. Typical dimensions might be product, time, and location. There are usually a limited number—four to six—of dimensions for a MOLAP data mart.

After the dimensions are created for the data mart, the data can be summarized along any number of dimensions. After the summarizations have been created, the data can then be *drilled down*, from summarization to detail within the confines of the data mart.

The essence of a MOLAP data mart is a very high degree of flexibility and performance when the data has been loaded. Ironically, in order to achieve a highly flexible structure, the data must be subjected to a highly inflexible amount of processing in order to prepare the data for entry into the multidimensional data mart.

ROLAP Data Marts

The second kind of data mart is a ROLAP data mart. The processing is much more general in a ROLAP data mart than in a MOLAP data mart. The aim of ROLAP is to provide a multidimensional view of data using proven relational DBMS—two-dimensional—technology (Oracle, Informix, Sybase, etc.). In contrast, a MOLAP data mart facilitates this using specialized multidimensional DBMS technology. The amount of transformation and preparation of the data prior to entry into the ROLAP data mart is significantly less than the preparation required for entry into the MOLAP data mart environment.

It is of interest that many MOLAP data marts relate to the financial area because of the simplicity of business dimensions—few and stable—and demands for fast and predictable performance. In contrast, ROLAP data marts have become very popular in areas that are willing to trade off predicable performance for the flexibility to manage and quickly alter large numbers of complex dimensions. ROLAP data marts are generally found in the areas of marketing, sales, and service.

A given department may have both a MOLAP and a set of ROLAP databases contained in the data mart. Indeed, there may be many different types of data mart databases and analytic tools within a department.

Star Join Schema and Data Marts

The physical database design structure known as a star join schema has a particular affinity for the data mart in support of ROLAP (see Figure 8.4). Star join schema organizes data so that it is easy to navigate and visualize. As a result, this database design technique greatly facilitates the simple and speedy access of analysis of data.

A star join schema is made up of fact tables and dimensions. The fact table represents the types of data that occur in great volume. The dimension tables represent smaller tables that are prejoined to the data in the fact table by means of a foreign key relationship. Because a star join schema generally entails some physical denormalization, there is the implication that star join schemas are optimal for only one type and class of processing (i.e., a star join schema is not

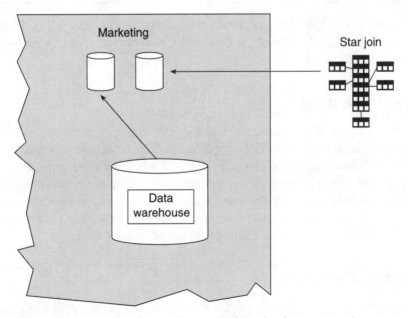

Figure 8.4 Star join schemas fit very nicely in the data mart environment.

a structure that is useful for a general representation of data). Such an observation is true because a star join schema optimizes processing for one user or set of users and deoptimizes access of data for all other users.

This trade-off of optimization and deoptimization is indeed an accurate statement of facts. But because a data mart is built for a department, a general pattern of access and analysis can be predicted for the department. The database designer is safe in specifying what the design of the star join schema will look like.

Note that such a proclamation cannot be made for data warehouses. Because so many different kinds of people are using a data warehouse, it is almost impossible to say that there is a dominant usage pattern for the data in the warehouse. That is why the star join schema is generally not a good fit for the data warehouse. Stated differently, when the data warehouse is structured under a star join or snowflake structure, the data warehouse will provide optimal access for one group of people at the expense of everyone else. This produces a severe diseconomy of scale that is felt across the organization.

Such is not the case at all for a department. A much more homogeneous pattern of data processing exists for a department, because there are fewer people, and those people have a similar interest and perspective in the execution of DSS processing.

Processing at the Data Mart

There are many kinds of processes that occur at the data mart. Figure 8.5 shows one way of classifying the processing that occurs there, as either repetitive or unpredictable.

Repetitive Processing

One type of processing that occurs at the data mart is repetitive processing; it is predictable and typically done by farmers. The repetitive processing can be done in a daily cycle, a weekly cycle, and so forth. Repetitive processing is generally found where companies are tracking key performance metrics that measure the overall health of the corporation. These metrics provide corporate decision makers insights into product profitability, customer churn, customer lifetime value, market share, fraud growth, and so forth.

Unpredictable Processing

The second style of processing done at the data mart is unpredictable processing. This occurs when a farmer starts to become curious and starts to turn into

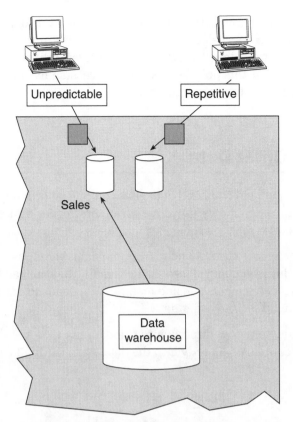

Figure 8.5 Two basic kinds of processing are found in the data mart environment: repetitive processes and unpredictable processes.

an explorer. The unpredictable processing that occurs in this case can be of many varieties, from a simple addition of variables that have not been regularly added before to the selection and comparison of information over time that has never before been considered. Very often the unpredictable processing that occurs at the data mart leads to the need for drill-down processing, which occurs when a unit of summary data requires explanation. In drill-down processing, questions are asked, such as:

- What data went into this summarization?
- What data was excluded from this summarization?
- When was the summarization made?
- What formula was used in this summarization?

The simplest basis for drill-down starts with data that is found in the data mart, assuming a calculation has been made there. However, drill-down does not have to stop with data found in the data mart. It can continue by asking the following questions: What data was selected in the data warehouse for the data mart? How was the selection done? How was customization done as data passed into the data mart? At this point, drill-down processing has proceeded down into the data warehouse from the data mart.

First Order, Second Order Data

Two types of data are stored and managed in the data mart: first order data and second order data. Figure 8.6 shows the creation of first order and second order data in the data mart.

Data that is placed directly into the data mart from the data warehouse can be called first order data. But when placed into the data mart, the data can be further manipulated. Subsequent calculation and manipulation leads to data in the data mart that can be called second order data.

External data can legitimately flow directly into the data mart, as seen in Figure 8.7. When external data flows directly into the data mart, the implication is

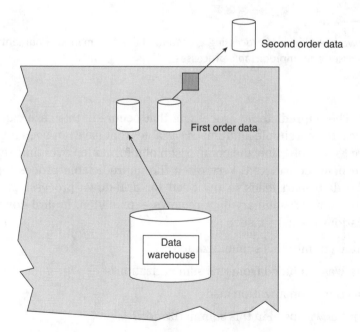

Figure 8.6   Two types of data are found in the data mart: first order data and second order data.

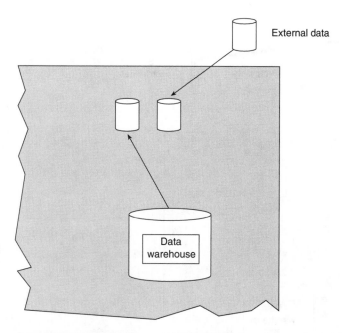

External data

Figure 8.7 External data can be loaded into a data mart directly when there is no other corporate use for the external data.

that the external data has no other use or application for any other data mart. If there is another use of the external data, it needs to first flow into the data warehouse and then flow from the data warehouse into the data mart.

Metadata

Another type of data found in the data mart is that of metadata. Data mart data does not have the rigid, formal metadata infrastructure that data warehouses have. Instead, metadata at the data mart comes in the flavor of metadata that is trapped and stored in the tools of access and analysis that are found in the data mart. Figure 8.8 shows that metadata is an integral part—if informal—of the data mart environment.

Metadata can be a very important part of the data mart environment. It can be useful to the farmer on those occasions when a farmer wishes to turn into an explorer. However, metadata, at the data mart, must be a natural and unconstraining part of the environment. The farmer at the data mart needs to have a great deal of autonomy and does not need a technology that limits what processing can and cannot be done.

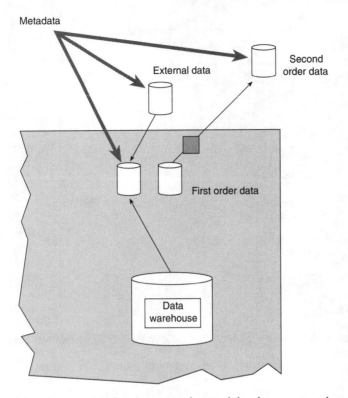

Metadata

External data

Second order data

First order data

Data warehouse

Figure 8.8 Metadata is a normal part of the data mart environment.

In some cases, it is desirable to have metadata control and management over more than one data mart. There can be a central data mart metadata controller that sits over more than one data mart, as suggested by Figure 8.9.

Summary

As data warehouses grow, another structure becomes attractive at the departmental level: a data mart. A data mart is a customized subset of data taken from the data warehouse; each department creates its own data mart.

In the final analysis, data marts provide business units the control and ability to interpret data warehouse data as needed to address their evolving business needs. In addition, data marts provide business units the autonomy to select and employ best-of-breed techniques and technology as their needs dictate. With this control and autonomy comes responsibility and accountability. Departments can no longer work independently. These business units must become active members of the corporate information community. They must be prepared to help define and enforce the use of data as a corporate resource.

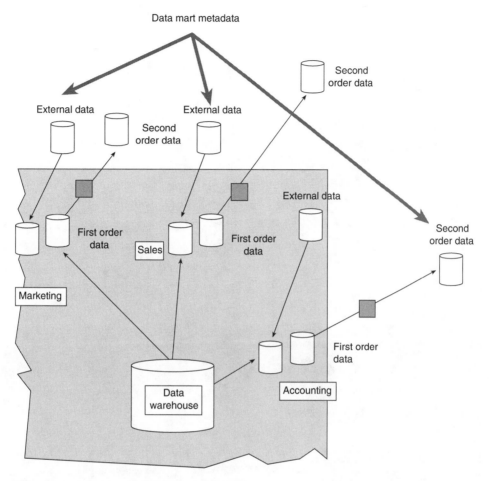

Figure 8.9   One possibility is for there to be a "super" metadata structure for more than one data mart.

There are three popular kinds of data marts—sample/subset/summary, MOLAP, and ROLAP. Each of these has its own unique characteristics.

Processing within the data mart can be classified as either repetitive or unpredictable against data that is primary or secondary. Metadata is seamlessly integrated into the DSS analyst environment and provides details necessary to understand, navigate, and use data mart data.

Now that we have talked about the components of the corporate information factory that integrate data—I & T layer and the data warehouse—and deliver information—the data mart—in support of strategic decision making, let's take a close look at cousins to the data mart, the *exploration warehouse* and *data mining warehouse*.

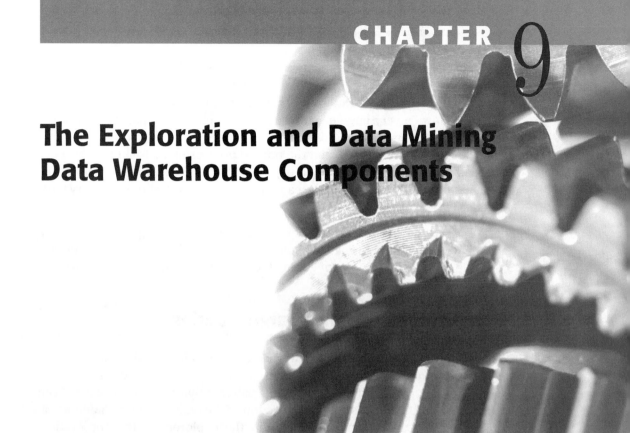

CHAPTER 9

The Exploration and Data Mining Data Warehouse Components

To understand the need for the exploration warehouse, consider the stance of the data warehouse administrator when faced with a large query—say a 72-hour query (as seen in Figure 9.1).

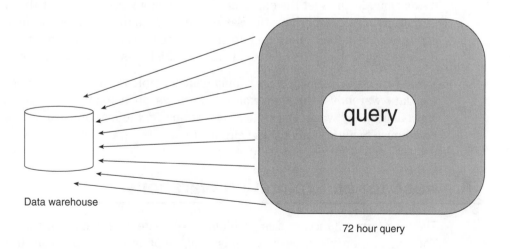

Data warehouse

query

72 hour query

Figure 9.1 What happens when the 72-hour query attempts to execute against the data warehouse?

The normal data warehouse administrator takes a firm stand and does not allow the large query to execute against the data warehouse. The rationale the data warehouse administrator offers is plausible. If the data warehouse administrator allows a very large query to go into execution against the data warehouse, everyone will suffer from poor performance. The large query will drain huge amounts of resources, and the normal processing that all other users of the data warehouse have come to expect will not be possible. Therefore, the administrator tells the analyst she cannot use the data warehouse for very large queries.

Is this a reasonable stance? From the standpoint of the average user of the data warehouse, this is rational and reasonable. With that said, this stance is not reasonable from the standpoint of getting the full value out of the warehouse.

How the Explorer Handles Large Queries

There are legitimate users of the warehouse (typically called explorers) who submit large queries. Explorers are usually "out of the box" thinkers—they are very unpredictable and look for business patterns that have never before been discovered. Although it is a natural reaction of the data warehouse administrator to protect the data warehouse from the explorers of the corporation, reserving the data warehouse for only the people who submit small requests and queries limits the potential of the data warehouse environment.

One stance the data warehouse administrator can take is to not let the explorers into the data warehouse at all. Another stance the data warehouse administrator can take is to let the explorers into the data warehouse over the annual Christmas break, or perhaps the Easter break. Yet a third stance is to make the explorers break their query up into small pieces and allow the explorer to run the query from the hours of 1:00 A.M. to 5:00 A.M. for as many nights as it takes.

These Draconian measures are simply unacceptable for the long-term usage of the data warehouse by the explorer. Perhaps on a temporary basis, these approaches may work. But on a long-term basis, the explorer cannot use the warehouse facilities under these circumstances.

The Need for an Exploration Warehouse

The long-term solution to this problem is to create an exploration warehouse. The exploration warehouse is a physically separate structure from the data warehouse. It is a facility dedicated exclusively to exploration processing. The exploration warehouse is a place where the explorer can turn to in order to do as much exploration processing as desired. There is no performance conflict with the regular users of the data warehouse, because the explorer isn't using it. The exploration warehouse then is a place where the explorer has a unique and dedicated facility for exploration processing, undisturbed by other influences.

The Evolution of the Exploration Warehouse

The evolution of the exploration warehouse and data mining warehouse has predictable evolution, as shown in Figure 9.2.

The origins of the exploration warehouse go back to the data warehouse itself. The data warehouse contains detailed and historical data that forms a foundation for exploratory processing. In the early days of exploration processing, the

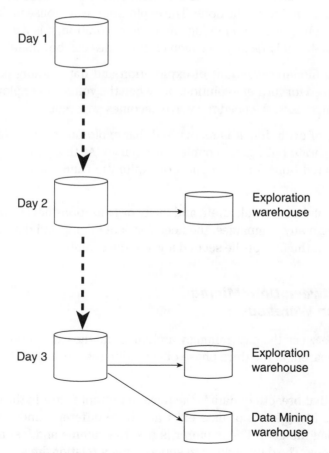

Figure 9.2   There is a predictable progression that companies follow when building the exploration warehouse and the data mining warehouse.

data warehouse served as an adequate foundation. Today, as long as the corporation is doing only a minimal amount of exploration processing, the data warehouse suffices.

But when the exploration community becomes more sophisticated, the data warehouse has some shortcomings, including:

- It contains no or scant external data.
- It undergoes periodic refreshment independent of the needs of the explorer.
- It is quite restrictive as to the hours when exploration can be done

For these reasons, as the exploration community matures something else is needed.

The second step in the evolution is the creation of an exploration warehouse. In this phase, the exploration warehouse is a general-purpose database in which exploration and data mining can be done. The exploration warehouse makes little or no distinction between data mining and data exploration; it is a granular, temporary, statistic-friendly facility to which large queries can be submitted.

As long as only a moderate amount of exploration and data mining is done here, there is no need for further evolution, but when the volume of exploration and data mining increases, the need to evolve becomes apparent.

In the third phase of evolution, it is recognized that exploration and data mining are indeed separate but tightly coupled disciplines. At this point separate databases are created—one for the support of exploration and one for the support of data mining.

Nowhere is the evolution a quick affair, and many organizations never arrive at the third level. For many companies, the need for data mining and data exploration can be met at the first or the second level of the evolution.

Differences between Data Mining and Exploration Warehouses

The differences between the data mining warehouse and the exploration warehouse become apparent at the third phase of evolution (as illustrated in Figure 9.3).

Figure 9.3 shows that breadth of data is the most important factor in the exploration warehouse. Many kinds of data exist and have different kinds of relationships entwining the data. The explorer is free to examine and test a wide range of possibilities. The data is there to support many relationships.

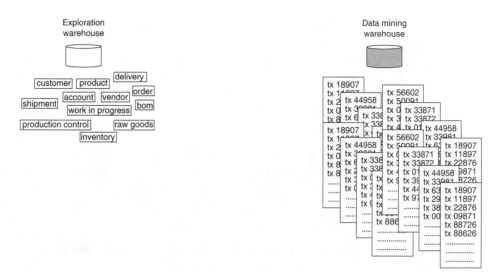

Figure 9.3   The differences between the data mining warehouse and the exploration warehouse.

The data miner, on the other hand, has a database in which many occurrences of data exist. There is very little variation in the data type found in the data mining warehouse, but many occurrences of data exist.

The differences between the types of data found in the two types of warehouses are shaped by the different needs of the explorer and the data miner. The explorer looks for patterns of data and formulates hypotheses and assertions about why the patterns exist. The data miner takes those hypotheses and assertions and tests the validity of them. There are then very different activities done by the explorer and the data miner, even though the activities are tightly interrelated. The databases that support the different, but related, cast of characters reflects the basic differences.

Feeding the Exploration Warehouse

The exploration warehouse is fed from three sources: external data, the data warehouse, and alternative storage.

External data is especially valuable to the explorer because it gives the explorer perspective from outside the corporation. After the outside perspective is developed, it can be contrasted to internal information. The effect of contrasting external data to internal data can be very dramatic and very useful.

The second source of data for the exploration warehouse is that of the data warehouse itself. The data warehouse contains both detailed and historical data, but seldom is the data warehouse merely copied to the exploration warehouse.

There are several reasons why the data warehouse is not just copied to the exploration warehouse. The first reason is that the data warehouse contains many types of data that simply are not germane to the analysis being done by the explorer. If the explorer is doing an analysis of the efficiency of production, it is unlikely that they will want to see data about human resources, finance, and sales promotions. The explorer can eliminate whole categories of data that reside in the data warehouse.

The second reason why data is not merely copied into the exploration warehouse from the data warehouse is that the data warehouse administrator (DWA) recognizes that some amount of simple, limited transformation will be beneficial. For example, the data warehouse administrator may wish to create "convenience" fields in the exploration warehouse.

Suppose the data warehouse contains the following data elements:

- Gross sales amount
- Sales tax
- Sales commission
- Shipment charges

The DWA knows that the explorer is interested only in the net sales amount, so she creates a new field in the exploration warehouse called "net sales." Net sales is calculated by:

net sales = gross sales amount − (sales tax + sales commission + shipment charges)

The data warehouse administrator places only the net sales field in the exploration warehouse because she knows that this value is the only thing the explorer wishes to see. In doing so, the data warehouse administrator saves the explorer the work of having to make a calculation every time the exploration warehouse database is accessed.

This simple transformation of convenience can save a great deal of time and confusion.

These practices illustrate why it is said that the data warehouse is not merely a copy of the exploration warehouse.

A third source of data for the exploration warehouse is alternative storage, in which older and bulk data residing in the corporate information factory is kept. Alternative storage is a treasure trove of data for the exploration warehouse. Data can pass directly to the exploration warehouse, rather than going through the data warehouse in order to move it to the exploration warehouse environ-

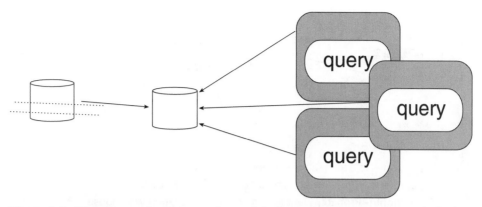

Figure 9.4 When the exploration warehouse is built, as many long queries as desired can be run against the data warehouse with no ill effects.

ment. Instead data can be passed directly to the exploration warehouse from alternative storage.

The fact that data can be passed directly to the exploration warehouse may seem inconsequential. It is anything but inconsequential. By moving data directly to the exploration warehouse from alternative storage, huge amounts of infrastructure costs are avoided.

Isolating Explorer Processing

Figure 9.4 shows that after the exploration warehouse is built, explorer processing is isolated from the data warehouse environment. The explorer can execute as many long-running queries as desired with no consideration for the damage to performance for the regular users of the data warehouse environment.

When Is the Exploration Warehouse Needed?

One of the interesting aspects of the exploration warehouse is that of the immediacy of the need for an exploration warehouse. Some companies need an exploration warehouse more than others. The need of a corporation depends entirely on how many long-running queries they execute. Figure 9.5 shows a simple chart that determines the degree of need for the exploration warehouse.

Figure 9.5 shows that if a company executes long-running queries infrequently, it will not need an exploration warehouse, but frequent long-running queries will make an exploration warehouse necessary.

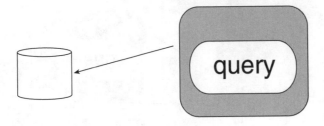

1 per year—No exploration warehouse needed
1 per quarter—Probably no exploration warehouse needed
1 per month—Probably want to consider an exploration warehouse
1 per week—Need an exploration warehouse
1 per day—Cannot get by without an exploration warehouse

Figure 9.5 How many long-running queries can be run against a data warehouse before an exploration warehouse is needed?

Why Are Explorer Queries So Long?

One of the interesting aspects of the expoloration warehouse environment is the question, why are explorer queries so long? Are explorer queries so long because the explorer doesn't know how to write queries efficiently? In most cases, the answer is no. There is a very good reason why explorer queries are so long. Explorer queries must look at:

■ Detailed data

■ Historical data

■ Data that has been configured in an unusual way

The result is a long-running query. When you multiply

$$\text{detail} \times \text{history} \times 14 \text{ ways joins/merges}$$

The result is a long running query.

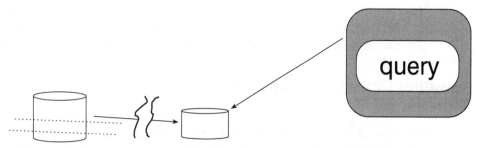

Figure 9.6 One feature of exploration warehouses is that they often require the data being analyzed to be *frozen*. Any update done to the data will ruin the capability of iterative analysis.

Freezing Exploration Data

One unique feature of exploration warehouses is the need to *freeze* data inside the exploration warehouse during analysis. Figure 9.6 illustrates this unique feature.

In most database environments, it is desirable to have as up-to-date data as possible. Updates are done as soon as the corporation is aware of a changing condition. But exploration warehouses require almost the exact opposite treatment.

One type of analysis done against exploration warehouses is *iterative analysis.* In an iterative analysis, the analyst tries first one analysis and then another. One result leads to the next analysis. In this manner an analyst proceeds through complex and large amounts of data. Because the results of one analysis set the stage for the next analysis, the analyst wants the data to remain stable.

As a simple example, suppose that the explorer wishes to calculate the number of adjustment requests made to phone bills during a day. The analyst determines that approximately 56 phone adjustment requests come in during the day. Now suppose that the explorer wishes to analyze how many adjustment requests are subsequently authorized by the telephone company. The analyst finds out that 75 adjustments are authorized. How can it be that 56 adjustment requests are entered each day, and the phone company authorizes 75 of them?

The problem is either in the data or in the fact that the data has changed from one analysis to the next. One possibility is that the explorer has defined an adjustment request one way for the first analysis and another way for the second analysis. If that is the case, then the explorer needs to determine a consistent definition for the data. Another possibility is that the data has been updated from one analysis to the next. The first analysis was done mid-month, and the second analysis was done at month's end. Between mid-month and month's end, a large number of adjustments were made. Because the data changed, the explorer cannot tell what is what.

In order for the explorer to be able to do an effective analysis, the data must be stable. After the explorer has completed an analysis, the data can be updated, but during the analytical process itself, it is dangerous to update the data.

Granular Data in the Exploration Warehouse

Another characteristic of the exploration environment is the need for granular data for analysis. Figure 9.7 shows that granular data makes up the fabric of the data base for exploration.

Granular data is so important for the exploration warehouse environment for several reasons. The first reason is that the more summarized the data is, the less chance that the explorer will find the patterns that are of interest to her. Summarizing data masks important details.

The second reason why the analyst needs granular data is because the data that is being analyzed must be looked at one way; then in the next analysis the very

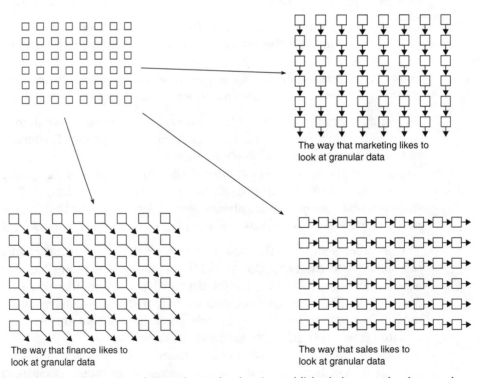

The way that marketing likes to look at granular data

The way that finance likes to look at granular data

The way that sales likes to look at granular data

Figure 9.7 When a foundation of granular data is established, the granular data can be examined in many different ways.

same data must be looked at another way. The only way the data can be this flexible is for the data to be stored at the lowest level of granularity, along with attributes of data that allow the data to be reoriented.

Loading Data into the Exploration Warehouse

In conjunction with the need to periodically freeze the loading of data into the exploration warehouse is the need to carefully manage the loading of the data into the exploration warehouse. Figure 9.8 shows the iterative approach to loading data into the exploration warehouse.

When an analyst finishes one phase of work, she often discovers that more data is needed. More data may be needed because:

- A different type of data is needed. More attributes must be added.

- More occurrences of data are needed. There is not enough of the data in the current version of the exploration warehouse to form a statistically meaningful opinion.

- Fresh new data is needed to keep the analysis as relevant is possible.

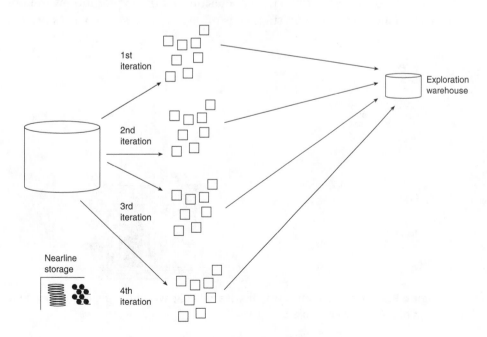

Figure 9.8   The exploration warehouse is loaded incrementally.

When the analyst deems that the exploration warehouse can be expanded, more data is added. For this reason, the exploration warehouse is built in iterations.

Skunk Works–the Only Way to Fly

In addition, the exploration warehouse is built as a *skunk works* or "under the covers" project in most instances. Figure 9.9 shows the ad hoc nature of the exploration warehouse.

The main reason why exploration warehouse projects are often built "under the covers" is that the costs are often hard to justify. The reason why they are so hard to cost justify goes back to the very nature of exploration processing itself.

In many ways, the explorer is like a baseball player—in particular a home run hitter. A home run in baseball is a spectacular event. But the reverse side to the glory of hitting a home run is that this hitter often strikes out.

Similarly, explorers sometimes achieve spectacular results, but often they fail to find anything terribly startling or useful for the corporation. When an explorer finds nothing, managers feel foolish in sponsoring the exploration warehouse effort. Furthermore, explorers often find it impossible to predict what they will find. The explorer simply "has a hunch." Business men don't like to invest in uncertainty. Sponsoring an exploration warehouse is simply too risky. All of which leads to the conclusion that the exploration warehouse—at least in the small, nascent stages—is often built as a *skunk works* project.

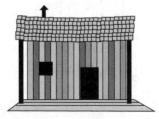

Figure 9.9 Most exploration warehouses are built away from the corporation in the form of a skunk works project.

Data Marts and the Exploration Warehouse

To an outside observer, the data mart and the exploration warehouse appear to have a great deal in common. In fact it has been suggested that the data mart and the exploration warehouse are the same thing. This is not the case at all. From an architectural standpoint, significant differences exist between the data mart and the exploration warehouse. Some of the differences between the exploration warehouse and the data mart include:

- **Granularity.** The exploration warehouse contains highly granular data; the data mart contains highly denormalized data.
- **Requirements.** The data mart is built after requirements have been gathered; the exploration warehouse is built because requirements are not known.
- **Technology.** The exploration warehouse is supported by statistically oriented analytical technology; the data mart environment is supported by end-user accessible technology.
- **Users.** The data mart user is typically a mid management decision maker; the exploration user is a statistically oriented mathematician.
- **Permanency.** The data mart is a permanent structure; the exploration warehouse is (usually) a temporary structure.

As you can see, there are in fact many differences between the data mart environment and the exploration environment.

Exploration Warehouses and Technology

The exploration environment can operate on a variety of technologies. One option is to operate on standard relational technology, which is fine for small, cursory analytical efforts. After the analytical effort grows in size and sophistication, however, other technology is in order.

Figure 9.10 illustrates some other technologies that are commonly used for exploration processing and data mining. (For an in-depth treatment of these two technologies, please refer to the book *The Exploration Warehouse*, by W. H. Inmon, R. H. Terdeman, and C. Imhoff, John Wiley, New York, NY 2000. This book goes into detail about the exploration.)

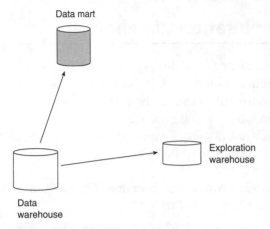

Figure 9.10 Significant differences exist between a data mart and a data warehouse.

Some Not So Obvious Benefits of the Exploration Warehouse

One benefit of the creation of the exploration warehouse (shown in Figure 9.11) is that the farmers and the explorers of the corporation are separated, naturally separating the workload. The small queries end up in the data mart and the data warehouse environment; the large queries end up in the exploration warehouse. Performance can now become optimal. The systems programmer can tune the data mart, data warehouse, and exploration warehouse environments optimally.

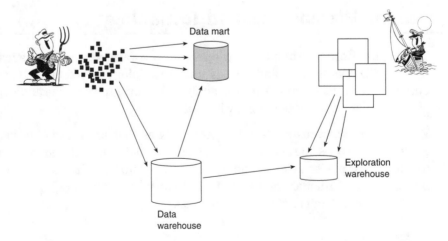

Figure 9.11 One effect of the exploration warehouse is the separation of farmers from explorers.

Summary

The exploration warehouse is born of the need to manage very large queries. As a rule, a data warehouse environment is not able to support a significant amount of large queries. Instead, a separate facility is built for a company to do **statistically analytical** processing.

This separate facility is called an exploration warehouse. At the beginning of the company's analysis, both exploration and data mining are done in the database and data warehouse or to a lesser degree, in the data mart. As time passes and the amount of exploration and data mining grow, some organizations create both an exploration warehouse and a data mining data warehouse.

The exploration warehouse is a structure rich in different types of data, but the data mining data warehouse is a structure rich in occurrences of data. Explorers find and interpret patterns in the exploration warehouse and form assertions and hypotheses. Data miners test the validity of these assertions and hypotheses.

So far, we have danced around a key storage component to the CIF, the *alternative storage*. It is here that the vast majority of infrequently used history is maintained. Let's now take a closer look at this adjunct to the data warehouse in more detail.

CHAPTER 10

The Alternative Storage Component

We have now talked about the components of the Corporate Information Factory (CIF) that help us analyze data contained in the data warehouse: data marts, operational data store, and exploration/data mining warehouse. These components also enable the warehouse to scale and extend its reach across the corporation. Now let's take a look at a component of the CIF that enables vast amounts of detail and history to be maintained in the warehouse efficiently and cost effectively—alternative storage.

Before we talk about alternative storage, we must first understand what is driving the need. As time passes, two realities strike corporations. The first reality is that the data volumes that collect in the data warehouse are overwhelming. The second reality is that as the volume of data grows, so does the cost of the infrastructure.

There are some powerful reasons why data in the warehouse grows at a rate never before witnessed by most corporations:

- Detailed data takes up more space than summarized or aggregated data.
- Deep history found in the data warehouses multiplies the size of the warehouse.

- Data warehouses are built with unknown requirements. This means that some data put into the warehouse will never be used.

- Summarized data is as important as detailed data. Summarized data is stored in data marts as well as the data warehouse.

As you can see, there are some very good reasons why data warehouses attract a lot of data. With the growth in data volumes come a host of new issues, including:

- Cost of the infrastructure

- Query and load performance issues

- System availability issues

Another issue related to growth of data is organizational acceptance and understanding of how to manage this data. The techniques and technology that worked well in the operational world, where there was only a modicum of data, simply do not apply to the world of data warehousing. The organization finds that it must learn how to function on a whole new terrain to cope with the data warehouse environment.

Growth of Dormant Data

Dormant data is data that is placed inside a data warehouse and is either never infrequently accessed. Dormant data exists at various levels of granularity—table, column, and row. In the early days of a data warehouse, when the volume of data is small, there is very little, if any, dormant data. But as the volume of data grows, the percentage of data used actually decreases and the amount of dormant data grows quite large, as depicted in Figure 10.1.

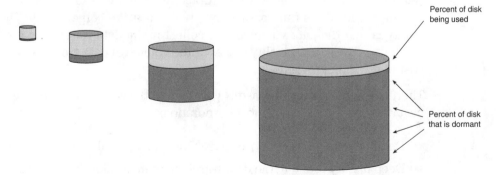

Figure 10.1 As data volume grows, the actual amount of disk storage being used decreases.

There are some fairly powerful reasons that data grows dormant in a data warehouse. Some of those reasons are:

Overestimation of the need for historical data. When the warehouse is first designed, the data demand is for five years of historical data. After the designer delivers five years of history, the user learns that for most processing only one or two years of history are needed.

Inclusion of data that is never needed for analysis. The data warehouse is designed to handle one sort of analysis that never bears fruit. As a consequence certain types of data are simply never accessed.

Creation of summary data that is used only once. It is very common for summary data to be placed in the warehouse. Unfortunately, few plan for managing these summary tables. As a result, the DWA doesn't know what summary tables to remove and plays it safe by not removing any of them.

The phenomenon of dormant data is one that is a normal and natural phenomenon. It simply happens that as the data volume grows, some data becomes dormant. At the rate that warehouses grow, a large amount of data grows dormant rather quickly. Now lets take look at a strategy for managing dormant data.

Managing Dormant Data

The solution to this problem is for the company to identify what data is dormant and move it away from data that is being actively used. Figure 10.2 shows that the bulk of the data is getting in the way of a small portion of the data that is being actively used.

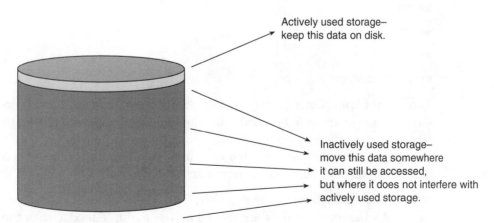

Actively used storage–
keep this data on disk.

Inactively used storage–
move this data somewhere
it can still be accessed,
but where it does not interfere with
actively used storage.

Figure 10.2 Dormant data gets in the way of data that is being actively used.

There are *many* benefits to performing the physical separation of active and inactive data including:

- Performance is greatly improved by moving dormant data away from actively used data.

- The cost of the warehouse drops dramatically by moving dormant data to a low-cost storage medium.

- The data can be designed to accommodate a very fine granularity of data.

- The warehouse can effectively extended to infinity.

These benefits will be examined in depth later in this chapter. But first, an important question must be answered: Where is the dividing line between actively and inactively used data?

Finding the Dividing Line

One approach to moving data to alternative storage is to simply pick an arbitrary dividing line and move all data over the line to alternative storage. For example, a company may pick 18 months as the dividing line. Any data earlier than 18 months stays in actively used storage and any data older than 18 months goes to alternative storage. Such a strategy is better than nothing at all. But picking an arbitrary dividing line is a very crude, and ultimately inefficient, thing to do. A much better approach to determining what should and should not be in actively used storage is to use an activity monitor. The activity monitor provides insight into data usage so that a more quantitative decision can be made regarding what data belongs in active storage versus inactive storage.

In order to be effective, the activity monitor needs to track data usage a several levels:

- Row level
- Table level
- Column level

There are implications to each of the different ways of examining dormant data. If a dormant table is found, then the table can be moved whole, to alternative storage. In the case of summary data, indeed, whole tables are found to be dormant. But the more normal case for dormant data is that rows of data and/or columns of data become dormant.

If rows of data are found to be dormant, they can be moved to alternative storage. But when rows of data are moved across multiple media, then the table exists on multiple media. There are some fairly severe technical implications to this splitting of data within the same table across different types of storage.

The third case is where entire columns of data are dormant. This is very common. Unfortunately, removing a column (or columns) of data very difficult in most database management systems (DBMSs) because such a removal requires a complete reorganization and redefinition of the data residing in the table. However, in some cases this type of reorganization is easily worth the resources expended.

One of the issues of monitoring the actively used storage component is the overhead and complexity of the monitoring itself. As a rule, every data unit needs to be monitored. Monitoring only sample information really does not do the job. In addition, if the monitoring software is complex, the software ends up needing as much management as the data warehouse itself. When looking at monitoring software, keep in mind the efficiency and simplicity of execution. The less intrusive the monitoring software the better.

Where the Activity Monitor Fits

Figure 10.3 shows that the activity monitor sits between the users of the system and the DBMS. The activity monitor looks at Structure Query Language (SQL) queries entering the DBMS and looks at the result set as it passes back to the end user.

When selecting an activity monitor, it is important to consider these questions:

- How much overhead does it require?
- How simple or complex is it to use?
- What level of detail and types of detail does it tape into?
- What technology does it work on?
- What does it cost?
- Can it be turned on permanently or only at selected moments?
- How many administrative resources are required to use it, and at what skill level?

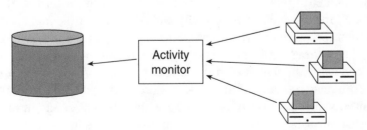

Figure 10.3 The activity monitor fits between the data warehouse and end user.

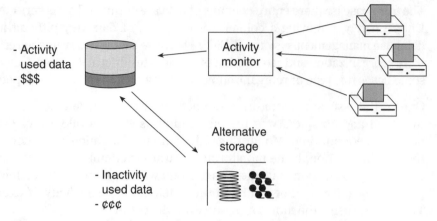

Figure 10.4 Moving dormant data to alternate storage.

Once the activity monitor is in place, the next step is to identify and move dormant data to alternative storage. This step is shown in Figure 10.4.

The activity monitor is used by the data warehouse administrator to identify dormant data. The dormant data is then moved to alternative storage. Once the data is moved to alternative storage, the high-performance disk environment is freed up. The only data left on high-performance disk storage is data that has a high probability of access.

Alternative Storage Technology

The alternative storage environment can be made up of (at least!) two types of technology, as depicted in Figure 10.5. These technologies can be classified as:

- Secondary storage (or "fat storage")
- Near-line storage

Secondary storage is disk storage that is slower, less cached, and less expensive than high-performance disk storage. Near-line storage is siloed tape storage, which has its origins in the mounted tape drives of yesterday. However, today's siloed tape is managed robotically and is much more compact and reliable than the tape drives of yesteryear. Siloed tape storage is less expensive than secondary storage. And both siloed tape storage and secondary storage are less expensive than high performance disk storage. One of the components necessary to managing data on alternative storage is that of a contents directory. A contents directory is an index as to where the data content is located inside alternative storage. In order for alternative storage to function properly, a contents directory must be part of the environment.

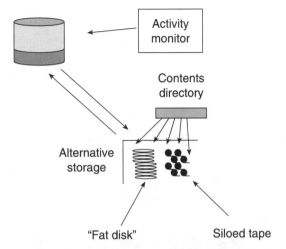

Figure 10.5 Alternative storage technology has one of two forms—secondary disk storage (also known as "fat storage") and near-line storage.

Meta Content Data

In order for alternative storage to be effective there needs to be a special type of data—meta content data. Meta content data describes the contents of data inside alternative storage. In many ways meta content data is like an index into the contents of alternative storage. The contents need to be made available to the cross media storage manager. It is through the meta content data that a query knows where to go inside alternative storage.

Cross Media Storage Manager

Although alternative storage is a powerful concept on its own, another technology is required in order for alternative storage to function. That component is generically called the cross media storage manager. Figure 10.6 shows where the cross media storage manager fits in the corporate information factory.

Cross media storage management entails seamlessly crossing the high-performance disk to alternative storage boundary. The cross media storage manager has the job of managing the flow of traffic to and from high-performance disk to alternative storage. When data is not being used frequently, the cross media storage manager moves the data to alternative storage. When there is a request for data from alternative storage, the cross media storage manager finds the data and makes it available to the requesting party.

Figure 10.6 illustrates how the cross media storage manager operates. Note: This example shows one way that cross media storage management can be

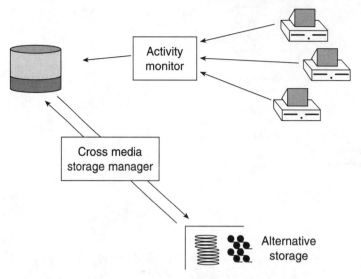

Figure 10.6 An essential component of the alternative storage environment is the cross media manager.

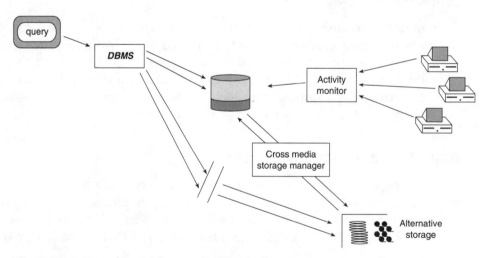

Figure 10.7 How data can be accessed inside alternative storage.

done. There are many variations to the implementation of cross media storage management.

In Figure 10.7, a query is submitted. The query sends its text to the DBMS. Once at the DBMS, the DBMS decides what data needs to be accessed. The DBMS sends different fetches to get the data. At this point the cross media storage manager intercepts those requests for data and adjusts the addresses for those pieces of data that reside in alternative storage. The requests are then sent either to the disk manager or to the alternative storage manager depending on where the data is located.

Figure 10.8 shows that after the data is located, the data is sent to the DBMS, which in turn sends it back to the query initiator as a result set.

Of course, if the request for data had not included data residing in alternative storage, then there would be no need to go to alternative storage. The effect of the activity monitor is to ensure that a minimum number of trips will have to be made to alternative storage.

Alternative Storage and Exploration Processing

The primary interface to alternative storage is to the data warehouse. This enables data to move back and forth between active and inactive storage mediums as usage should dictate. However, another important interface for alternative storage exists, between alternative storage and the exploration warehouse. Figure 10.9 shows this interface.

Data can be passed directly from alternative storage to the exploration warehouse. There is no need to place the data inside the data warehouse from alternative storage then move the data to the exploration warehouse.

Availability of data from alternative storage directly to the exploration warehouse greatly simplifies the job of the data warehouse administrator (DWA). The DWA does not have to worry about requests for data, which are used only

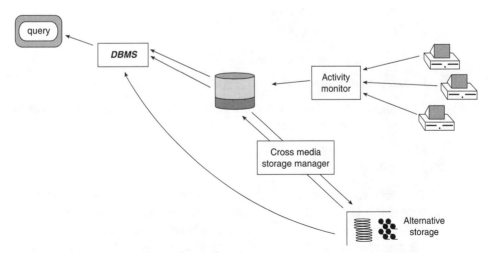

Figure 10.8 When located in alternative storage, data is returned directly to the DBMS.

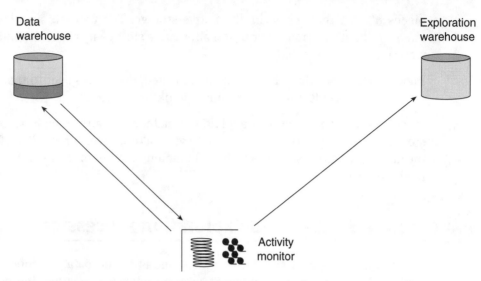

Figure 10.9 Interface between alternative storage and the exploration warehouse.

once in a blue moon, passing through high performance disk storage in order to get to the exploration warehouse. Instead, when explorers have their own environment, the high performance data warehouse remains free to process regularly occurring queries.

Why Use Alternative Storage?

Companies look at a variety of factors when determining whether or not to use alternative storage, including:

- Cost
- Optimizing query performance
- Level of granularity needed

The following sections look at these factors and demonstrate the advantages of moving to alternative storage.

Saving Money

The first reason companies use alternative storage is the cost differential between a large high-performance disk implementation of a data warehouse and an implementation where data is spread across high-performance disk storage and alternative storage. Depending on the type of alternative storage, there may be as much as two orders of magnitude difference between the costs of the two implementations. In a word, going to alternative storage for the placement of dormant data brings the cost of data warehousing down dramatically.

But significant cost savings is not the only reason that alternative storage is so appealing.

Better Query Performance

The stage is now set for optimal performance for the data warehouse. Figure 10.10 illustrates what happens when alternative storage has been loaded with dormant data and the space formerly occupied by dormant data is freed up.

The two queries shown in Figure 10.10 do exactly the same thing. The only difference is that they operate on different foundations of data. One query operates where all data is maintained on high-performance disk storage. The other

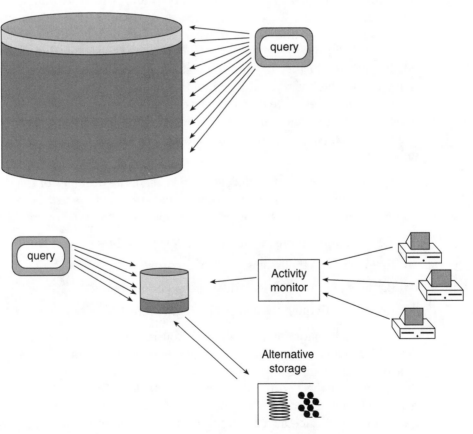

Figure 10.10 Contrast a query performance accessing active data in an environment with and without alternative storage. The latter is substantially faster.

query operates in an environment where dormant data has been moved off of the high-performance disk storage to alternative storage.

The query that operates on all high-performance disk storage uses a large percentage of its resources looking at and passing over dormant data. As much as 95 percent of the resources expended by this query is used scanning through data that is not germane to the analysis.

The query that operates on high-performance disk storage where dormant data has been removed operates *much* more efficiently than the other query. This query operates in an environment that does not contain dormant data; as a result the response time for queries in this environment is much faster.

Keeping Lowest Level of Granularity

Cost and performance are not the only reasons why companies go to alternative storage. Another important reason is its ability to store data at the lowest level of granularity. To control costs, it is common for a data warehouse implementation—without alternative storage—to limit detail history to the last twelve months and to summarize history beyond that point. Unfortunately, our ability to trend history beyond the last 12 months is constrained by what we knew about the business at the time the summary data was created. As time passes on, it is inevitable that summaries that were useful 12 months ago are no longer relevant business indicators worth tracking in the data warehouse. This leaves the company with summary data that is out of context and only marginally useful.

However, when alternative disk storage is used, the designer of the data warehouse has much more freedom to design the system at the lowest level of granularity. There are a number of industries that face this issue of granularity:

- Telecommunications, with their call-level detail records
- Retailing, with their sales and sku records
- Banking and finance, with their transaction records
- Airlines, with their passenger and flight records

With alternative storage, the data warehouse designer is free to go to as low a level of detail as is desired. This ability, in some ways, is the most important reason that organizations must include alternative storage as a foundation technology for their corporate information factory. Stated differently, an organization building a corporate information factory that chooses to use *only* high performance storage as a basis for storing data greatly limits the potential of their corporate information factory.

Vendor Implementations

Now that we have spent a bit of time discussing alternative storage and cross media management, let's take a look at some vendors have implemented these technologies.

Alternative Storage: Filetek

Alternative storage would only be a dream were it not for the software that allows data to be stored and managed on both disk storage and alternative storage. Following is a description of one of the software vendors for alternative storage.

FileTek's StorHouse® fits strategically in the corporate information factory architecture by uniquely combining relational database technology with the management of multi-level storage media. It is comprised of two components, StorHouse/SM and StorHouse/RM. Together the components comprise a comprehensive system for automating the management of massive amounts of detailed data and providing selective, row-level access to data through industry standard methods. Customer relationship management (CRM), e-business, enterprise resource planning (ERP), and enterprise data warehousing initiatives put ever-increasing demands on conventional database technologies. With the demand for data projected to grow over 100 percent per year for next several years, enterprises are searching for new approaches to managing and accessing information. StorHouse addresses the performance, data management, and economic challenges facing enterprises that need to deliver the right information to decision-makers, customer-care personnel, vendors, and customers too.

The corporate information factory architecture identifies databases and tools designed for specific functions. Operational data stores (ODS), data warehouses, exploration databases, data marts, on-line analytical processing (OLAP) tools, and alternative storage systems, among other technologies, comprise the CIF. StorHouse fits in the CIF architecture as the atomic data repository that uses alternative storage technologies. And detailed, atomic-level data—the fundamental transactions of the business—are at the heart of the CIF. Atomic data is defined as the detailed transaction data generated during the course of every business day. Atomic data appears in many places in the world of corporate business.

For a telecommunications company, call detail records represent atomic data. Retailers collect point-of-sale transactions and banks generate atomic data in the form of ATM, credit card, and teller transactions, to name a few. Increasingly, e-businesses are collecting clickstream details that identify customer patterns of interacting with Web sites. Atomic data is generated and collected in large volumes—typically date specific—may be structured or unstructured, and is most valuable when retained over time. An effective data storage strategy for the CIF will make these transaction-level details affordable, available, and manageable.

Affordability

StorHouse manages a hierarchy of storage devices, including cache, redundant arrays of independent disks (RAID), erasable and write-once-read-many (WORM) optical jukeboxes, and automated tape libraries. However, unlike conventional hierarchical storage management (HSM) systems, StorHouse provides direct, row-level access to data it manages, even when that data is stored on removable media such as tape. The financial benefits of managing large amounts of transaction-level details and other types of relational data that are infrequently used are significant. The current economics of storage media suggest that storing data on tape is approximately seven percent of the cost of magnetic disk. Automated tape library systems offer a practical way to store historical atomic data for many years if necessary. But it is not enough merely to store data. Applications that use the CIF architecture need to access data quickly and efficiently. Traditional database implementations use tape to back up and restore entire databases or portions of the database system. In this sense, tape is a "passive" medium that it is not used for direct data storage and querying. In contrast, StorHouse closely integrates the relational database management system (RDBMS) with storage management to make "near-line" storage behave as online devices.

Compatibility with an organization's investments in other databases and analytical tools also affects affordability. StorHouse integrates with the most commonly used relational database systems such as Oracle, DB2, and SQL Server. For instance, StorHouse transparently extends Oracle databases to give users access to StorHouse tables from Oracle-based applications. StorHouse tables can be defined as database links to the Oracle database using standard Oracle database administration and ODBC tools. As with other Oracle database links, administrators can build views of StorHouse tables and use table synonyms. Views and synonyms shield the user from having to know where database tables actually reside.

Similarly, StorHouse can extend a DB2 database using IBM's Data Joiner. DB2/Data Joiner manages metadata that describes the location of different data items and the capabilities of the StorHouse data source. When it receives a DB2 query, Data Joiner parses the query and develops a query access plan. Elements of this plan become queries to DB2 and StorHouse. Data Joiner then combines and further refines the result sets returned by the data sources and passes the answer set back to the application. Database transparency protects an organization's investments in applications as well as database administration tools and methods.

Availability

StorHouse processes industry-standard SQL '92. SQL is used to selectively "filter" the data required to satisfy an application or user's request for information. When StorHouse processes a query, it does not reload complete files to a database. Rather, it accesses rows directly from the storage media upon which they are stored. In many cases, a single large table may span more than one type of storage media such as RAID and tape. The StorHouse architecture greatly improves the availability of corporate data by making it accessible from multiple diverse applications and platforms. StorHouse supports industry-standard gateways such as ODBC, JDBC, and OLE/DB ADO. Commonly used ETL, OLAP, and query generation tools use these standard APIs. StorHouse also supports the IBM DRDA interface so that mainframe-based DB2 applications can transparently access StorHouse-managed data.

StorHouse-managed data is accessible through a variety of interfaces and applications. But it is not enough to bring tape online as a part of the CIF architecture. Data is a corporate asset that needs to be protected over long periods of time in spite of hardware failures that inevitably occur in storage devices of all kinds. StorHouse automatically duplexes data across multiple storage libraries. Even when a failure to an optical or tape library or drive occurs, a second copy of data is available to the application. A third, backup copy can also be created. StorHouse does not require any other backup procedures since they are handled automatically by the system.

Routine database maintenance can also make the data managed by those databases unavailable for extended periods of time. Database reorganization, backups, and database version upgrades that require data conversion are among the maintenance events that take data offline. StorHouse databases avoid these issues. StorHouse does not require database reorganization and automatically creates its own backup copies. Data written to a StorHouse server can be copied, rather than converted, to storage devices with new form factors. These capabilities and others are designed to maximize the availability of StorHouse-managed data.

Manageability

In addition to making data available through standard relational database techniques, StorHouse is a comprehensive data management solution. StorHouse/

Control Center is the system administration interface for systems and database administrators. It continually monitors the performance and reliability of the StorHouse server and its storage hardware devices. Administrators use Control Center to create databases and their schema, set storage management policies, and generate usage statistics and reports.

StorHouse differs from HSM systems in many respects. One of the storage management policies StorHouse administers is the automatic movement of data through the storage hierarchy. StorHouse migrates data from high-performance, higher cost storage media, to lower cost storage devices based upon the age and usage characteristics of the data. Data that is most frequently used is retained in the StorHouse performance buffer or on RAID while less active data moves to optical or tape. Likewise, when the StorHouse system detects that data stored on tape is becoming more frequently accessed, it will temporarily move it to RAID to improve its performance characteristics. StorHouse also provides the flexibility to separate indexes from the data those indexes represent. Indexes typically require rapid access and can be retained on higher performance storage longer than the data if necessary.

StorHouse solves other management issues associated with large data volumes. One of these is the sheer data volume that an atomic data store component in the CIF must load and index every day. StorHouse is capable of loading data in multiple parallel streams to meet throughput requirements. StorHouse supports concurrent loading of a single StorHouse table and can also load separate tables from a single load stream. StorHouse also builds its indexes "on-the-fly" to speed the data loading and indexing process. Other databases first load data, then create indexes in place. While this method is satisfactory for smaller data volume systems, it usually does not meet the needs of the enterprise CIF atomic data store. StorHouse loads data and builds indexes an order of magnitude faster than other conventional RDBMSs.

StorHouse includes other features that enhance its performance and manageability. These include a patented range index that speeds access to other indexes (i.e., value and hash). The system also sorts indexes based on data placement on storage volumes so that all the data required to satisfy a query is read from a volume before it is unmounted. Without this level of intelligent indexing and look-ahead queuing, systems that use removable media storage thrash as volumes are randomly mounted and unmounted while data is accessed.

StorHouse is a specialized server for managing and providing access to corporate information. It combines the flexibility and openness of a relational database with comprehensive data management capabilities. Enterprises use StorHouse to manage historical atomic data that "fuels" other informational and operational systems. For example, a telecommunications company uses StorHouse to feed data to an exploration warehouse that models customer network usage habits. Another company uses StorHouse to transparently extend a primary database for customer care applications. In both cases, the StorHouse system stores, manages, and provides access to the enterprise transactions—the atomic data. It sits at the heart of the CIF architecture to deliver economical and timely access to enterprise data assets of all types.

Cross Media Management: Unitree

There has been the notion of managing data on multiple storage media for many years. It is not a new idea. What is new is the notion of the granularity at which data has to be managed over the different media. For a number of years there has been what is called hierarchical storage management (HSM). In HSM, data resides on different storage media based on its probability of access.

But data is moved to one storage media or another based on entire tables or databases of data. The tables and databases that are found in a data warehouse are so large that it is simply unthinkable to manage them at this very gross level of granularity.

Instead, it makes much more sense to manage the movement of data at the row or block level. In a given table or database there will be many, many rows and blocks of data. An example of this style of data management across multiple storage media comes from Unitree. With Unitree, a row of data or a block of data can be moved from one storage media to another if its probability of access warrants. In doing so, a table or a database can be managed where some of the data resides on disk storage and other parts of the table or database reside on near line or secondary storage.

The Unitree software allows queries to be executed in a transparent manner. When issued the query it has no idea that the data it is looking for resides on anything but disk storage. The DBMS simply thinks that it is going to get data. Only the system software knows that some of the data being retrieved resides one place and other of the data resides elsewhere.

Of course, data still needs to be managed with the Unitree software. Data with a high probability of access needs to be placed in disk storage and data with a low probability of access needs to be placed elsewhere. And there needs to be constant monitoring of data to make sure the balance is kept equal over time.

Summary

In this chapter, the concept of alternative storage was introduced. Alternative storage becomes critical to the performance and cost effectiveness as the amount of dormant data grows in your data warehouse environment. Benefits to alternative storage include:

- Lowering the cost of ownership
- Extending the depth and breath of historical detail data that can be managed
- Improving query performance for everyone

Alternative storage takes two forms: secondary storage and near-line storage. Each of the physical form of storage has its own set of considerations.

Now that you are familiar with the components of the corporate information factory responsible for collecting, storing, and using data, let's take a look at the communication fabric that binds these components together—the *Internet/intranet*.

CHAPTER 11

The Internet/Intranet Components

T he components of the corporate information factory (CIF)—external world, applications, integration and transformation layer (I & T layer), operational data store (ODS), data warehouse, data marts, and exploration/data mining warehouse—do not stand alone. The different components of the architecture pass data in an orderly manner between themselves by means of a communications fabric. One way of thinking about this fabric is in terms of the Internet/intranet, though networks as a means to pass data actually existed long before the creation of intranets. The advent of the Internet/intranet has led to the formalization and categorization of the various types of intercommunications among the different architectural entities.

The Internet/intranet—from the perspective of the CIF—is the line of communication along which data flows and the different components interact with each other. Figure 11.1 shows that the Internet/intranet handles those communications that occur within the confines of the CIF.

The purpose of this communications fabric is to:

- Transport data
- Distribute processing

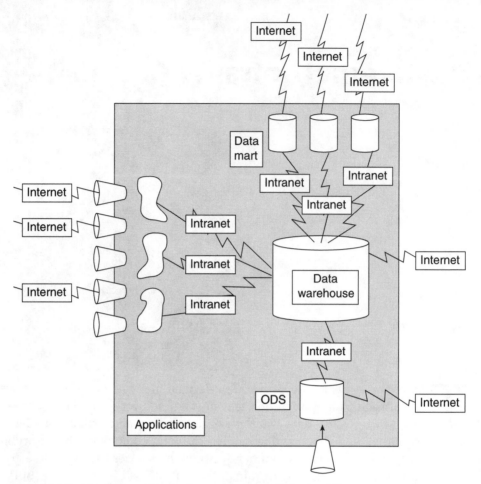

Figure 11.1 The different kinds of transmissions within the CIF.

- Schedule and coordinate activities
- Deliver status within the architecture
- Provide architectural connectivity
- Expose CIF capabilities to the external world

Issues of Communication

The communications between the different components of the CIF are governed by many factors:

- Volume and speed of data
- Capacity of network
- Mode of transport
- Cost of telecommunication lines
- Nature of the transport
- Availability of the fabric

Volume of Data

The first consideration is the volume of data that can be passed through the communications fabric, as shown in Figure 11.2.

The volume of data that must be pushed through the intranet is of great concern in the CIF because of the amount of data that is found there. The data warehouse, in particular, contains huge volumes of data that have passed from the applications or the ODS environment. In considering the proper technology for the communications fabric, the architect must first keep in mind the massive amount of data that must pass through the environment, and the people and processes that drive the movement of data.

Speed of Data

The second consideration is the speed with which data will pass through the intranet. Figure 11.3 shows that the speed of transmission is important, because

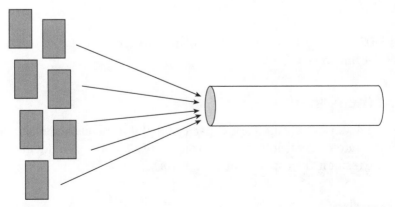

Figure 11.2 The volume of data to be transmitted–bandwidth–is the first parameter of interest to the CIF architect.

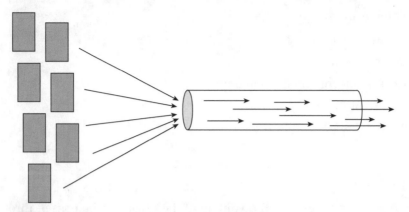

Figure 11.3 The speed of transmission is the second parameter of interest to the CIF architect.

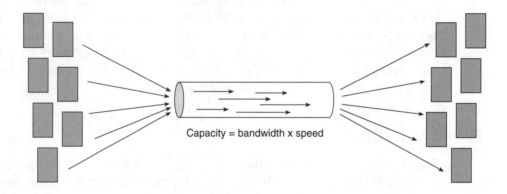

Capacity = bandwidth x speed

Figure 11.4 Line capacity is the third parameter of interest to the CIF architect.

of the ODS (that is, Class I ODS) and the need to accommodate the regular flow of massive amounts of data.

Capacity of the Network

Figure 11.4 shows that network capacity for the intranet is another concern. When the rate of data flow and the volume of data are in tandem with each other, the result is the capacity of the network.

Mode of Transport

Although capacity is a primary concern, it is not the only consideration in the overall architecture. The mode of transport is also a concern. Some communi-

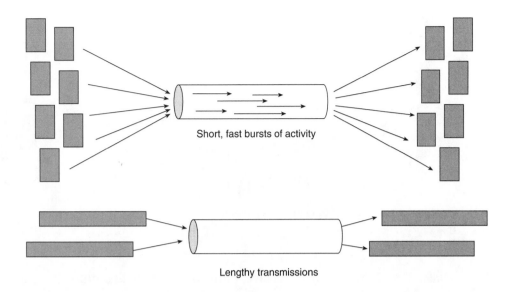

Short, fast bursts of activity

Lengthy transmissions

Figure 11.5   Some types of lines are geared for short bursts of activity; other lines are geared for bulk transmissions.

cations are of a bulk type and other transmissions are of a burst type. Figure 11.5 shows these different types of transmissions.

A bulk type of transmission is one where large amounts of data are transmitted all at once. The communications fabric is loaded and tied up for a lengthy amount of time as long transmissions of many bytes flow in all at once.

The burst kind of transmission is fundamentally different; in this type, many short transmissions are made. The types of technologies employed to support these different types of transmissions across the communication fabric are quite distinct.

Cost of Telecommunication Lines

Cost is another factor the architect must take into consideration. Figure 11.6 shows that the cost of telecommunication lines is a function of capacity and line type. An organization can always satisfy the needs for capacity if it is willing to spend enough. The trick is to satisfy the communications needs of the company and to do so economically.

Nature of the Transport

Another consideration of the intranet technology is the nature of the transport. Some transport technologies are very effective at transmitting *bulk* amounts of

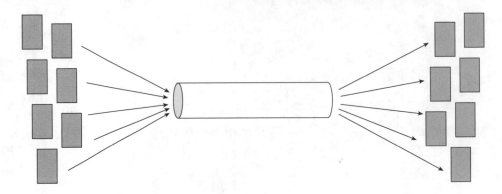

Figure 11.6 Cost of transmission infrastructure.

data but are relatively expensive, difficult to set up, and difficult to maintain. Some of the more popular networks of this type are Asynchronous Transfer Mode (ATM), Fiber Distributed Data Interface (FDDI), HPPI, and Fiber. Alternatively, other networks are very good at managing *burst* volumes and are relatively inexpensive, easy to set up, and easy to maintain. The most popular network type in this category is Ethernet. As your solution evolves, you are likely to find a combination of these transport technologies will make up your communication fabric. The final mix will be based on your needs and the cost and maturity of the transport technology. Figure 11.7 shows that some transport technologies are suitable for burst transmissions, while others are geared for *bulk* transmissions.

Availability of the Fabric

A final concern of the architect is the hours of availability of the communications fabric. Figure 11.8 depicts this issue.

All of the issues must be taken into account by the architect who is in charge of weaving together the different components of the CIF.

Who Uses the Communications Facilities?

One of the interesting ways to understand the needs of communications facilities inside and outside the CIF is in terms of who the end users are. Figure 11.9 shows who the different users of communications facilities are.

Direct and indirect customers are the users of the communications facilities as the data enters the CIF applications. Once the data enters the CIF, the next set

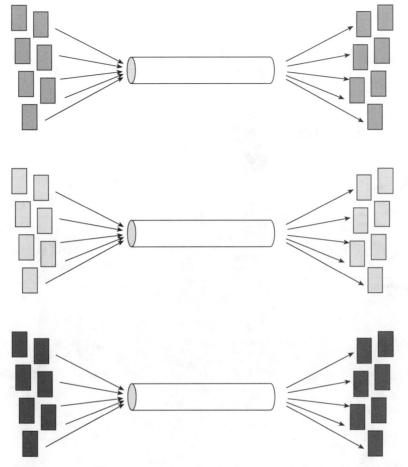

Figure 11.7   Different transport technologies are optimized to support different transmission needs.

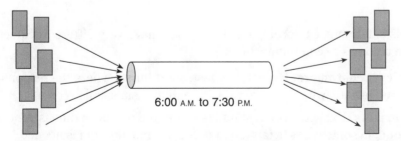

6:00 A.M. to 7:30 P.M.

Figure 11.8   The hours of availability are yet another concern of the CIF architect.

of users consists of farmers and explorers. As data passes out of the CIF (or into the CIF from nondirect facilities), the end users are tourists.

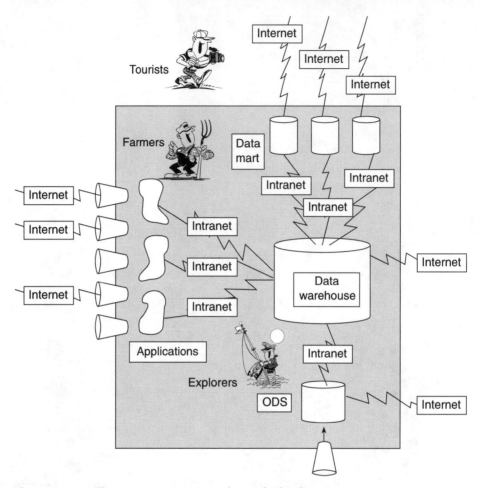

Figure 11.9 Different users are scattered over the landscape.

Tourists, farmers, explorers, and direct users have very different expectations when it comes to communications:

- **Direct customers.** Expect very fast, short bursts where the response time is immediate, with very few massive bulk transmissions.

- **Farmers.** Expect short, fast bursts where the response time is generally good. In some cases, a fair amount of data transmission is needed.

- **Explorers.** Expect very infrequent transmissions of large amounts of data.

- **Tourists.** Expect sporadic transmissions of large and small amounts of data from a wide variety of sources.

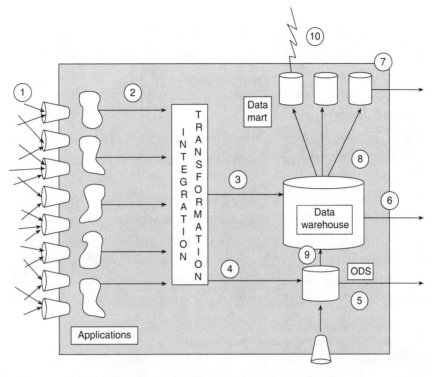

Figure 11.10 The different types of facilities are contained in the communications fabric.

Fortunately, the different classes of users are separated, and there is little overlap in the type of communications facility that is required. Figure 11.10 shows the different types of communications facilities that are required across the CIF.

A categorization of the different characteristics of the communications technologies is shown in Table 11.1.

Communication outside the CIF is accomplished by means of the Internet, as shown in Figure 11.11. Essentially, two types of transmissions are made here:

1. Transmissions between one CIF and another CIF

2. Transmission from a CIF to a Web site

Each of these types of transmissions has its own set of characteristics.

A CIF-to-CIF transmission may be one where one corporation is communicating with another corporation, or one where two parts of the same corporation are communicating, but each part is served by different CIFs.

Table 11.1 Characteristics of Communications Facilities

	SPEED	VOLUME	CAPACITY	FACILITY TYPE
1. Entry into applications	high	moderate	moderate	burst
2. Applications to I & T	high	high	very high	bulk
3. I & T to DW	high	high	very high	bulk
4. I & T to ODS	very high	low	high	burst
5. ODS to DSS	low	low	low	bulk & burst
6. DW to DSS	low	low	low	bulk
7. Data mart to DSS	very low	very low	very low	burst
8. DW to data mart	low	moderate/ low	moderate/ low	bulk
9. ODS to DW	low	moderate/ low	low	bulk
10. Internet	low	low	low	burst

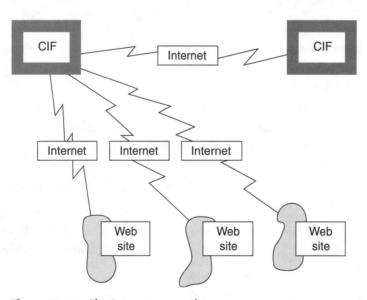

Figure 11.11 The Internet connections.

Summary

The communications between the different components of the CIF are accomplished by means of Internet/intranet transmissions. Intranet transmissions are those that occur within the CIF versus Internet transmissions that occur from/to the CIF and other external agencies. Some of the architectural issues are:

- Volume of data to be transported
- Capacity of networks
- Cost of telecommunications lines
- Nature of the transport
- Availability of the fabric

Different types of users have different transmission needs. Farmers are found in the data marts, the data warehouse, and ODS; explorers are found in the data warehouse and occasionally in the ODS; and tourists are found on the Internet.

We have now covered all aspects of the corporate information factory necessary to give end users visibility into the data. However, this is not enough. The data lacks legibility to all but the most experienced end users. A final component is needed that describes the data in terms of definition, structure, content, and use. This component of the corporate information factory is the *metadata* and will be discussed in the next chapter.

CHAPTER 12

The Metadata Component

The most important yet most ambiguous, most amorphous component of the Corporate Information Factory (CIF) is the metadata. From the standpoint of cohesiveness and continuity of structure across the many different components of the CIF, metadata is easily the most important component.

What Is Metadata?

A very common way of thinking about metadata is that it is data about data. An alternate way of describing metadata is that it is everything about data needed to promote its administration and use. These two widely accepted definitions of metadata, however, do not do justice to what metadata really is. A more practical approach to describing metadata by citing some examples:

- **Date layout.** The customer-record layout contains the list of attributes, and their relative position and format of data on the storage media.
    - Cust-id   char (15)
    - Cust-name   varchar (45)
    - Cust-address   varchar (45)
    - Cust-balance   dec fixed (15, 2)

- **Content.** There are 150,000 occurrences of transaction X in table PLK.
- **Indexes.** Table XYZ has indexes on the following columns:
  - Column HYT
  - Column BFD
  - Column MJI
- **Refreshment scheduling.** Table ABC is refreshed every Tuesday at 2:00 P.M.
- **Usage.** Only 2 of the 10 columns in table ABC have been used over the past six months.
- **Referential integrity.** Table XYZ is related to table ABC by means of the key QWE.
- **General documentation.** "Table ABC was designed in 1975 as part of the new accounts payable system. Table ABC contains accounts overdue data as calculated by . . . "

These examples of metadata only begin to scratch the surface of the possibilities. The final form will only be limited by your imagination and those needs that govern the use and administration of the CIF.

The reason why metadata is so important to the corporate information factory, and its different components, is that metadata is the glue that holds the architecture together. Figure 12.1 illustrates this role of metadata.

Without metadata, the different components of the CIF are merely standalone structures with no relationship to any other structure. It is metadata that gives the different structures—components of the architecture—an overall cohesiveness. Through metadata, one component of the architecture is able to interpret and make sense of what another component is trying to communicate.

The Conflict within Metadata

Despite all the benefits of metadata, a conflict exists: Metadata has a need to be shared, and a propensity to be managed and used, in an autonomous manner. Unfortunately, these propensities are in direct conflict with each other. Equally unfortunate is that the pull of metadata is *very, very* strong in both directions at the same time. Because of this conflict, metadata can be thought of as polarized, as shown in Figure 12.2.

Because the pull is so strong and so diametrically opposite, metadata is sometimes said to be *schizophrenic*. This leads to some fairly extreme conflicts within the CIF. As an example of the propensity of metadata to be shared, consider an architect who is building an operational database. If the operational database is to be integrated, the basic integrated, modeled design of the data

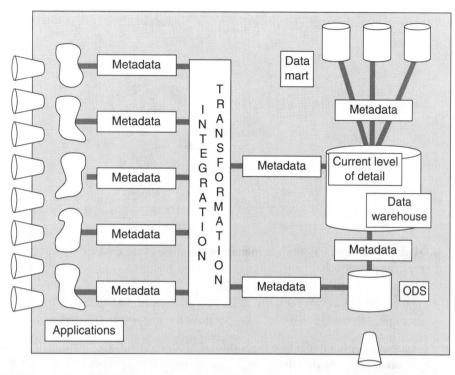

Figure 12.1 Metadata is the glue that holds the different components of the CIF together. Without metadata, there would be no cohesiveness across the CIF.

Figure 12.2 Metadata is stretched by two opposing forces.

needs to be shared from the data modeling environment. As the data ages and is pushed off to the data warehouse, the structure of the data needs to be shared within the data warehouse. As the data is moved into a data mart, the data once again needs to be shared. If there is to be any consistency across the corporate information factory, then metadata must be shared.

Is Centralization the Answer?

In response to the need for a central, unified source of data definition, structure, content, and use across the corporate information factory, the notion of a central repository arises (see Figure 12.3).

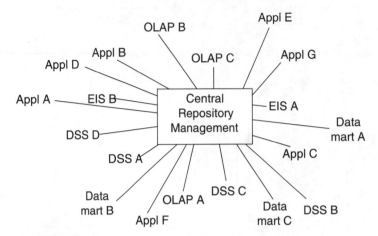

Figure 12.3 One approach to managing metadata is the data dictionary or the central repository approach.

The central repository approach is a good solution to the needs for sharability of metadata. However, is a central repository the answer to the organization's needs?

Consider the scenario of a DSS analyst working on Excel who is deep into solving an analytical problem. At 2:17 A.M. the DSS analyst has an epiphany and makes changes to the Lotus spreadsheet. Does the analyst need to call the data warehouse administrator and ask permission to define and analyze a new data structure? Does the DSS analyst need permission to derive a new data element on the fly? Shouldn't this new data structure and new data element be documented in the metadata repository?

Of course, the DSS analyst does not need or want anyone telling him or her what can and cannot be done at an early morning hour in the middle of a creative analysis of a problem. The DSS analyst operates in a state of autonomy and the central repository is neither welcome nor effective. The repository simply gets in the way of the DSS analyst using Excel. The DSS analyst does what is needed to bypass the repository, usually ignoring updates to the metadata in the repository.

The need for autonomy at the DSS analysis level is so overwhelming and the tools of DSS access and analysis are so powerful that a central repository does not stand a chance as a medium for total metadata management.

Is Autonomy the Answer?

If a powerful case can be made for why a central repository is not the answer, consider the opposite of the central repository where everybody "does their own thing," as shown in Figure 12.4.

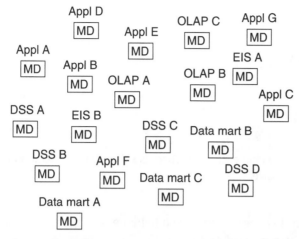

Figure 12.4 The autonomous approach to metadata management.

In the figure, autonomy exists in that every environment and every tool has its own unique facility for interpreting metadata. Because no constraints of any type can be found anywhere in the environment, complete autonomy is in place. The autonomy suggested by the figure is pleasing to the DSS analyst in that no one or no authority is telling the DSS analyst what to do. However, the following questions arise:

- What happens when one DSS user wants to know how data is defined and used elsewhere?

- What happens when a DSS user wants to know what a unit of data means?

- What happens when one DSS user wants to correlate results with another DSS analyst?

- What happens when a DSS analyst needs to reconcile results with the source systems providing the data for analysis?

- What happens when data is not interpreted consistently? What profit figures are correct?

The result is chaos. There simply is no uniformity or cohesiveness anywhere to be found in the autonomous environment. The purely autonomous environment is as impractical and unworkable as the central repository environment.

Achieving a Balance

Neither approach is acceptable in the long run to the architect wanting to make the corporate information factory a professionally organized environment.

In order to be successful, the CIF architect must balance the legitimate need to share metadata with the need for autonomy. Understanding the problem is the

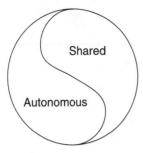

Figure 12.5 The metadata within each component is either shared or autonomous. The categories are mutually exclusive.

first step to a solution. In order to achieve a balance, a different perspective of metadata is required, *distributed* metadata.

The structure for metadata suggested in Figure 12.5 states that there must be a separation of metadata at each component in the architecture between metadata that is sharable and metadata that is autonomous. Metadata must be divided at each component of the CIF:

- Applications
- Operational Data Source
- Data warehouse
- Data mart
- Exploration/data mining warehouse

Furthermore, all metadata at an individual node must also fit into either a shared or autonomous category. There can be no metadata that is neither sharable nor autonomous. Likewise, metadata cannot be sharable and autonomous at the same time.

But Figure 12.5 has other ramifications. The metadata that is managed at an individual component must be accessible by tools that reside in that component. The tools may be tools of access, analysis, or development. In any case, whether the metadata is sharable or autonomous, the metadata needs to be available to and usable by the different tools that reside at the architectural component.

Another implication of the figure is that sharable metadata must be able to be replicated from one architectural component to another. Once the sharable metadata is replicated, it can be used and incorporated into the processing that occurs at other components of the corporate information factory.

Differentiating Sharable and Autonomous Metadata

The following are examples of sharable data:

- The table name and attributes shared among applications and the data warehouse
- Some definitions of data shared among the enterprise data model, the data warehouse, and the data mart
- Physical attributes shared among the applications and the ODS
- Physical attributes shared from one application to another
- Description of how shared data is transformed as it moves through the integration and transformation (I & T) layer

Ultimately, very commonly used metadata needs to be sharable.

An example of autonomous metadata might be the indexes a table has for its use in an application. At the data mart level, the results of a given analysis might be autonomous. At the data warehouse level, the metrics of the table content may well be autonomous data. At the ODS level, the response time achieved in access and analysis of the ODS is a form of autonomous metadata. In short, many varied forms of autonomous metadata exist. In general, much more autonomous metadata can be found than shared metadata.

Defining the System of Record

In order to make the structure workable as suggested in Figure 12.5, there needs to be a clear and formal definition of the system of record (i.e., authoritative source) for shared metadata (see Figure 12.6). The system of record for shared

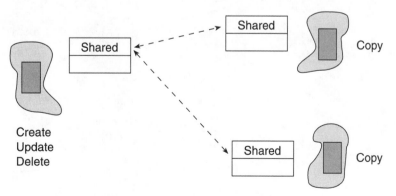

Figure 12.6   The system of record for the metadata.

metadata implies that each shared metadata element must be owned and maintained by only one component of the corporate information factory (such as a data warehouse, data mart, ODS, etc.). In contrast, this shared metadata can be replicated for use by all components of the corporate information factory.

For example, suppose that the definition of shared metadata is made at the data warehouse level (a very normal assumption). The implication is that the definition can be used throughout the CIF but cannot be altered anywhere except at the data warehouse. In other words, the data mart DSS analyst can use the metadata but cannot alter the metadata.

Establishing the system of record for metadata is a defining factor in the successful implementation and evolution of the CIF. Another important implication of the approach to distributed metadata is that there be an exchange of this meta object among the different architectural components (see Figure 12.7).

The sharable meta object needs to be passed efficiently and on an on-demand basis. One of the more important implications of this sharability is that it be shared across multiple technologies, as illustrated in Figure 12.8.

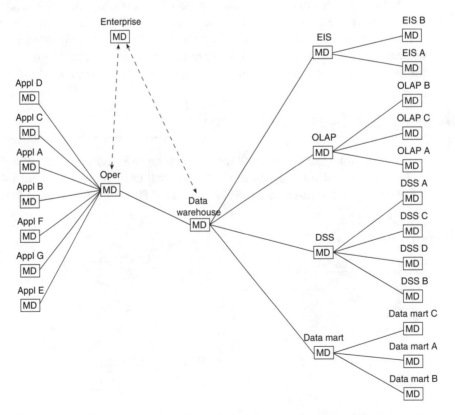

Figure 12.7 Metadata needs to be exchanged across the many different components of the CIF.

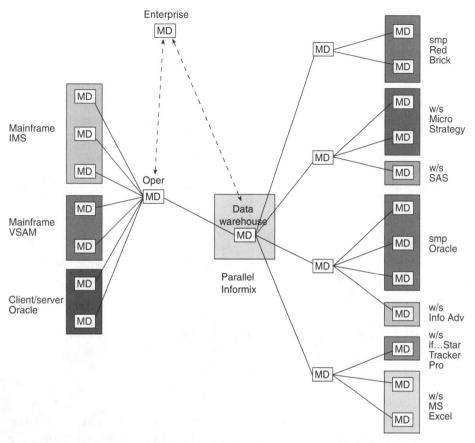

Figure 12.8 One of the main challenges of sharing metadata across the CIF is that many different platforms must be serviced.

Using Metadata

The whole notion of sharing metadata across different components of the architecture along with the autonomy of metadata at each component level results in a larger architecture. The larger picture shown in Figure 12.9 shows that indeed a balance exists between sharability and autonomy. With this architecture, the end user has all the autonomy desired, and the CIF architect has all the sharability and uniformity of definition that is desired. The conflict between sharability and autonomy that is evident in metadata is resolved quite nicely by the architecture outlined in Figure 12.9.

Consider the usage of this architecture in Figure 12.10, where a DSS analyst at the data mart level desires to know the lineage of attribute ABC in table XYZ. The data mart analyst recognizes that sharable information about table XYZ is

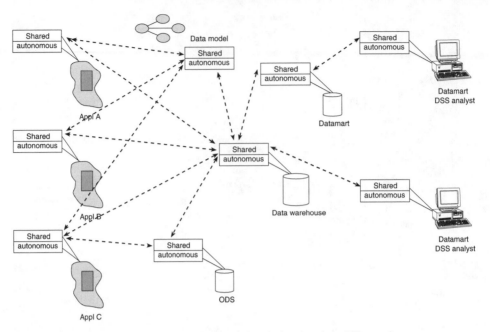

Figure 12.9   A larger metadata architecture that balances sharability and autonomy.

available. The DSS analyst asks the data warehouse what information is available. The data warehouse offers sharable information about the table and the attribute in question. If the DSS analyst has what is needed, the question is resolved. If the DSS analyst has what is needed, the question is resolved. If the DSS analyst is still unsure about the table and its attributes, he will push further into the network of sharable and go back to the application. The DSS analyst then learns even more about the metadata in question. If still further questions are being asked, the DSS analyst can look inside the I & T layer or even go back to the enterprise model to see more information about the table and attribute.

Another use of sharable metadata is that of impact analysis (see Figure 12.11). In the figure, an application programmer is getting ready to make a change to some part of the application. The CIF architect will ask the following questions:

- When was the change made in the application?

- What elements of data are going to be affected across the CIF?

With the formalized structure of metadata, it is a relatively simple matter to determine what data in what environment will be impacted by a change in the applications environment.

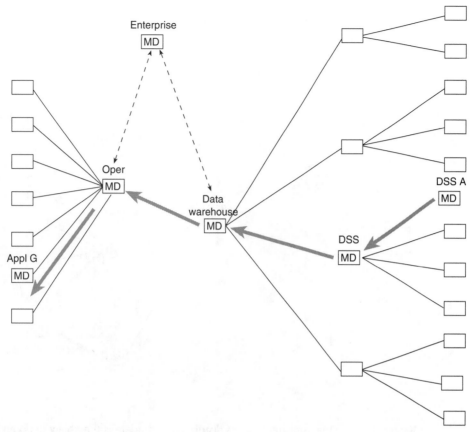

Figure 12.10 Metadata information all the way back to the applications environment is available to the DSS analyst at the data mart, if needed.

Operational versus DSS Usage

Metadata plays a very different role in the DSS and the operational environments. For example, after driving a familiar route for a period of time, drivers take road signs for granted and ignore their information because it's simply not needed.

If the same activity is repeated over and over, metadata can get in the way of the end user. After the tenth time that an end user repeats the same activity, the end user hardly glances at whatever metadata is present and may even complain that the metadata display gets in the way of doing his or her job.

However, when drivers are in unfamiliar territory, road signs make all the difference in the world. The same can be said for metadata in the DSS environment. When the DSS analyst is doing a *new* report, metadata is invaluable in

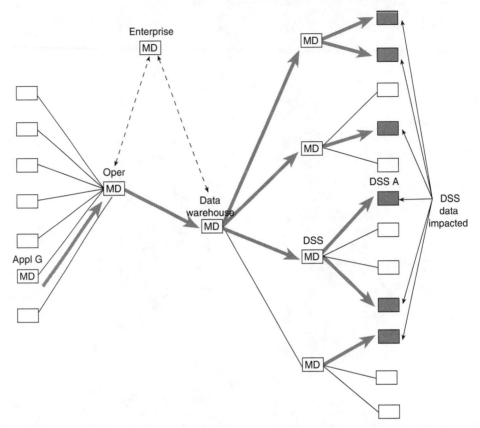

Figure 12.11 One important use of distributed metadata is the ability to do an impact analysis. In this case, the applications programmer has asked the question, "If there is a change in the applications data, which data marts are affected?"

telling the DSS analyst what he or she needs to know to get started and do an effective DSS analysis. Metadata plays an entirely different role in the world of DSS than it does in the world of operational systems.

Because of this difference, it is worth noting how metadata relates to the CIF based on the differences between operational processing and DSS processing. Figure 12.12 shows that metadata in the operational environment is a by-product of processing. In fact, metadata in the operational environment is of most use to the developer and the designer. Metadata in the DSS environment, on the other hand, is of great use to the DSS analyst as an active part of the analytical, informational effort. This is due largely to the fact that, in this environment, the end user has more control over how data is interpreted and used.

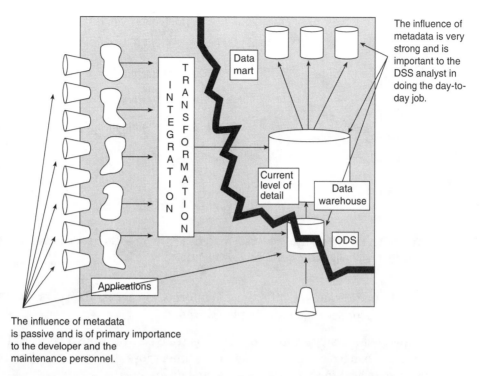

The influence of metadata is very strong and is important to the DSS analyst in doing the day-to-day job.

The influence of metadata is passive and is of primary importance to the developer and the maintenance personnel.

Figure 12.12 The role metadata plays throughout the CIF is quite different.

Versioning of Metadata

One of the characteristics of the data warehouse environment is that it contains a robust supply of historical information. It is not unusual for it to contain 5 to 10 years' worth of information. As such, history is a dimension of the data warehouse that is not present or important elsewhere in the CIF.

Consider the DSS analyst who is trying to compare 1996 data with 1990 data. The DSS analyst may be having a difficult time for a variety of reasons:

- 1996 data had a different source of data than 1990 data.
- 1996 data had a different definition of a product than 1990 data's definition.
- 1996 had a different marketing territory than 1990's marketing territory.

Potentially many different factors may make the data from 1996 incompatible with data from 1990. The DSS analyst needs to know what those factors are if a meaningful comparison of data is to be made across the years. In order to be

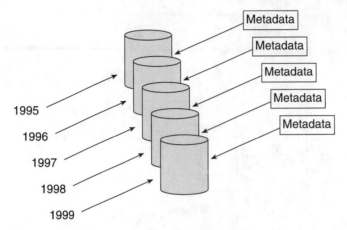

Figure 12.13 Versions of metadata must be kept in order to track changes in data structure that naturally occur in the data warehouse.

able to understand the difference in information across the years, the DSS analyst needs to see metadata that is *versioned*.

Versioned metadata is metadata that is tracked over time. Figure 12.13 shows that as changes are made to data over time, those changes are reflected in the metadata as different versions of metadata are created.

One of the characteristics of versioned metadata is that each occurrence of it contains a from-date and a to-date, resulting in a continuous *state* record.

Once the continuous versions of metadata are created, the DSS analyst can use those versions to understand the content of data in its historical context. For example, the DSS analysis solicits answers to such key questions as the following:

- On December 29, 1995, what was the source of data for file XYZ?
- On October 14, 1996, what was the definition of a product?
- On July 20, 1994, what was the price of product ABC?

Versioned metadata for the data warehouse adds an extremely important dimension of data.

Archiving and Metadata

In the same vein as versioned metadata, the CIF architect must consider the role of metadata as data is archived. When data is removed from the data ware-

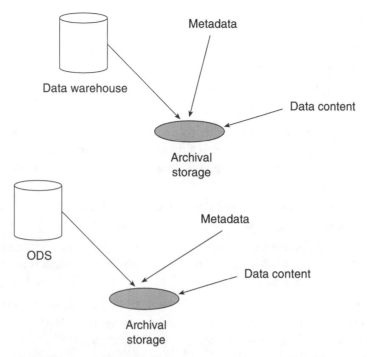

Figure 12.14 When data is archived, metadata is stored directly on the archival medium with the actual data content.

house, data mart, or the ODS, it can be discarded or, more likely, archived onto secondary storage. As this happens, it makes sense to store the metadata relating to the archived data along with the archived data. By doing this, the CIF architect ensures that at a later point in time, archival information will be available in the most efficient and effective manner. Figure 12.14 shows that metadata should be stored with the archival information.

Capturing Metadata

The Achilles heel of metadata has always been in its capture. When applications were built in the 1960s, no documentation or captured metadata existed. Organizations realized in the late 1980s and early 1990s that no metadata had been developed for the systems that were written years ago. Trying to go back in time and reconstruct metadata that was attached to systems that were written decades ago was a daunting task. The obstacles of trying to reconstruct metadata 20 years after the fact were many:

1. The people who wrote the systems originally were not available because:
   - They had been promoted.
   - They had left for another job.
   - They had forgotten.
   - They never understood the data in the first place.
2. The budget for development had dried up years ago. Trying to show management tangible benefits from a data dictionary project or a repository project required a huge imagination on the part of the manager footing the bill.
3. Physically gathering the metadata information was its own challenge. In many cases, source code had been lost a long time ago.
4. Even if metadata could be recovered from an old application system, only some metadata was available. A complete picture of metadata was almost impossible to reconstruct.
5. Even if metadata could be recovered from an old legacy system, as updates were made to the system, keeping the updates in synch with the metadata manager—a dictionary or a repository—was almost impossible.

For these reasons and more, capturing applications' metadata after the fact is a very difficult thing to do.

A much better alternative is the capturing of metadata during the active development process. When a tool of automation is used for the development process and is able to produce metadata as a by-product of its code that is produced, then the possibility of creating metadata automatically arises.

Figure 12.15 shows a tool that produces metadata as a by-product of the creation of code. This approach has many advantages:

- Metadata creation does not require another budgetary line item—it comes automatically.
- Updating metadata as changes are made is not a problem.
- Metadata versions are created every time a new version of code is created.
- Programmers do not know that they are creating metadata.
- Programmers think they are building systems. The creation of the metadata comes spontaneously, unknown to the programmer.
- The logic of transformation can be trapped. The transformation tool can understand exactly what conversion and reformatting logic is occurring.

The automatic creation of code offers many advantages in the capture of metadata—ultimately, productivity.

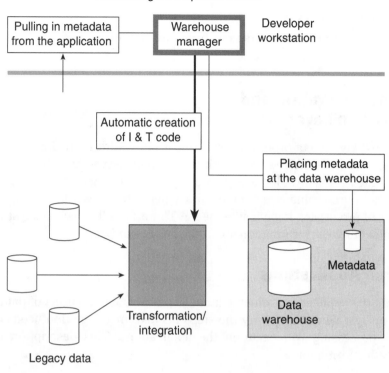

Metadata is developed as an interactive product of designing and
developing the data warehouse environment:

    It is complete.
    It is done every time.
    It is done automatically.
    It is not an afterthought.
    It is not optional.
    It requires no extra effort—manually or otherwise.

Figure 12.15   Capturing metadata to support integration and transformation. The same
process can apply for development and capture in the application environment.

Meta-Process Information

While metadata is undoubtedly the center of attention in the CIF, other types
of meta objects are available for usage. One such type of meta object is meta-
process information. Although metadata is descriptive data about data, meta-
process information is descriptive information about code or processes.
Meta-process information is useful anywhere there is a large body of code. The
three most obvious places in the CIF where this occurs are:

1. At the I & T layer

2. Within the applications

3. As data passes to the data mart from the data warehouse

Uses at the Integration and Transformation Layer

The I & T layer meta-process information is interesting to the DSS analyst as he or she tries to determine how a unit of data was derived from the applications. When the DSS analyst looks at a value of $275 in the data warehouse and sees that the source value was $314, he or she needs to know what was going on in terms of processing logic inside the I & T interface. The DSS analyst needs to see meta-process information about the I & T interface.

Uses within Applications

Within the applications, much editing, capturing, and updating of data occurs. The analyst who will specify the steps needed for integration needs to know what processing will occur in the applications. This description is meta-process information.

Uses from the Data Warehouse to the Data Mart

As data passes from the data warehouse to the data mart, it is customized and summarized to meet the individual demands of the department to which it is being shipped. This process is very interesting to the DSS analyst who must do drill-down processing. In drill-down processing, the DSS analyst goes to successfully lower levels of detail in order to explain to management how a unit of summarization came to be. The DSS analyst, or the tool he or she is using, occasionally needs to drill down past the data mart into the data warehouse. At this point, the DSS analyst needs to see meta-process information about the interface between the data mart and the data warehouse.

Summary

Metadata is the glue that holds the CIF together. Without metadata, the CIF is just a collection of components that manage and use data with no continuity or cohesiveness.

Metadata presents different challenges in that it needs to be both autonomous and sharable at the same time. Unfortunately, these goals are mutually exclusive. In order to be successful, however, both goals need to be simultaneously achieved.

One approach to sharability is through a central repository. It satisfies many of the needs for sharability but does not satisfy the need for autonomy. Another approach to autonomy of metadata is for "everyone to do their own thing." This approach achieves autonomy, but there is no sharability.

An alternate approach is *distributed* metadata. In distributed metadata, some data is shared and other metadata is autonomous. There needs to be a rigorously defined system of record (that is, an authoritative source) for the shared portion of distributed metadata.

One of the challenges of shared metadata is that of crossing many different lines of technology. Another challenge is the transport of meta objects.

Metadata plays a very different role in the operational environment than it does in the DSS environment. In the operational environment, the applications developer is the primary user of metadata. In the DSS environment, the end user is the primary user of metadata.

Now that we have taken a look at the basic building blocks to the corporate information factory, let's take a look at how these blocks are used to deliver *decision support capabilities*.

CHAPTER 13

Decision Support Capabilities

T he ultimate goal of the corporate information factory (CIF) is to get the right information into the right people's hands when they need it. Much of what we have discussed so far covers the design and implementation of the infrastructure to accomplish this goal.

In this chapter, we focus on how these components work together to enable decision support capabilities.

First, we cover the decision support capabilities available today that are used to solve a business user's difficult strategic and tactical problems. These capabilities use data marts for strategic analysis and oper-marts for tactical analysis. The foundation for the data marts is, of course, the data warehouse. The data warehouse not only supplies integrated, high-quality, static data to the marts, it also acts as the repository of strategic historical data. For these reasons and others, the data warehouse is a mandatory part of the strategic analysis infrastructure.

Data marts will be discussed next. These structures are subsets of strategic data provided by the data warehouse and have different database designs depending on the business problem(s) they solve. How and when to use the different types of data marts and data mart designs are discussed.

Next, we talk about two interesting forms of DSS applications coming to the fore in this environment: ERP applications and e-business. The ERP vendors are offering some interesting new strategic applications built from the strength of their integrated operational capabilities. As with any self-contained condition, some good things and some less than optimal considerations must be taken into account.

Additionally, we take a look at e-business. E-business is one of the most challenging business ventures we have seen in years. The CIF has a significant role in ensuring the success of a corporation using the Web to conduct its business. A natural fit exists between the CIF infrastructure and the "click and mortar" companies that you need to understand before implementing your e-business strategy.

We then turn our attention to the more tactical requirements for data. The interaction between the data warehouse and the operational data store is an often overlooked yet very important relationship. The need to obtain strategic information in a real-time mode is becoming more and more essential. Small amounts of pre-aggregated or pre-analyzed data must be available to the business user for immediate decision-making. We discuss a mechanism to satisfy the need for both strategic and tactical data in a high-performance situation.

This leads into our next discussion. Another new need is for tactical analyses performed on operational data. This need has been the genesis of a new structure called an oper-mart. Small subsets of operational data can be extracted and loaded into a multidimensional structure (hypercube or star schema) for instant analysis and tactical decision-making.

We end the chapter with a discussion of the "off-the-shelf," commercially available applications for both strategic and tactical decision support. The vendor community is beginning to offer generic DSS applications such as Risk Management or Customer Relationship Management (CRM) in which the database schema and access methods are already set up. All you do is add data. These off-the-shelf or commercial applications show great promise. However, you must be diligent in determining if these "data marts in a box" are appropriate for your company. Therefore, we offer as a last section a set of guidelines to use when selecting one of these commercial applications.

Putting the Role of the Data Warehouse Into Context

The key to the integrity and ease of maintenance of your decision support applications is to have a repository of high-quality, stable data. The data warehouse is an ideal foundation for building these data marts. The data warehouse contains the basic ingredients that ensure the success of your strategic analytical environment:

- Integrated data
- Historical data
- Easily accessible data

Each of these aspects beautifully supports the construction of data marts (Figure 13.1).

The foundation provided by the data warehouse is very strong. The integration of data is important when trying to achieve a corporate view. Without integration, a corporate perspective is difficult to achieve. When data is integrated on a one-time basis only (as is the case for a temporary "staging area"), an integrated view is possible, but repeated uses of the data are very unlikely. When an integrated foundation is created on a permanent basis (an enduring data warehouse structure), not only is an integrated perspective easily achievable and reusability of the data possible, but also different analyses performed over a lengthy period of time can be reconciled, should there be a need. It is from this stable foundation that we recommend you begin building your data marts.

The Data Warehouse Adds Depth to Data

The data warehouse provides data marts with integrated data that can be used to give data more "depth" that is otherwise not possible. As an example of the depth that can be created with integrated data, consider the CRM need to understand customers holistically. Figure 13.2 shows the need for a holistic approach to data. Every person contacting the customer (via the Customer Touch Zone), regardless of who it is, should start with their understanding of who the customer is, what interactions have happened in the past, and what value the customer brings to the business in the future—commonly referred to

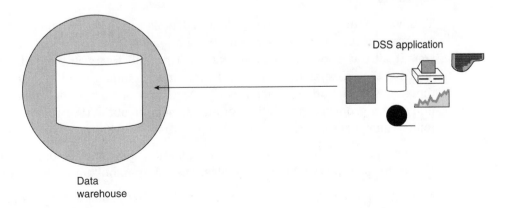

Figure 13.1 Why DSS applications find the data warehouse attractive.

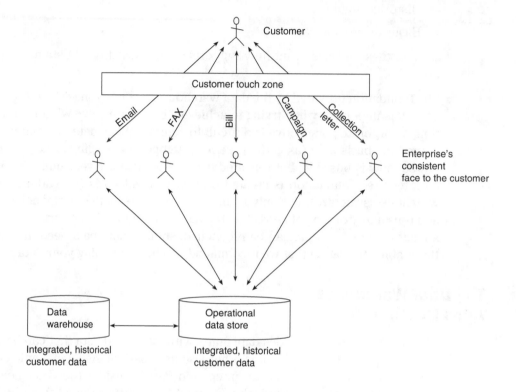

Figure 13.2 An integrated database of historical (data warehouse) and current (operational data store) data is used for very customer touch.

as lifetime value. This ensures that the corporation has a consistent voice to the customer.

To illustrate the usefulness of an integrated, holistic approach to managing customers, consider a salesperson with two prospects: Tom Jones and Barry Wilson. If all the salesperson knows about Tom and Barry is their name and address, the salesperson has a hard time understanding what will appeal to them, how he should approach them, and what products best suit them. Going into a sales proposition with little or no information about the prospective customers minimizes any chance of a sale or, worse, of irritating the customer.

But now suppose a host of integrated information about the customers is available to the salesperson before the sales. The salesperson knows the following:

■ Tom is single and has never been married. He has used the corporation's products consistently for four years. Tom rents an apartment and watches a lot of TV. Tom works as a clerk for the local electric utility and drives a motorcycle on the weekends. He calls his sister in Seattle every Sunday and pays his bills attentively, often correcting mistakes he finds in them.

- Barry is married to Susan and they have three children. Barry is the head of a 200-person law firm. He lives on a 10-acre estate on the outskirts of town. He is a new customer to the corporation and may not stay long if irritated with his service. Barry plays golf at the local country club and was a former golf star in college. He drives a luxury car and is often late in paying his bills.

Now that the salesperson has a lot of background information (depth) about Tom and Barry, he can formulate a strategy using the warehouse and marts as to what might work and what probably won't work when it comes to making a sale. He then uses the ODS to determine the best method of contact (email, phone call, fax, mailing, and so on) for each individual. The ODS supplies the most accurate contact information for the sales person as well as the best channel to use. The sales person determines the following strategy for each customer:

- Tom is unlikely to be interested in life insurance, but he may well want accident and injury insurance. Also Tom would like to receive a paper bill every month and prefers to pay his bill which a check. The sales person should contact Tom via phone.

- Barry, on the other hand, needs life insurance and he is a likely candidate for whole life insurance. He definitely would like to pay his bill via EFT rather than via a check. Barry should be contacted via email followed up by a personal letter or phone call.

The addition of integrated historical data about a prospect makes the sales effort efficient and directed. Without this background information, both Barry and Tom appear to be "flat." The integrated information brings out the differences, giving great depth to the individuals and understanding to the salesperson, thus greatly enhancing the prospects of a sale.

But integration of information is not the only desirable feature of data found in the data warehouse. The fact that the data warehouse contains historical data is equally important.

The Dimension of History

One of the defining characteristics of the data warehouse is its storage of historical data. This data is extremely useful in a number of data marts. As a sample of its usefulness, the following example is given:

In the CRM environment, historical data is very important in predicting the future. This ability to predict the future may be somewhat indirect and obtuse, but it is very valuable to your corporation. The reason why historical data is so useful in predicting the future is that customers (both individuals as well as businesses and governments) are creatures of habit. The habits formed early on tend to stick with us throughout our lives. It is very unusual for an individual or organization to undergo a dramatic and complete change of lifestyle. If lifestyles change at all, they change slowly and predictably. For example, the majority of individuals go through these life stages:

- Young college student or beginning wage earner
- Wage earner, no kids
- Wage earner with young kids
- Wage earner with college kids
- Empty nester
- Early retirement
- Late retirement

As a consequence of this nature of people, the past becomes a powerful predictor of the future when it comes to people and organizations. A high lifetime value or a potentially high lifetime value customer is an invaluable asset to your corporation. A low lifetime value customer may not be someone you should spend your time on. You need to understand what type of customer you are interacting with and deal with them appropriately. By having this robust source of historical data, your analysts can predict the next life stage that customers are most likely to go through, customize their products/campaigns for that stage, and cross-sell appropriate products according to the prediction.

For example, a married couple with two teenage children is likely to be looking for ways to fund their kids' college expenses. A savvy CRM person would know this and offer loans (second mortgages, signature, and so on) appropriate for the couple's impending change in life stage. For this reason then, the historical data found in the data warehouse becomes very useful to the world of data marts.

Easily Accessible Data

Finally, the data warehouse brings disparate data together into a consistent format and technology. By storing the data in an open, easily understood environment, it becomes a simple process to dip into this data pool and extract what you need over and over for your particular analytical needs.

The metadata that goes along with the data warehouse is invaluable in determining what data you should use in the ultimate analytical environment. The enterprise view is upheld by the metadata definitions and descriptions of each entity and attribute in the warehouse.

This stable repository can also serve to improve the quality of the data you offer to your business community. The data warehouse can be researched, analyzed, and scoured for data defects. Monitoring it for quality is the single best way to determine which of your operational systems is producing low-quality data.

Now that we have established that the data warehouse is the perfect foundation for data marts, let's turn our attention to analytical applications. First, we will discuss strategic ones (the data marts) and then we will examine the tactical ones (ODS and oper-marts).

Putting the Data Mart into Context

The data mart is customized or summarized data that is derived from the data warehouse and tailored to support the specific analytical requirements of a given business unit or business function. It utilizes a common enterprise view of strategic data and provides business units more flexibility, control, and responsibility. The data mart may or may not be on the same server or location as the data warehouse.

If your company has a few tangible, documented business requirements to tackle, and you are reasonably sure that a new data mart will do the trick, you may be asking yourself how to strategically integrate the new data mart into your organization. Even though the answer depends on the specifics of your situation, you'll probably end up with a data mart that resembles one of two proven types. Our nomenclatures for the two types are DSS Application and Departmental. The following definitions may help you understand the differences between these two types of marts.

Departmental Data Marts

The definition of a departmental data mart is a decision support database that belongs solely to a particular department or division within your organization. For example, the sales department may want to create a decision support database containing sales data specifically. These data marts are fairly generic in functionality and serve as repositories of historical data for use by that department's personnel only. The design must be fairly generic as well, that is, not focused on any particular functionality or process. In other words, departmental data marts generally have a broad focus and a narrow audience.

DSS Application Data Marts

DSS application data marts have a very different focus. Their focus is on a particular decision support process such as risk management, campaign analysis, or head count analysis, rather than generic utilization. Because of their universal appeal in the company, they also are seen as an enterprise resource. They can be used by anyone within the organization that has a need for its analytical capability. Another way of saying this is that DSS application data marts have a narrow focus but broad user community usage.

Similarities and Differences between Marts

Both departmental data marts and DSS application data marts emanate from the data warehouse. DSS applications differ from departmental data marts in several respects. Table 13.1 summarizes the difference between a departmental data mart and a DSS application one.

In short, although certainly similarities exist between departmental and DSS application data marts, certain differences are notable as well. Determining the type of data marts results from the answers to three basic questions: What does it do, who is it for, and who is paying for it?

What Does It Do?

First and foremost, the answer to the question should be that it efficiently solves the tangible, documented business requirements. In addition, if the nature and scope of the requirement are clearly comprehensive or universally

Table 13.1 DSS Application versus Departmental Data Mart

	DSS APPLICATION DATA MART	DEPARTMENTAL DATA MART
Focus	Highly focused	Broad, generic focus
Outputs	Standard analyses and repetitive reporting	General analyses and reports, some ad hoc reports
Usage	Highly structured	Unstructured
Pattern of access	Predictable	Unpredictable
Audience	Multiple departments or divisions	Single department or division

used, then a DSS application data mart is in order. If the nature and scope is limited and even proprietary, then a departmental data mart is probably better.

■ For departmental data marts, don't forget to determine whether other departments have the same requirement; that is, they would be interested in sharing the benefits and the costs. This may lead you to change the scope of the mart.

■ For either data mart type, manage user expectations. Make sure that everyone understands what the data mart will and won't do. Famous last words: "Our new data mart will answer all our questions."

Who Is It For?

Although the roster of users who access the data mart is important, this question goes to the politics of the situation and to performance-based compensation. The real question is who will ultimately benefit the most from the data mart's success? If the answer is business analysts and executives of a single department, then the data mart should be departmental. If the answer is the people at many levels throughout the organization, then make it a DSS application data mart.

Once you've identified whom it is for, invite them to be the project sponsor(s). If you can't sell them on the role, then consider delaying the implementation until you can, because if they won't fight for the project at the start, they may fight against it later.

Who Is Paying for It?

Although budgeting practices differ widely and IT departments often function under their own budgets, you should maximize the association between costs and benefits. So, if only one department is willing to cover the costs, a departmental data mart is needed. If the budge sponsor(s) have overall or inclusive responsibilities or include many departments, then a DSS application data mart is the right one to build. If the senior project sponsors don't have budget authority, consider whether the ultimate benefactor is actually higher up in the food chain.

Once you've answered the three questions, you should compare the answers to the inherent features of each type and evaluate which approach is needed.

Pros and Cons of Each Type of Data Mart

When deciding whether to build a departmental or DSS application data mart, several factors must be considered. First and foremost, you should be aware of the pros and cons of each structure. At least then you are going into the implementation knowing the strengths and the weaknesses of each type of data mart.

Departmental Data Marts

Departmental data marts have a number of attributes that are to your advantage when constructing analytical capabilities:

- You have a good chance of delivering what the department wants. The users are usually very involved in the design and usage of this mart.
- You can get good funding since the department owns this mart.
- Most IT projects are founded this way—one department paying for its own system—so it is easy for the department to build a business case.
- The department controls the mart and therefore can make it perform almost all of the department's proprietary analyses.

On the other hand, you should be aware of the pitfalls to these types of marts:

- Performance issues can arise due to the data mart not being optimized for any set of queries—or worse, being optimized for some queries that cause performance problems for other queries.
- Redundant queries can run on different data marts throughout the organization although the result sets from these may not be consistent! This is somewhat mitigated by having the data warehouse feeding all the marts, but it is certainly not guaranteed that two marts will produce the same numbers, and so on.
- A minimal sharing of findings between departments can occur.
- No desire exists for supporting an enterprise view of the information.
- You face a difficulty in getting funding for the data warehouse (an enterprise resource).

DSS Application Data Marts

DSS application data marts have the advantage of an enterprise-wide appeal and reusability. Other advantages include the following:

- It is possible to create standard analyses and reports from these marts.
- An analytical functionality is created only once and is used by the business community in much the same fashion.
- The data mart is easy to tune and the capacity is predictable.

- Many vendors today offer specific DSS applications that can plug into your data warehouse environment, thus speeding up the implementation of analytical applications.

These types of marts also have disadvantages:

- It may be difficult to customize the views or queries into the mart enough to satisfy the diverse set of users.

- Funding must come from an enterprise source rather than a single department.

- It can be hard to get the business community to agree on the overall design of this application.

- Some of the analyses may be suboptimized due to the nondepartment specific nature of the mart. That is, the mart may satisfy only 80 to 90 percent of a department's needs because it is an application for the entire enterprise.

Database Designs for Data Marts

Without a doubt, the most popular designs include the star schema and its variations. There is good reason for this. The star schema is great for supporting a multidimensional analysis in data marts with known, stable requirements, fairly predictable queries with reasonable response times, recurring reports, and so on. Not surprisingly, multidimensional tools have earned a strong position in the marketplace as well.

The techniques for building star schemas are perhaps the most elegant, well-explained, and useful techniques for determining business requirements, dimensions, keys, and, when necessary, physical database schemas. Numerous projects have successfully applied these techniques and concepts.

However, other issues relate to the data warehouse environments besides dimensionality:

- The cost of ownership is now an issue confronting many data warehouse shops. Does the return equal the ongoing investment?

- Queries that do stock processes but do not open the data up for exploration risk creating an environment that does not generate adequate return.

It seems reasonable to conclude that unique combinations of processing requirements and types of data demand different structures. In other words, one approach or structure isn't always best.

Experience indicates that the "universe" of data warehouse processing types is diverse. It includes data mining, statistical analysis, data exploration, and more. The decision support users performing these types of analyses often search for unexpected data relationships.

So, if your entire data warehouse environment consists of a single structure, then your ability to analyze your data is limited to the subset of analyses that the structure best supports. To maximize your data warehousing return on investment (ROI), you need to embrace and implement data warehouse architectures that enable the full spectrum of analysis.

The usage of the data warehouse for the purpose of business intelligence is usually accommodated by the integrated, historical data found in the data warehouse and the construction of DSS application or departmental data marts. In the case of the data marts, the data must be reformatted to meet the needs of the particular business requirement and the tool used for that requirement. Figure 13.3 shows the support of business intelligence by the data warehouse.

The data found in the data warehouse is at a very granular level. For most DSS applications, it is necessary to restructure the data to facilitate the use of the tools found in business intelligence. Some of the ways that data can be restructured to meet the needs of business intelligence are as follows:

- **Merging or aggregating the data.** Small units of data are joined together to form a cohesive whole that makes sense to the business intelligence analyst. Generally, the database design is in the form of a star schema or snowflake schema.

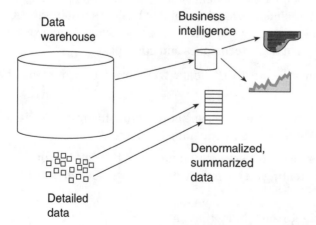

Figure 13.3 Business intelligence is supported by derailed data that is restructured to meet the analyst's needs.

- **Summarizing the data.** Many detailed units of data are summarized so that the business analyst can see the forest for the trees.

- **Cubing the data.** The detailed data found in the data warehouse is presented and stored in a specialized multidimensional database structure.

- Statistical subsets of data. Unbiased sets of data are created for mining or exploration.

The restructuring of the data that occurs as data is moved from the warehouse to the tools of business intelligence usually is thought of as going from a normalized structure to some form of denormalized design. In general, the data found in the data warehouse is normalized (or if not perfectly normalized, it is very close). The data needed for business intelligence on the other hand is denormalized. Many different flavors of denormalization are available:

- Summarization

- Aggregation

- Star schemas

- Snowflake schemas

- Hierarchical structures

- Data sets

- Flat files

The denormalization that is done as data approaches the business intelligence environment is done in accordance with the requirements of the business community seeking answers and the particular business intelligence tool chosen for each application.

For many statistical, data mining, or exploratory analyses, there must be no hint of a bias or an arbitrary establishment of data relationships. The value of these exploratory algorithms depends on the absence of predefined relationships. These applications are searching for *unknown* relationships rather than the known relationships established by star schemas or hypercubes. By definition, the star schema must have predetermined, physical relationships, thus maximizing the straightforward, multidimensional queries but hampering any ability to look for unknown or unexpected data relationships.

For a low-latency data warehouse (one with rapid update cycles), the star schema offers restrictions in update speed and insertion capabilities. Many of the mission-critical, large-volume data warehouses now appearing require rapid insertion capabilities.

The truth is that database structures vary across a spectrum of normalized to denormalized to flat files of transactions. The ideal situation is to craft the schemas after the requirements are established. Unfortunately, the database structure/solution is often selected before the specific business needs are known. How often have you heard members of the development team debating the merits of star versus normalized schemas before even starting the business requirements analysis? For whatever reason, architects and data modelers latch onto a particular design technique—perhaps through comfort with a particular technique or ignorance of other techniques—and force all data marts and even the data warehouse to have that one type of design. This is similar to the person who is an expert with a hammer—everything they see resembles a nail.

Commercial Decision Support Applications

Now that we have an understanding of how the DSS application data mart differs from the more traditional departmental data mart, let's take a closer look at some of the more common DSS applications: ERP and e-business.

ERP Analytical Applications

One of the most important DSS applications comes from the ERP world. Figure 13.4 shows that ERP activity begins in the transaction application environment. Once the ERP transaction has been executed, it flows into one or more ERP

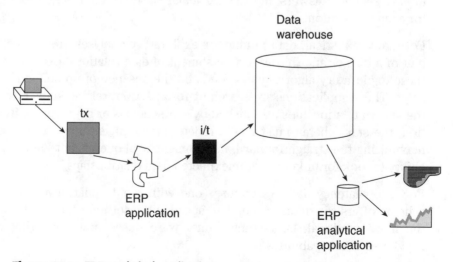

Figure 13.4 ERP analytical applications.

application databases. As the data ages, it is pulled from the ERP transaction database into the data warehouse. However, before it can be put into the data warehouse, the ERP data may need to be integrated with other sources of data into meaningful units.

This form of integration is somewhat different from the integration found among the various operational or legacy systems supplying data to the data warehouse. This is because the ERP data often is stored in many tables that are highly fractured. This is done to help the OLTP performance of the ERP system. However, to be meaningful to the DSS analyst, the ERP data must be reconstructed or reintegrated back into meaningful units. Generally, this means merging tables together or "normalizing" the database design. Figure 13.5 demonstrates the reconstruction of the ERP data into meaningful units of data.

The reintegrated ERP data is then placed into the data warehouse. Once inside, the ERP data is available for DSS analytical processing and reporting. The kinds of reporting that typically are done by a DSS analysis application include the following:

- Simple reporting
- Key performance monitoring
- Checkpoint monitoring
- Summary reporting
- Exception reporting

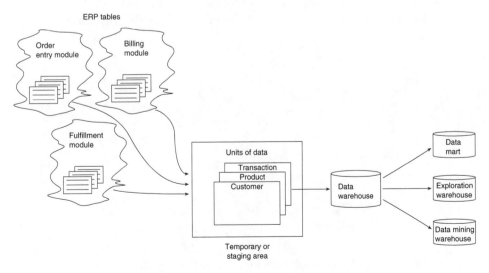

Figure 13.5 ERP data reconstructed into meaningful units of data.

In addition, ERP data in the data warehouse can be placed in exploration warehouses or mining warehouses where it can be freely interrogated along many different parameters.

The incorporation of ERP data into a data warehouse is an issue that can be addressed in more than one way. Figure 13.6 shows the three common ways that ERP data can enter a data warehouse. One option is to create a data warehouse within the ERP environment and to pull non-ERP data into the ERP data warehouse. This approach requires you to convert the non-ERP data to ERP-like data. In addition, this approach may constrain the DSS analyst to using the data within the confines of the ERP environment. The ERP environment typically enables access of the data only through ERP-specific structures. Unfortunately, in a DSS environment, the DSS analyst often wants to see the data through multiple technologies and the ERP-specific data structures may not permit this freedom of analysis. The proprietary nature of the ERP's data warehouse environment may limit your ability to satisfy all of the business community.

A second limitation affects the tools the ERP vendor supports for DSS analysis. If the organization has its own favorite and customary set of tools and the ERP vendor does not support those tools, then a fundamental problem will occur with building the data warehouse within the confines of the ERP environment.

A second approach is to build two types of warehouses. One warehouse is built for non-ERP data in a conventional warehouse environment. Another ERP-specific warehouse is built just for ERP data. Much analysis can be done in either environment. However, if a combination of the two warehouses is needed, the data must either be pushed to the non-ERP data warehouse where it is merged and compared in a conventional manner with conventional tools or the non-ERP data must be introduced into the ERP warehouse structure.

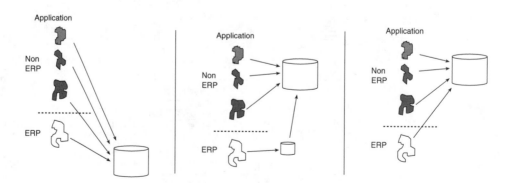

Figure 13.6   Three possibilities for merging ERP and non-ERP data.

A third approach is to take the ERP data and move it directly out of the ERP environment and into a non-ERP data warehouse. The issue here concerns pulling the data out of the ERP environment. In order to do so it is advisable to use a commercial tool designed for that purpose.

e-Business Analytic Applications

Strictly speaking, e-business is not a DSS application, but many aspects of e-business relate to a DSS analysis. A very natural relationship exists between the Web site (which supports e-business) and the corporate information factory. Figure 13.7 shows that the fit with the data warehouse-centric CIF is tight and comfortable. The Web site feeds data to the data warehouse through a granularity manager. The granularity manager is a component of the Web interface that reduces, aggregates, and organizes very low-level detail created in the Web site (such as click streams) as the data passes into the CIF. In turn, the Web site may receive small amounts of aggregated, analyzed data originating from the data warehouse and fed into an ODS. The last direct interface the Web site has with the CIF is through the fulfillment process, which is the order-processing component of the CIF. When the Web site encounters an order, the

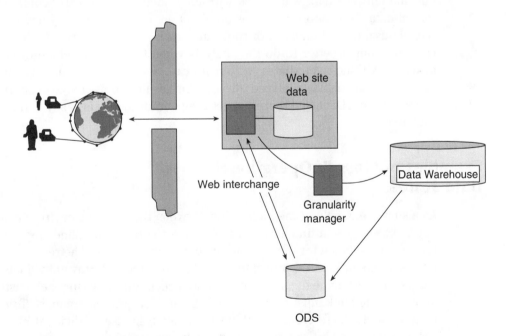

Figure 13.7 The essential components of the web and the CIF.

information needed to complete the order is passed directly into the operational systems of the corporation.

Interaction of the Data Warehouse and the Operational Data Store

One aspect of the CIF that is often overlooked or ignored is the interaction between the data warehouse, data marts, and the operational data store. This interaction calls for small amounts of pre-aggregated or pre-analyzed data to flow from the strategic decision support environment into the ODS for use with more tactical applications. By placing the results of a strategic analysis in the ODS, we can rapidly access key strategic information while performing operational tasks. This new addition to the ODS evolution is called a *Class 4 ODS*.

Once the strategic results are stored in the ODS, online real-time support of important strategic information is possible. In doing so, the data warehouse can be said to support online high-performance access of data when that access is needed.

This is a valuable and important concept—an indirect approach to strategic information. The data warehouse with its associated data marts contains historical data. To support a conclusion about a customer, you may have to analyze thousands or hundreds of thousands of historical records. If that is the case, it is much better to do the analysis when plenty of machine cycles are available with no rush, that is, within your strategic decision support environment. After the data is analyzed through, the result of that analysis can then be placed in the ODS. Once there, this strategic information is easily and quickly available.

Examples of Class IV Operational Data Stores

As a simple example of the interaction between the strategic environment and our ODS, suppose a financial institute wants to create an online environment for loan acceptance for the regular customers of the bank. The requirement is for instantaneous loan approval for valuable and credit-worthy individuals. The analysis to determine the individual instant acceptance limit for each customer known to the bank must be performed in the appropriate data mart. To determine an individual's credit worthiness, the analysis uses individual historical transaction data, information about each customer's assets and liabilities, demographic data, and other integrated information to determine what the

Table 13.2 Results of Instant Loan Amount Analysis

CUSTOMER ID	INSTANTANEOUS LOAN AMOUNT
0010199	$100,000
0010200	$150,000
0028971	$75,000
0190432	$25,000
2159801	$200,000
And so on	. . .

bank is willing to risk in the way of an instantaneous loan to each individual. The net result of this analysis is shown in Table 13.2.

The results of the pre-aggregated, analyzed data are loaded into the ODS. In other words, the bank is willing to give customer 0010199 a loan of up to $100,000 instantly; 0010200, $150,000; 0028971, $75,000; and so on. Obviously, when customer 0010199 walks into the bank and requests a loan, he or she should get instant approval for any amount up to $100,000. The problem comes in accessing this critical information. Certainly, the loan officer does not want to run this lengthy analysis every time someone asks for a loan. Even if the results set is stored in an easily accessible report, he still does not know who each of these IDs refers to. He has little or no other information about these results other than the customer's ID. Obviously, he would like to go to one place to look up the current, integrated data about his customer and get immediate access to this strategic piece of information as well.

Therefore, this small amount of data from the strategic analysis is matched up with the same customer IDs in the ODS and the results are stored with each customer's record. The ODS customer information looks like Table 13.3.

Now the loan officer can simply look up a particular customer in the ODS to determine their individual loan limit. If the customer requires more than the pre-approved amount, then the bank must go through its normal loan routine to ensure her credit worthiness for the higher amount.

This is only one example of how critical strategic information can be fed to the ODS. We can think of numerous other examples of strategic information that would be good candidates for this new class of ODS. Table 13.4 has a few of these suggestions.

The Operational Data Store has evolved many times to new and critical roles within the operational world. This latest (but not last?) evolution is one in

Table 13.3 Strategic Data Stored in the ODS

CUSTOMER ID	NAME	ADDRESS	PRE-APPROVED LOAN AMT	PHONE NUMBER
0010199	Ron Powell	101 Main St.	$100,000	555-2342
0010200	Jean Schauer	53 Maple Ave.	$150,000	555-7896
0028971	Jon Geiger	23 Center St.	$75,000	555-4326
0190432	Claudia Imhoff	10 D Court St.	$25,000	555-7654
2159801	Joyce Norris	1908 Phillips St.	$200,000	555-3452
And so on	...	...	...	...

Table 13.4 Examples of Strategic Results That May Be Populated into the ODS

STRATEGIC RESULT	DEFINITION
Customer LTV Score	This analysis of determining the customer's overall lifetime value to the organization
Segmentation Score	The analysis determining the customer's market segment score
VIP Indicator	A determination of VIP status based on a customer's other relationships (is he or she a CEO of an important commercial account?), household status (son of important investor?), and so on

which the need to access small amounts of strategic information drives the incorporation of this information into the ODS from the strategic decision support environment. The ability to access this strategic information in a real-time mode has proven to be an appreciated and highly successful new twist in a well-established component of the CIF.

What Is an "Oper-Mart"?

Over the years since the publication of *Building the Operational Data Store*[1], we have learned a great deal about the utilization and construction of this

---

[1] Inmon, Imhoff, and Battas. *Building the Operational Data Store*, John Wiley & Sons, 1996.

important component of the CIF. Furthermore, we have discovered a new structure, heretofore unknown that is used for tactical analysis. This structure is called an *oper-mart*. Yes, it is similar to the data mart in that it is a smaller subset of data available in the ODS, but it differs significantly in its currency, its usage, and the business community members using it. The characteristics of an oper-mart are as follows:

- It is a small subset of operational data-store data used in tactical analysis.
- It is stored usually in a multidimensional manner (star schema or hypercube).
- It is updated by transactions occurring in the ODS (no history stored here!).
- It may be created in a temporary manner and dismantled when no longer needed

Oper-marts are created when current operational data needs to be analyzed in a multidimensional fashion. For example, a banker may want to get a quick idea of how many and what types of loans have been issued in a particular market segment for commercial customers today. He may need to slice this data in several different ways to get a current understanding of the bank's operations. He needs immediate access to current data in an easy fashion, yet he cannot impact the functioning of his operational systems. He needs an oper-mart that is quickly constructed, easily understood, and constantly updated as the day's business progresses.

We are starting to see oper-marts being built off ERP systems, from ODS implementations, and even from some legacy systems. Like all things, these should be used conservatively and have a rational plan in place for their construction, maintenance, and eventual destruction. They are not all-purpose tools and should never be used to replace strategic data marts or the data warehouse.

Off-the-Shelf Applications

Many vendors today are developing pre-designed applications for both strategic and tactical applications. These vendors have studied and implemented the needs of both vertical industries (financial services, telecommunications, retail, utilities) and horizontal applications (risk management, fraud analysis, CRM applications) and have developed everything needed for generic applications. These applications include the data models, database schemas, maps to specific ERP systems, and even the transformation rules necessary to integrate the data—all that is needed to create an application. All you add is your data.

Guidelines for Choosing the Right Off-the-Shelf Decision Support Application

The DSS industry is moving toward more and more pre-built, pre-designed decision support applications. As an example of these "data marts in a box," you can find vendors selling risk management applications, profitability marts, CRM demographic profiling and lifetime value applications, and so on. As a final part of this chapter, we offer the following guidelines to help you choose the best off-the-shelf applications for your corporation.

- Diligently determine the business requirements for the application. Create a document that clearly and concisely states the business problems that will be solved by the commercial application.

- Determine whether the application will be used by only a department (departmental data mart) or whether it will be used by many departments (DSS application data mart). This determination may affect the interface into the mart and the security of the data within.

- Determine the match between the commercial application and the documented business requirements. No commercial mart will satisfy all the requirements, but it should support at least 80 percent of the known requirements.

- Determine the technological fit with your existing warehouse environment. If the commercial mart requires new technology, you may want to reconsider. Will it fit into a feed from the warehouse easily and with minimal disruption to the current flow of data?

- Determine the performance criteria for the new capability. This will require you to determine the immediate number of users, the growth of these users over the next two years, the performance expectations from the business community, and so on.

- Consider the data volumes the application may have to handle and ensure that it can support these volumes.

- Create a prototype of the application to test it out in your environment. Nothing is more important than ensuring that the application will work in your particular environment.

- Determine the entire costs of the application (include hidden costs such as technical support, upgrades, and so on). Make sure you have done a solid cost/benefit analysis to justify the cost.

- Obtain references from the vendor of similar installations. You may even want to do a site visit with the references.

Buying rather than building an analytical application has several advantages:

- The time for implementation can be greatly shortened.
- There may be functionalities in the commercial mart that your users did not consider.
- The commercial mart forces an amount of standardization that you may not be able to achieve if you build the application.

Buying the commercial mart has deterrents as well:

- The functionality may not be customizable, so what you get is all you get.
- Since it is a generic application, there may be functionalities that you don't want or need, and there may be concessions that your business communities may make to accommodate the application.
- Your competitor may have the same application, thus destroying any strategic advantage you may think you will get.

Summary

The data warehouse serves as an excellent source of data for data marts. It not only supplies integrated, high-quality data, but it also serves as a repository of valuable historical data for use in decision support analyses.

Two types of data marts can be built—those for a specific department that are rather generic in purpose and design and are used only by one department—and DSS applications that are used by multiple departments and have a very specific design and purpose. Each type of mart has advantages and disadvantages associated with it. Your job is to determine which mart type best suits your corporation's business needs.

Data mart designs come in many flavors:

- Multidimensional ones using star schemas, snowflake schemas or hypercubes
- Reporting ones that simply use subsets of relatively static, normalized data
- Exploration ones that require denormalized flat files with minimal data relationships

You must fit the design to the business problem identified and the access tool selected.

The data warehouse and data marts also have a very nice interplay with the operational data store. Small amounts of pre-aggregated or pre-analyzed data may flow from the warehouse into the ODS for use in tactical decision-making. This interaction enables critical strategic data to be accessible in a real-time, fast access mode. The ODS may also spawn oper-marts, current subsets of data used for tactical multidimensional analysis.

Finally, a number of vendors offer commercial applications that can truly speed up the implementation time. Care must be taken to ensure that these applications are right for your organization and business community. The set of guidelines given will help you determine whether to buy or build your data mart functionality.

Congratulations! You have now covered a broad spectrum of concepts ranging from what components comprise the corporate information factory to how these components are used in the delivery of decision-support capabilities. Now, let's take a look at *variations* to implementing the corporate information factory and the associated risks to the long-term viability of your information ecosystem.

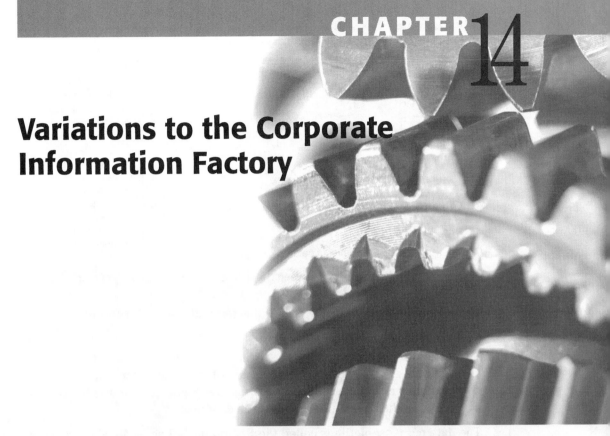

Variations to the Corporate Information Factory

A policeman won't blow his whistle and arrest you if you violate the design guidelines of the corporate information factory (CIF). However, when you choose to build your systems outside of the architecture suggested by the CIF, a price must be paid. In some cases, the price is a large one; in others, it is not. As long as the architect is aware of the stakes and the potential disadvantages of a design that violates the CIF, nothing prevents the architect from following the CIF design.

The CIF and its different components have been specified as they are for a reason. If they are built in a manner other than that outlined in this book, something important may suffer. This chapter will suggest several popular alternatives to the CIF and point out the price for not having followed the design principles specified.

Should We Build the Data Mart or the Data Warehouse First?

The classical structure for delivering business intelligence contains two levels of data that are of interest—the data warehouse data and the data mart data. The data warehouse, often called the *current level of detail*, contains the bulk

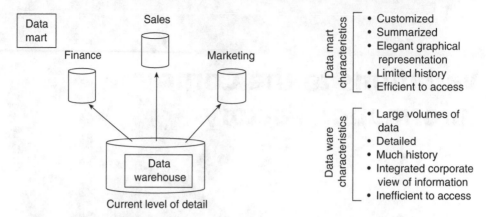

Figure 14.1 The relationship between the data warehouse and the data mart.

of the detailed data that has been collected and integrated from the applications environment.

The data mart is a departmental subset of the current detailed data that is shaped to meet the DSS processing needs of that particular department. The source of data mart data is the data warehouse. Figure 14.1 shows the relationship between the data warehouse and the data mart.

The data mart—sometimes called the Relational Online Analytical Processing (ROLAP) or the Mulitdimensional Online Analytical Processing (MOLAP) environment—contains a subset of the current level data that has been customized for the department. Typically, the finance, marketing, and sales departments have their own data marts. The data mart usually contains data that has been distilled to meet the performance, analytic, navigation, and visualization needs of a particular department. Data marts are generally very small compared to the data warehouse. This is due to the fact that data marts generally contain a sample or subset data, or data that has been aggregated by predefined set business dimensions (such as, product, time, channel, etc.) and metrics (revenue, profit, usage, counts, etc.).

The new data warehouse contains a massive amount of integrated data and represents a truly corporate understanding of information. Because of the massive volumes of data found in the data warehouse, and since it serves many different departmental data marts, the data warehouse is not terribly efficient to access.

One of the most important questions the data warehouse architect faces is that of the order in which to build the data marts and the data warehouse. Two basic choices exist:

1. Build the data marts before the data warehouse is built.

2. Build the data marts in conjunction with the data warehouse.

The decision to do one or the other does not *appear* to be an important decision, but this decision is one of the most important and strategic decisions that the architect will ever make. The CIF dictates that the data marts be built in conjunction with the data warehouse, but nothing can keep the data marts from being built first, directly from the applications environment.

Building the Data Mart First

One choice the CIF architect has is to build the data marts first, directly from the applications environment.

The data mart shown in Figure 14.2 is built directly from the applications. When the diagram is as simple as that shown in the figure, no problem occurs with building the data mart as the first part of the architecture. Building the data mart directly from the applications first appears to be cheap, easy, and fast.

However, some very real reasons dictate that building the data marts directly from applications is a poor idea and that the price to pay is severe. It is not at all obvious at the moment of building the first one or two data marts. Instead, the price becomes obvious as soon as the third or fourth data mart is being built. It takes a while for the organization to discover that building a data mart in a manner not suggested by the CIF can have tremendous consequences. This price is usually paid as the complexity of the interface increases, or when considering the placement and interpretation of data. We will discuss this price shortly.

Building the Data Mart in Conjunction with the Data Warehouse

The alternative to building data marts as the first part of the architecture is to build the data warehouse first and then build the data marts on top of the data

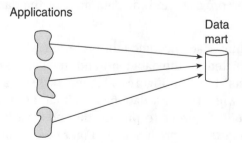

Figure 14.2 Building the data mart directly from the applications.

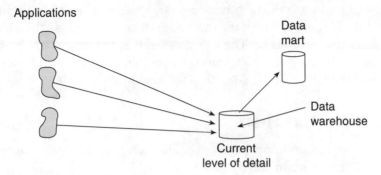

Figure 14.3 Building the data mart from the data warehoused data.

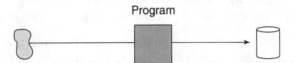

Figure 14.4 The interface program must be written, maintained, and executed.

warehouse (see Figure 14.3). This alternative is expensive, slow, and difficult. Compared to the ease of building data marts directly from the applications first, it is reasonable to ask why anyone would choose this approach.

Complexity of the Interface

In order to answer this question, left's shift focus to the interface between the applications and the data mart or the data warehouse itself. In Figures 14.2 and 14.3, a simple line represents the flow of data from the applications to the data mart or the data warehouse. The interface shown in Figure 14.4 is anything but simple. Rather, a program must be written, maintained, and provide resources every time it is executed.

In short, much development and many mechanical resources are required every time the line between the program and the data mart or the data warehouse appears.

The resources required by the interface become more relevant when we consider that the environment depicted for the data mart and the data warehouse is hardly realistic. The diagrams shown in Figures 14.2 and 14.3 represent the world of business intelligence when the *first* data mart is built, not the world when the *last* data mart is built. In order to picture the more realistic and mature environment of data marts and applications, Figure 14.5 shows that many source applications and many data marts exist; each of the data marts has its own user or department.

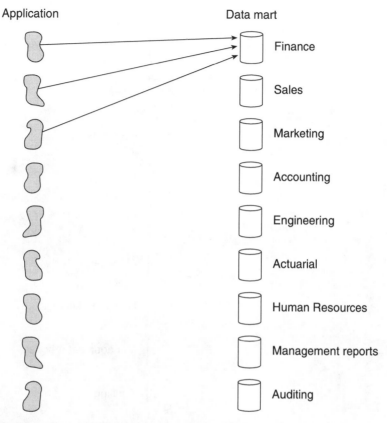

Figure 14.5 A much more accurate picture of the information environment with many applications and data marts.

By the same token, when the data warehouse is built first, multiple sources of data and multiple data marts will be built in conjunction, as shown in Figure 14.6.

The reality of this environment is that many application sources and many data marts will be built. The perspective shown in Figures 14.2 and 14.3 is merely the perspective of the very first of the data marts that will be built. As such, the environment shown in these figures is an extremely short-term view of the world.

Figure 14.7 shows that the interface between the applications and the data marts is a very complex one. *Many* programs provide interfaces for the two environments that must be built and maintained. In addition, the amount of hardware required to move the data along all of the interfaces is considerable. In fact, the number of interfaces required can be expressed mathematically. If m applications exist and if n data marts are needed, then $m \times n$ interfaces will have to be built and executed.

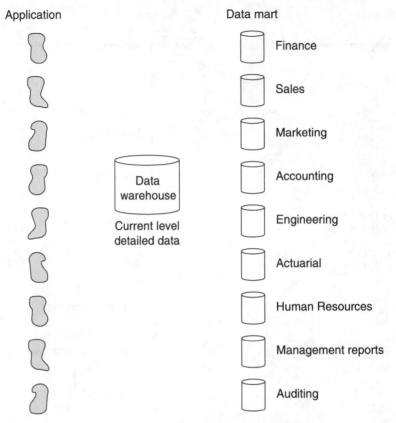

Application

Data mart

Finance

Sales

Marketing

Accounting

Engineering

Actuarial

Human Resources

Management reports

Auditing

Data warehouse

Current level detailed data

Figure 14.6 A much more accurate picture of the information environment where many applications and data marts are integrated via the data warehouse.

The scenario described in Figure 14.7 is one that is reminiscent of the classical operational *spider web environment*.

The complexity and chaos of the applications-to-data-mart approach is in stark contrast to the order and discipline that is achieved by building the data mart in conjunction with the data warehouse. Figure 14.8 displays this alternative.

Of course, interfaces are required in the building of the data warehouse first. However, a very orderly approach to creating interfaces can be taken, as shown in Figure 14.8. The number of interfaces that are required can be expressed mathematically. If there are m applications and n data marts, then building the data warehouse in conjunction with the data mart requires $m + n$ interfaces.

Since the direct data mart approach requires $m \times n$ interfaces and the data warehouse approach requires $m + n$ interfaces, the conclusion can be drawn

Application

Data mart

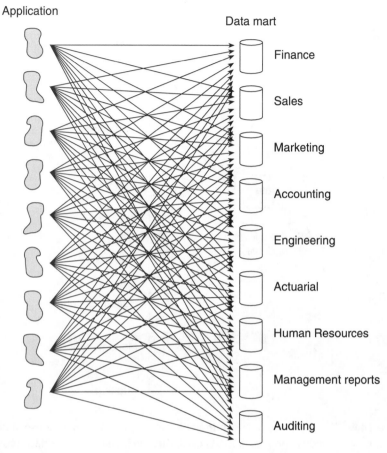

Finance

Sales

Marketing

Accounting

Engineering

Actuarial

Human Resources

Management reports

Auditing

Figure 14.7 The interfaces between applications and data marts. If m applications and n data marts exist, there will be $m \times n$ interface programs.

that the more complex and larger the application environment is and the more data marts there will be, the more complex the interface between the data mart and the application becomes. Indeed, the complexity increases geometrically with an increase in scale.

Placement of Data

The interfaces between the different environments is not the only reason why building the data marts directly from the applications environment is a bad idea. A second reason is because of the dilemma caused by deciding where to place common and unique data.

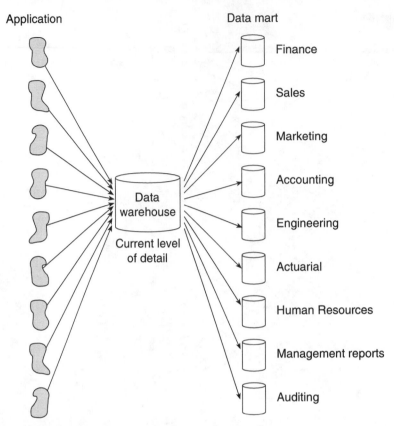

Application

Data mart

Finance

Sales

Marketing

Accounting

Engineering

Data warehouse

Current level of detail

Actuarial

Human Resources

Management reports

Auditing

Figure 14.8 The interfaces between the applications, the data warehouse, and the data mart. If *m* applications and *n* data marts exist, there will be *m* + *n* interface programs.

Figure 14.9 shows the data warehouse is a very convenient place to hold the common corporate data. The data marts are good places to hold the data that is unique to the department that owns the mart. The architecture shown in Figure 14.9 provides for a clean and convenient positioning of corporate and departmental data.

Figure 14.10 shows that where data marts are built directly from the applications, placing common corporate data in every data mart is needed.

Each data mart contains its own collection of unique data and common detailed data. The massive redundancy of data that results from every data mart "doing its own thing" is shown in Figure 14.11.

Common data is grossly redundant across the different data marts. Furthermore, the data that is redundant is the most voluminous of all the data a corporation has. This is a very expensive proposition from both a data storage and processing perspective.

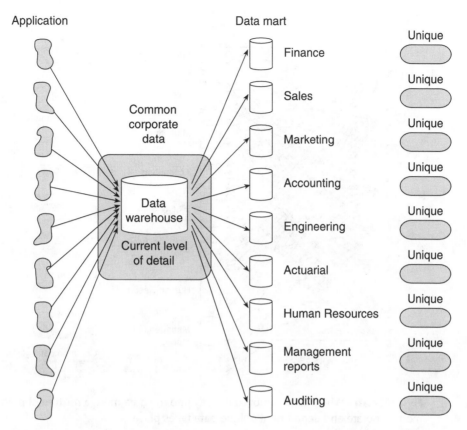

Figure 14.9 A very nice division exists between common corporate data and departmentally unique data.

Interpreting the Number of Customers

Yet another reason proves that building the data marts directly from the applications is a bad idea, and that reason is illustrated by asking the question, "How many customers does the corporation have?" Figure 14.12 shows that when the data marts are built directly from the applications, each different department has its own answer to the question of how many customers the business has. Trying to make a coherent business decision based on the wildly differing interpretations of how many customers is impossible.

Contrast the chaos of Figure 14.12 with the discipline in Figure 14.13.

Figure 14.13 shows a single definition and a single occurrence of a customer in the current level of detail. Each customer record contains a single, integrated definition of what a customer is. The customer record has qualifying attributes that allow the distinction to be made between different classes of customers.

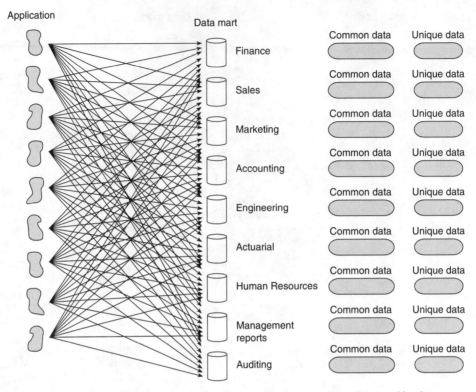

Figure 14.10 Where data is moved directly into the data mart, a mixture of both common corporate and department unique data takes place.

The attributes typically contain data about old, new, and potential customers; about large and small customers; about Italian, English, American customers; and so forth. Because of the single integrated definition, the departments can clearly identify exactly what customer category is being considered, something that is not possible when the data marts are built directly from the applications.

Once the departments can tell what data they are talking about, making distinctions between the different categories of customers is easy. Once the distinction between customers can be made, making business sense out of the data becomes a real possibility.

Should We Combine the Data Warehouse and the Operational Data Store?

Another architectural possibility that conflicts with the specifications of the CIF is that of trying to combine the operational data store (ODS) and the data

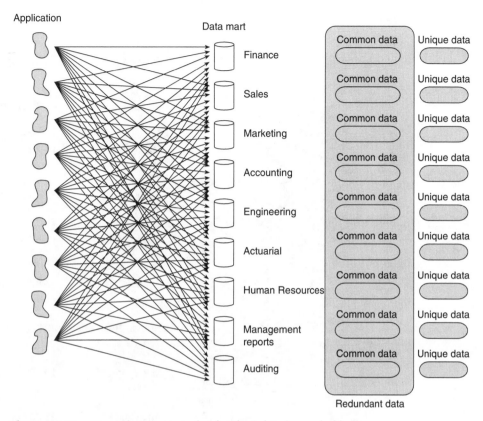

Figure 14.11 A massive amount of redundant data is needed here.

warehouse into the same structure. It is theoretically possible to build such a structure, and under very limited circumstances, such a combination structure can be made to work.

With a very small amount of data and processing, as well as an abundance of processing power, it is possible to merge an ODS and a data warehouse into the same structure. The capacity levels for the processor should not exceed more than 5 or 10 percent under the normal hours of utilization in order for the merger to function properly. Unfortunately, it is not economically feasible to purchase a powerful and versatile machine and use it so sparsely. Figure 14.14 shows the merging of the ODS and the data warehouse into the same structure.

There are many reasons why the ODS and the data warehouse should not be combined. Some of the reasons are very large and important; others are smaller and represent only inconveniences. However, taken together, the reasons all add up to the same thing—the data warehouse and the ODS need to be physically separate entities and environments in order to ensure long-term viability of your information ecosystem.

Application

Data mart

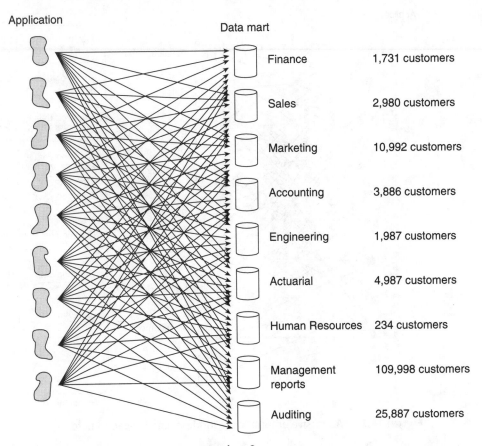

Finance	1,731 customers
Sales	2,980 customers
Marketing	10,992 customers
Accounting	3,886 customers
Engineering	1,987 customers
Actuarial	4,987 customers
Human Resources	234 customers
Management reports	109,998 customers
Auditing	25,887 customers

Figure 14.12 How many customers are there?

The Combination of Incompatible Transaction Types

Figure 14.15 shows that online transactional processing (OLTP) and analytical transactions are mixed together when the ODS and the data warehouse are combined.

OLTP transactions and analytical transactions are as different as transaction types can be. When they are separated, many advantageous things happen:

- System block sizes can be optimized for one type of transaction or the other.
- Buffers can be optimized for one type of processing or the other.

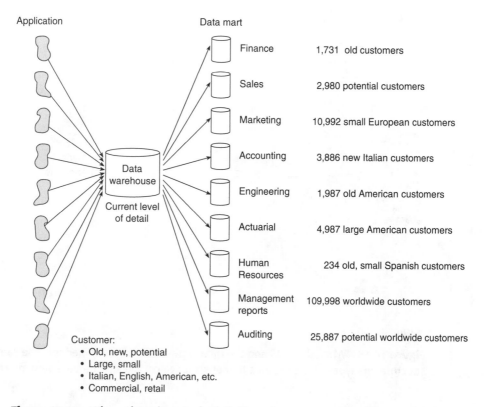

Figure 14.13 Where there is a single definition of a customer, the different variations can be understood.

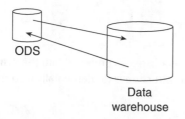

Figure 14.14 Another possibility for the CIF is the merging of the ODS and the data warehouse.

- System initialization parameters, such as FREESPACE, can be optimized for one type of activity or the other.
- Data can be distributed across system resources (central processing unit [CPU], disk, and so on) for one type of processing or the other.

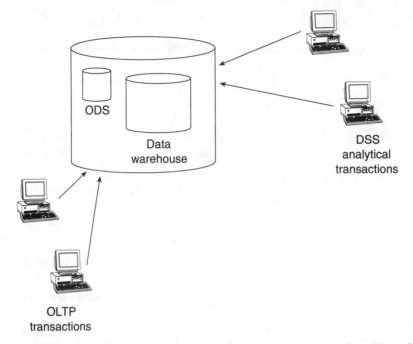

Figure 14.15   When the ODS and the data warehouse are combined into the same structure, the types of transactions that are run against the structure are very mixed.

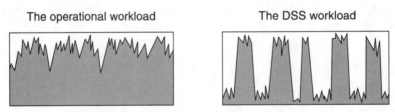

Figure 14.16   When the ODS and the data warehouse are combined into the same structure, the workload that operates against the structure is fundamentally incompatible with itself.

The Forced Combination of Incompatible Workload Types

Figure 14.16 shows that very different workload patterns take place in the OLTP environment and the analytical environment.

The OLTP workload is one with peaks and valleys, but within it the mean system utilization is a descriptive number. The OLTP workload is one that can be predicted and managed, and the analytical workload is essentially a binary workload. Either the system is being used heavily or not being used at all. This workload is not predictable and the mean utilization of the system is a useless number in most circumstances. When the ODS and the data warehouse are mixed in the same environment and technology, the two workloads are forced into the same box.

Figure 14.17 shows two approaches to mixing ODS and data warehouse processing in a single machine/database.

The DWA can buy a very large box to try to contain the workload. The strategy is to buy a box with sufficient capacity that the analytical workload can be accommodated without impacting the OLTP workload. Given the unpredictable nature of the analytical workload, this results in a machine with a significant amount of idle capacity (more than 50 percent). This approach yields reasonable performance (not optimal) with an unreasable price tag.

A large processor

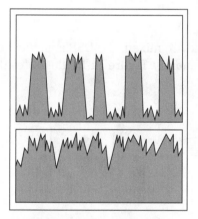

A small processor

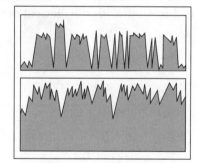

One way to resolve the conflict in the pattern of processing is to buy a mammoth amount of capacity. When you do this:

- The unit price of the hardware is as expensive as it gets.
- You have excess capacity left over.
- The end user is happy with response time.
- The financial manager considers the purchase to be a disaster.

Another way to resolve the conflict presented by mixing incompatible workloads is to buy a small machine and to cram all processing in the small machine. When you do this:

- The machine is used at 100% capacity.
- The end user declares the system unusable.
- The financial manager loves it because it is cheap and the machine is being used at 100%.

Figure 14.17 There is no good way to mix incompatible workloads.

Alternatively, the DWA can combine the workload in a small machine. This pleases the finance manager (especially when the finance manager finds out that the machine is being used close to 100 percent of the time). The user community is far less enthusiastic about this configuration. Watching a query complete in this environment is like watching paint dry. Quickly, users become disenchanted and go elsewhere. This approach yields unreasonable performance with a reasonable price tag.

Given that you can live with either of these approaches, consider a few additional things before taking the historic step (one way or another) of mixing workloads.

Style Incompatibility

The system cannot be tuned or optimized for any style of processing. This workload incompatibility is resolved by separating the ODS and the data warehouse.

Mixing of Communities

When the ODS and the data warehouse are mixed, the DSS analytical community is thrown in with the clerical community. Figure 14.18 illustrates this phe-

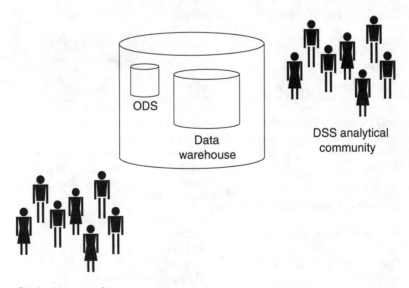

ODS

Data
warehouse

DSS analytical
community

Clerical community

Figure 14.18 When the ODS and the data warehouse are combined into the same structure, the different communities they serve are lumped together.

nomenon. When enough people start to use the combined structure, they start to step on each other's toes.

Transmissions Are Incompatible

Figure 14.19 shows that when workload is combined the transmissions across the communications lines are mixed as well.

On the left-hand side of Figure 14.19, the transmission types are not mixed because the ODS and the data warehouse are separated. On the right-hand side, the transmission types are mixed together. In order to achieve a uniform and efficient flow, there needs to be a separation of the different transmission types.

Mixed Current and Historical Data

Figure 14.20 shows that ODS current data is mixed with data warehouse historical data.

When current data is mixed with historical data, a problem arises concerning data access. Current data typically has a much higher probability of access than historical data, but when they are mixed together, current data can *hide* behind historical data, making current data hard and inefficient to access.

No clear distinction exists between dynamic summary data and static summary data, as shown in Figure 14.21.

When the ODS and the data warehouse are separated, a very real barrier is created between dynamic summary data and static summary data. When the two are combined, chances are that *no* distinction will be made between the two

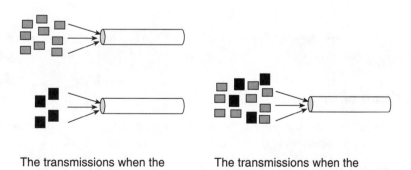

The transmissions when the ODS and the data warehouse are separated.

The transmissions when the ODS and the data warehouse are combined.

Figure 14.19 Mixing combined workloads across the communication lines.

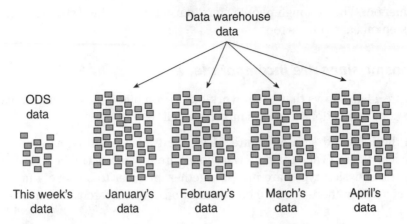

Figure 14.20 Current data is mixed with historical data when the ODS is mixed with the data warehouse.

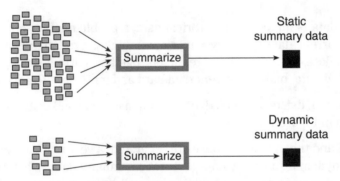

Figure 14.21 When the ODS is mixed with the data warehouse, dynamic summary data is mixed with static summary data.

types of summary data. Unfortunately, this blurring of distinctions can cause real confusion.

Overhead of Updates

Figure 14.22 shows that when the ODS and the data warehouse are mixed together, every transaction pays the price for overhead of updates.

The overhead of an update shows up as check pointing, rollback, the logging of transactions, and committing data. When an update is a possibility, all transactions that are in execution pay the same price of overhead. Even when only one in a thousand transactions actually does update, *all* transactions that are operating pay the price of overhead. When the ODS is separated from the data ware-

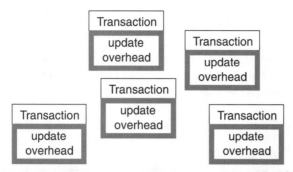

Figure 14.22 All transactions may pay the price for overhead of updates, even when they don't do any updates.

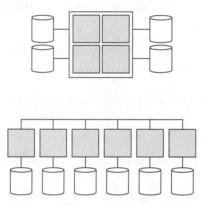

Figure 14.23 No optimal hardware architecture for the ODS and the data warehouse is available when they are mixed.

house, it is very convenient to separate update processing from access processing. Update processing is regularly done in the ODS environment while access-only processing (which is very efficient) is done in the data warehouse environment.

No Optimal Hardware Architecture

Figure 14.23 shows that when the ODS and the data warehouse are mixed, no optimal hardware architecture is available.

When the ODS is separated from the data warehouse, the ODS operates optimally on an MPP architecture. Depending on the size and the processing done, the data warehouse may or may not run optimally on an MPP architecture. Indeed, the data warehouse may operate optimally on an SMP architecture.

When this is the case, the mixing of the two environments causes a dilemma for the CIF architect.

These, then, are reasons why the ODS and the data warehouse workloads should be split. The DWA *can* violate the CIF and combine workloads, but if this is done, there is a price to be paid.

Summary

The CIF and its different components can be built in many different ways. The architecture suggested by the CIF is not without its variations, though problems can arise when these variations exist. As long as the system architect is aware of these potential problems and the price of these problems, then the CIF architecture can be violated at will.

As an example of a price to be paid, when the data marts are built from the applications environment, some severe drawbacks occur:

- The interface between the applications and the data marts turns into a nightmare.
- There is no integration foundation.
- A tremendous amount of redundancy and inconsistent interpretations of data are introduced.

As another example of violating the CIF, the ODS and the data warehouse can be built together as a single structure. But when a single structure is created, the following occurrences take place:

- OLTP is freely mixed with analytical transactions.
- The workload is mixed.
- Analytic users are mixed with clerical users.
- Mixed transmission types are forced into the same communications link.
- Current data is mixed with historical data.

This completes our review of an architecture that will embody the information ecosystem of tomorrow's business leaders, the *corporate information factory*. In the next chapter, we will discuss considerations for building the corporate information factory.

CHAPTER 15

Building the Corporate Information Factory

Now that we have reviewed the components of the corporate information factory (CIF) and trade-offs associated with the variations, it is a good time to discuss building it. The information ecosystem that the CIF embodies is very much like any ecosystem in that:

- It feeds from a common source of energy, in the form of data, provided by the application environment and external sources.

- It transforms this data, through a series of complex processes, into food (that is, information) consumed by end users of the ecosystem.

- It recycles end-user by-products to further enrich and strengthen the ecosystem.

- Its development is evolutionary in nature.

In building the corporate information factory, the phrase *"evolutionary in nature"* should be foremost in our minds. This is not to say a *strategic plan* doesn't exist. Arguably, even the ecosystem in which we live has a strategic plan that provides purpose. However, the CIF development should be driven by *strategic actions* aimed at tactical business needs crucial to the survival of the business ecosystem that it supports. With each strategic action—or iteration—the CIF evolves, in form and function, to deliver incremental value to the business. It is only through this iterative delivery that:

- Business value is quickly added and relevance is achieved.

- Business interest is maintained and heightened.

- Details of the strategic plan are materialized.

Through the effective use of a strategic plan complemented by strategic actions, we can expect to deliver a CIF that evolves to support both the short- and long-term needs of the business.

The Strategic Plan

The first step in building the CIF is to understand what competencies drive your business. Business competencies represent areas of proficiency needed to support the business processes (such as sales, marketing, service, and so on) as they will exist in tomorrow's business landscape. These competencies are usually a combination of people, processes, and/or systems. Though this may seem like a fairly simple exercise, it is very interesting to note that many existing competencies are being refined, and new competencies are being added, as companies move away from a business model that targets products to the masses to a model that tailors products to the customer.

In general, the following competencies are common or are becoming common in most companies:

- Transaction management

- Account management

- Product management

- Human resources management

- Distribution management

- Contact management

- Customer management

- Business intelligence

The next step is to align the different components of the CIF to these core competencies, as illustrated in Figure 15.1.

In this example, we see that five competencies have been identified: business intelligence, contact management, account management, human resource (HR) management, and customer management. In addition, we can see how these competencies are being positioned to support such business processes as marketing, sales/service, and billing. This overlay of competencies to business processes represents our *business vision*. With that said, let's take a look at how the different components of the CIF align to support this business vision.

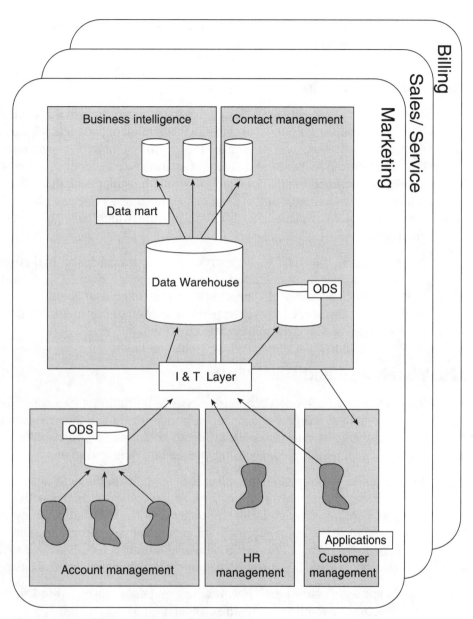

Figure 15.1 Aligning the CIF to the core competencies of the business.

Applications Environment

The applications align very nicely to support HR management and customer management. In both cases, there appears to be a single, integrated application to support each competency. In contrast, account management consists of three separate applications with no integration (probably one account management application per product line).

Operational Data Store

The operational data store (ODS) appears to have two users in this environment. The first use is as a vehicle to provide an integration of products within product management. Rather than waiting for this environment to be re-engineered, the ODS can be used to expedite delivery of an integrated account view to support immediate business needs. An example would be supporting the rollup of customer products into account(s) used in customizing service and billing. In addition, this construct provides a foundation from which re-engineering efforts can build.

A second use of the ODS is in support of contact management. In this situation, the ODS provides a consolidated view of application data for use during customer contact activities. In creating this part of the ODS, different contact channels can be assured that their need for customer information will not contend with the needs of the application environment.

Data Warehouse and Data Mart

The data warehouse and data marts seem to be fulfilling two roles. The first role is to deliver integrated data to support business intelligence capabilities. These capabilities support such strategic activities as profitability analysis, customer segmentation and scoring, product pricing, and so on.

In addition to these business intelligence capabilities, the data warehouse and data mart are also used to support the lead-generation activities within contact management. It is through these components of the CIF that planning and customer qualification are performed for campaigns and programs. Once a customer is assigned to a campaign(s) and/or program, the ODS is used to provide the operational details necessary to support the dialogue with the customer.

In this strategic plan, the data warehouse and data mart are used to discover and plan business action, while the ODS is used to take action.

The Strategic Action

The previous example is by no means definitive but should give a feel for the process used to derive a high-level strategic plan. It is from this plan that strategic action(s) will be taken.

The first step in determining a strategic action is to select from the business community what competency or competencies should be addressed first. This decision usually follows an assessment in which the high-level needs of each competency area are defined and evaluated. Consider these questions in selecting your competency:

- What needs are immediate versus long-term? What are the benefits versus the risks of meeting or not meeting these needs?
- How well do the current information systems align to these business needs and the competencies they represent? Are any of the current information systems positioned to support any of these competencies—full or in part? If not, what migration effort must occur?
- Are any of these needs part of a key corporate initiative?
- What is the cost to fulfill the need(s)? What funding is available?

Once the competency or competencies have been selected, strategic action can be taken to define the specific capabilities and to deliver/refine the necessary components of the CIF to support these capabilities. Simply put, a capability is a tool that enables the business community to derive value out of the CIF in support of a selected business competency. For example, a popular business intelligence capability would be one that supports profitability analysis. In addition, the necessary organization, technology, and procedures are employed to support administration and ongoing development.

Development Lifecycles

Many stark differences exist between the different components of the CIF. Perhaps the greatest difference is the development lifecycle used to implement the capabilities. Figure 15.2 outlines the different development lifecycles found in the CIF.

Two basic types of development lifecycles are available—the systems development lifecycle SDLC and the CLDS. The CLDS is in many ways the reverse image of the SDLC. The SDLC is often called a *waterfall* methodology because one phase feeds into the other. The classical stages of the SDLC are:

- Requirements gathering
- Analysis
- Design
- Programming

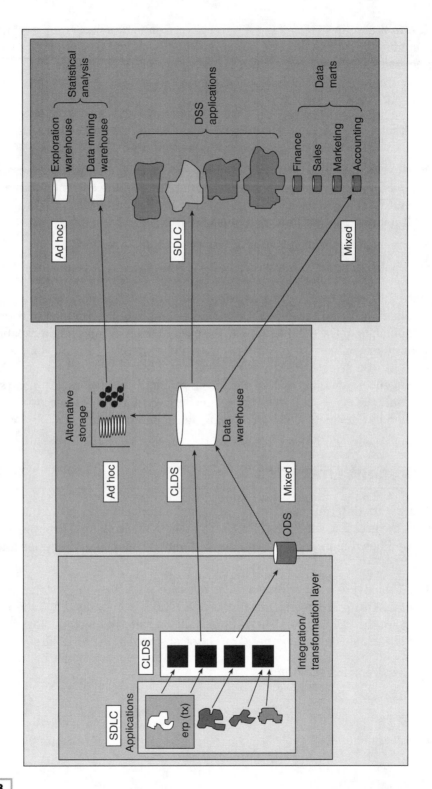

Figure 15.2 Very different approaches are used to develop the different parts of the CIF.

- Testing

- Implementation

The CLDS is an iterative approach to development and is quite different from the SDLC waterfall approach. Sometimes the CLDS is called a *spiral* methodology. The classical steps of the CLDS are as follows:

1. Start with implemented data, typically transaction data.

2. Probe and test the data.

3. Write some exploratory programs to determine what must be done in order to access and analyze the data.

4. Once the initial programs are written, do a formal design.

5. Analyze the results of the design, then go back and reformulate and reprogram.

6. As the final step, understand what the requirements are.

The SDLC is typically found in the applications arena. Because of the constant change that is endemic to the inegration and transformation (I & T) layer, the CLDS approach works best with the programs that must be developed there.

The ODS contains elements of both the SDLC and the CLDS. Because of this confusion, the ODS is the most difficult structure in the CIF to build successfully.

CLDS can apply to both the data warehouse and the data mart, but the development lifecycle on the data mart varies from the norm when in use by a farmer. The data warehouse is generally used by explorers. As a result, CLDS methodology proves to be very effective. In contrast, farmer activities are more repetitive and predictable. In this environment, the SDLC may prove to be more appropriate. Figure 15.3 makes the distinction between different kinds of development lifecycles.

Managing Different Organizational Units

Not surprisingly, different kinds of organizational units can be found scattered across the CIF. Figure 15.4 shows some of the more important organizational roles and where they are found.

System administrators are found in the management of the applications arena and in the administration of the network. Database administrators (DBAs) are found in the applications arena as well as applications programmers. Network administrators are found in the network management environment. Data warehouse administrators (DWAs) are located in the specification of the I & T layer and the data warehouse venue. The data administrator also is involved with the I & T layer. The ODS requires its own administrator. Finally, the data mart is

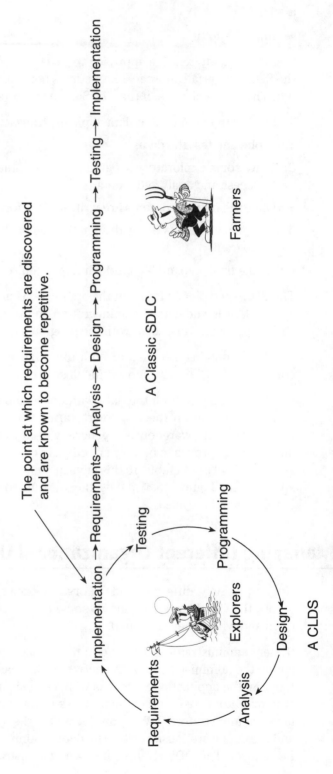

The point at which requirements are discovered and are known to become repetitive.

Implementation → Requirements → Analysis → Design → Programming → Testing → Implementation

A Classic SDLC

Farmers

Testing

Programming

Explorers

Requirements

Analysis

Design

A CLDS

Figure 15.3   An important relationship exists between the SDLC and the CLDS.

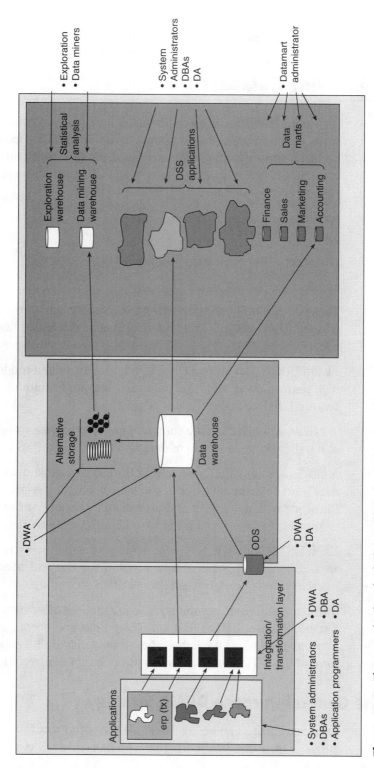

Figure 15.4   The organizational administrative roles across the CIF.

under the guidance of the departments that own the data mart itself with its own set of administrators and management.

Deploying Databases

Any number of strategies can be used for the deployment of database management systems across the components of the CIF. The first strategy is on a *niche* basis, where different DBMs are used for different components based on an ideal fit. In Figure 15.5, each part of the CIF has a different DBMS. In the applications arena, the following DBMSs are used:

- IMS
- IDMS
- VSAM
- CICS

These DBMSs are good at moving transactions and performing repetitive transactions. They can yield a high performance and a very high degree of availability.

At the ODS is Tandem's NON STOP SQL. For mixed-mode processing, where a high performance, update capabilities, and some amount of DSS processing are required, NON STOP SQL works very nicely.

Teradata and Informix are shown operating the data warehouse. They are good at handling large amounts of data and managing a DSS workload.

Multidimensional database and ROLAP tools are shown managing data at the data mart environment. These tools have a high degree of flexibility of processing along with an elegant end-user display. Finally, at the end-user workstation is Microsoft Access, an all-purpose DBMS for the workstation.

Each DBMS shown in the niche strategy has its own strengths and specialties. In addition, each is peculiarly adapted for the end user that it serves. Little overlap takes place between these DBMS technologies.

Though a different combination of databases may have been selected using Oracle, Sybase, DB2, Teradata, Red Brick, and so on, the point of the niche strategy is to select a database based on its ideal fit for each individual component of the CIF. The niche strategy is one that evolves naturally.

The General-Purpose DBMS Strategy

Other strategies can be used besides the niche strategy. Another is the *general-purpose* strategy. In Figure 15.6, the same DBMS is found in more than one

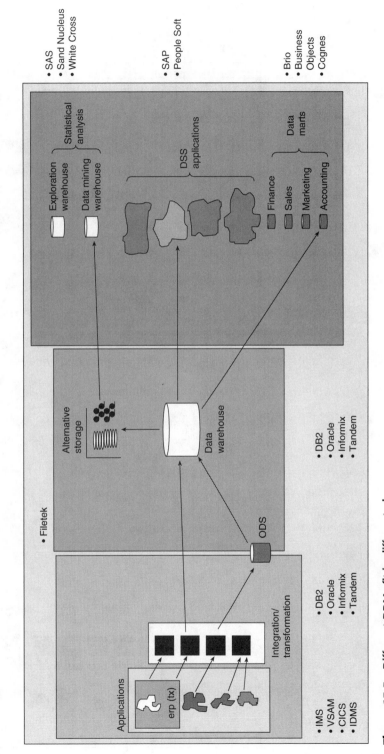

Figure 15.5 Different DBMs fit in different places.

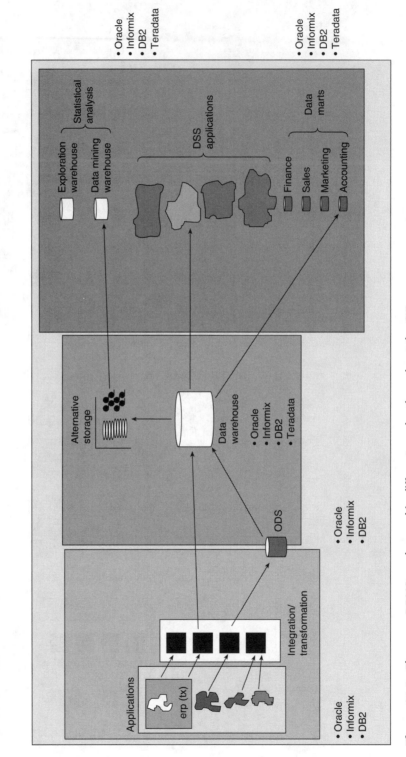

Figure 15.6 The same DBMS can be used in different modes throughout the CIF.

component of the CIF. At first glance, this appears to be a contradiction of the niche strategy, but upon a closer look, the general-purpose strategy ends up looking very similar to the niche strategy.

The reason why the general-purpose strategy looks a lot like the niche strategy is because even though the same DBMS is used in multiple places, the DBMS is configured very differently in different components. In other words, it may be Oracle in the applications arena and Oracle in the data warehouse, but the way that Oracle is configured in one place is not at all the way Oracle is configured elsewhere. In the applications environment, Oracle is configured for running transactions. In the data warehouse environment, Oracle is configured to manage a lot of data. In the ODS environment, Oracle is configured to manage a mixed workload.

A DBMS can be configured in many different ways to meet the peculiar needs of the environment that it is cast in, such as the following:

- Buffer sizes can be altered.
- FREESPACE can be modified.
- Transaction integrity can be turned off.
- Data can be partitioned.
- Checkpoints can be taken.
- Transactions can be governed.
- Processing can be prioritized.
- Buffers can be scanned sequentially.

The different environments can be optimized for their differing needs in hundreds of ways.

Different Hardware Platforms

Not surprisingly, different hardware platforms and hardware architectures work better in different parts of the CIF. The three types of hardware architectures, shown in Figure 15.7, are as follows:

1. Parallel MPP architectures: Multiple units of data are tied together by a common "backbone."

2. Parallel SMP architectures: Multiple processors are tied together in a shared memory configuration.

3. Uniprocessor architectures: A single storage device is controlled by a single processor, much as in a workstation on a mainframe processor.

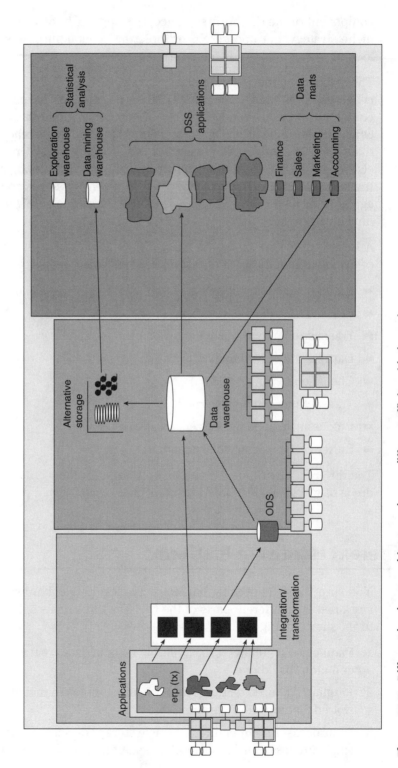

Figure 15.7 Different hardware architectures have a different affinity with the various components of the CIF.

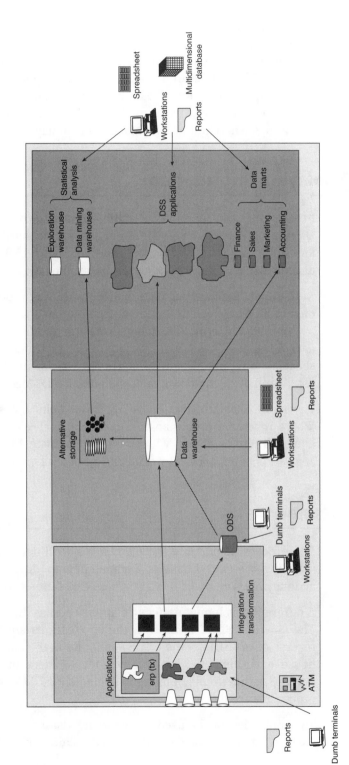

Figure 15.8 The different forms of display at the different components.

The applications environment uses a parallel SMP architecture as well; for smaller amounts of processing, a uniprocessor architecture is sufficient. The ODS environment has a particularly strong affinity for an MPP processing environment. The data warehouse environment operates well on a parallel MPP environment with a lot of data and on an SMP configuration with less data. Data marts work well with smaller SMP configurations and uniprocessor configurations where not much data is to be managed.

Displaying Information

In addition to the components of the CIF needing different DMBSs (or the same DMBS configured in very different ways) and hardware platforms, multiple kinds of information displays are needed. Figure 15.8 shows that information is displayed in a different mode throughout the CIF.

At the applications level, data is displayed using reports, dumb terminals, and on direct consumer interaction devices, such as an ATM. The ODS uses workstations, dumb terminals, and reports for the display of its information. The data warehouse has a wide variety of displays, such as workstations, spreadsheets, and reports. The data marts have the same display mechanisms as the data warehouse, including multidimensional DBMS.

The mode that information is displayed suits the style of data processing. Where repetitive processing is occurring, such as at the applications level, a dumb terminal suffices. With free-form, analytical processing, where iterative analysis is being done, powerful and flexible displays are in order.

Summary

The process of building the CIF begins with defining the strategic plan and selecting the first business competency to develop. From here, strategic actions are taken and valued business capabilities are delivered.

A different development lifecycle applies across the CIF to deliver capabilities. The classical SDLC is used in the applications and the ODS arena, and the reverse of the SDLC—the CLDS—is found in the data mart and the data warehouse environment. The explorer development lifecycle—the CLDS—turns into the farmer's development lifecycle—the SDLC—when the requirements of processing are discovered.

Two strategies can be used for deploying databases within the CIF. On a niche basis, a variety of specialized databases can be used to optimize performance within each component of the CIF. Alternatively, general-purpose databases can be tuned according to the varied processing demands of each component offering near-optimal performance.

Different hardware architectures support components of the CIF. MPP hardware environments fit very well with the ODS and occasionally with the data warehouse. SMP and uniprocessor architectures fit nicely with the data warehouse and the data mart environment.

In this chapter, we discussed people, process techniques, and technology considerations in building the CIF. In the next chapter, we review the key considerations in managing the CIF.

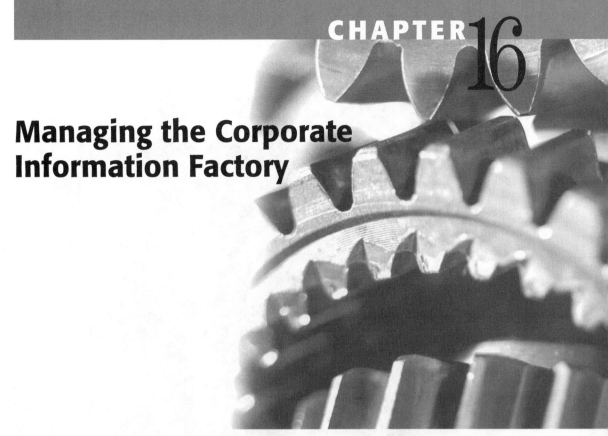

CHAPTER 16

Managing the Corporate Information Factory

O nce the corporate information factory (CIF) is built—in whole or in part—it requires ongoing systems management. Because of the diversity of processing that occurs within the CIF, it is no surprise that many different types of systems management tools are needed to monitor and run day-to-day operations. The CIF is simply much too big and diverse for any one suite of systems management tools to suffice. Indeed, the parameters of importance from one component of the CIF to another are so different that no one approach to systems management can be undertaken. Instead, the need for systems management must be considered on a component-by-component basis (see Figure 16.1):

- In the applications environment, systems management needs are characterized by transaction response time and availability.

- In the I & T layer, systems management needs are characterized by the ability to handle complexity, and the ability to gracefully and efficiently orchestrate maintenance with an ever-changing set of requirements.

- In the ODS environment, systems management needs are characterized by workload incompatibility and growth. As discussed earlier, this could easily become the most complex systems management task of all.

- In the data warehouse, systems management needs are characterized by volumes of data and an unpredictable workload.

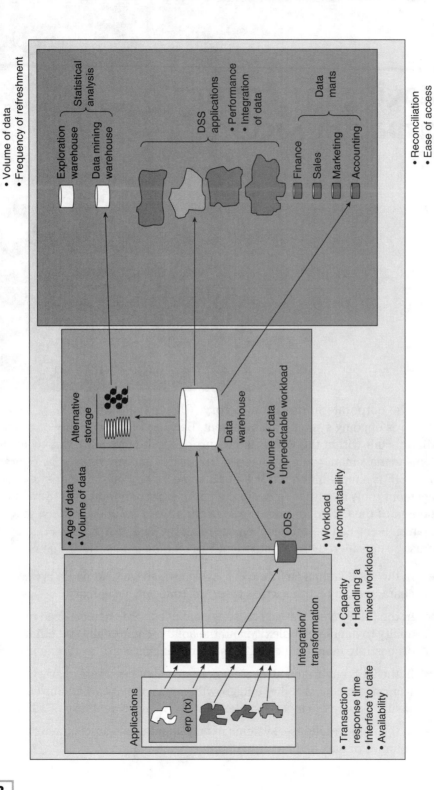

Figure 16.1 The characterization of systems management needs within the CIF.

- In the data mart environment, systems management needs are characterized by the reconciliation of data, and the ease of access and manipulation.

- In the Internet and intranet, systems management needs are characterized by network capacity and the ability to handle a mixed transmission workload.

Each of these issues of ongoing management will be addressed, component by component.

Ongoing Management — Applications

The primary issue of ongoing systems management for the applications arena is that of online response time and online systems availability. If the online system is not up and running, and if the online response time is not adequate, then the end user considers the application systems a failure. The desired response time is in the one- to two-second range. The systems availability desired is seven days a week, 24 hours a day—7 × 24.

Obtaining such a high degree of availability and responsiveness can be done in many different ways. The simplest way is to supply the applications environment with ample hardware resources. The problem with managing performance with resources is that it is very expensive and that, for some problems, additional systems resources do not improve performance or availability. Sometimes performance and availability are constrained by the software that uses the hardware. For example, let's say that you decide to upgrade your hardware environment from one CPU to two CPUs in an effort to improve transaction performance. It is possible that you may not realize any performance gain if the DBMS (the software) is not designed to distribute data and processing across multiple CPUs. Your only hope at this point would be to upgrade to a faster CPU or buy a new database.

A better long-term approach is to monitor the environment closely. With an OLTP monitor, two results can be achieved:

1. Hot spots and trouble areas can be identified and corrected before they become a major problem. Corrections could consist of simple software changes, or indexing and redistributing of data.

2. Capacity can be watched so that as soon as a legitimate need for more capacity arises, additional hardware can be procured.

Another approach to the optimization of the response time is to design applications so that an optimal response time can be achieved. In this approach, called the *standard work unit* approach, programs are written so that each uses a small and uniform amount of resources. Thus, the transactions that are created run through the system at a very efficient rate.

Another consideration of the ongoing success of the applications environment is that of placing the applications environment on the appropriate technology. Indeed, all CIF components need to be placed on top of technology that is optimal for their execution.

Ongoing Management—The Integration and Transformation Layer

Daily operations do not occur in the I & T layer in the same sense that they do in the applications environment or in other environments, yet the I & T layer needs to be managed just like any other component of the CIF. The following things are vital to the ongoing management of this layer:

- The maintenance of the code created for the I & T layer
- The efficiency of execution of the code inside the I & T layer
- The creation of metadata as a code by-product inside the I & T layer
- The creation of process and procedures to audit the I & T layer

The programs and processes within the I & T layer are notoriously dynamic because they sit in the crossroads between the applications environment and the data integration mechanisms of the CIF—the data warehouse and ODS. As a result, the I & T layer has the potential to change when

- The application environment changes
- The data warehouse changes
- The operational data store changes

To further complicate matters, the nature of data warehouse development is very iterative. As a result, changes occur frequently. As you can see, the I & T layer is subject to frequent change and therefore requires constant attention and maintenance.

Creating and Maintaining the Interface

One of the most effective approaches to managing the I & T layer is to use a tool of automation for the creation and maintenance of the interface. Instead of having manual programming as the basis for the creation of the I & T code, a tool of automation creates code for the interface automatically. This means that code is created and maintained much more quickly and cost-effectively.

Executing the Code

The efficiency of the code execution in the I & T layer is another ongoing challenge. There can be some gains in performance by carefully designing the programs and processes to effectively execute in the targeted hardware and DBMS environment. In addition, significant performance improvements can be realized by altering the means by which application *change* transactions are captured. Rather than sifting through the DBMS or DBMS backup file, the DBMS *log* can be used to capture application change transactions far more efficiently. The trade-off is that programs that read the log file tend to be fairly complex given the challenges involved in interpreting it. When log tapes are used as a source of refreshment:

- Only the data that has been added, changed, or deleted is considered for refreshment. It is not needed to pass massive amounts of data in the applications database looking for data that might be a candidate for refreshment.

- The log tape can be passed offline, not requiring the native DBMS to be up and active.

- The machine the log tape runs on can be a small machine where the cost of processing is not an issue. When the native DBMS must be read, the reading inevitably takes place on a large machine whose cost of processing is very high.

- The contention for resources with the operational systems is minimized.

The Production of Metadata

Although a powerful argument can be made for the usage of a tool of automation for productivity and maintenance, an even more powerful case can be made when it comes to the production of metadata as a by-product of creating code. When using a tool of automation to build the I & T layer, metadata about the processing is produced as a by-product of the creation of code. The programmer thinks that he or she is creating code that defines the interface between an application file and a data warehouse file when, in fact, that is exactly what the programmer is doing. After the programmer has finished the creation of the code, the tool of automation simultaneously produces relevant metadata.

When a tool of automation is used to create and maintain the I & T layer and metadata is produced as a by-product, then:

- The production of metadata is automatic, requiring no extra effort by the programmer.

- The metadata is produced for every new iteration of development, thereby keeping a complete historical version of the metadata applicable to the data in the warehouse.

- The metadata mappings are produced completely, so that no incomplete gaps exist in the metadata.

- No extra cost justification effort is required for the production of the metadata.

- The logic of transformation can be included as part of metadata.

- Standard business rules can be managed and reused.

Ongoing Management–The Operational Data Store

The ODS is easily the most complex and difficult arena for ongoing systems management because it is truly a mixed environment. Elements of OLTP, DSS/informational, and every other kind of processing the ODS contains. This results in an environment that supports high availability, one- to two-second transaction response times, and complex DSS queries. Because of this mixture, managing the ODS environment is difficult, even under the best of circumstances.

The only real way the ODS environment can be managed is to slice the ODS day into different segments and manage each segment differently from the others. At 10:00 A.M., the ODS is an OLTP. At 5:30 P.M., the ODS is a batch environment. At 2:45 A.M., the ODS is a DSS machine.

Because the ODS is, in fact, the same physical entity and the work that is done is only superficially governed by the time of day that processing is done, the ODS ends up not being optimal for anything. At best, the ODS is *acceptable* for all the roles it plays.

Some of the tools and approaches used to manage the ODS environment on an ongoing basis include:

- Monitoring the ODS using an OLTP monitor

- Monitoring the ODS using a DSS activity monitor

- Monitoring the ODS using a data monitor

Another approach is to use hardware optimal to the ODS environment. The ODS operates well on an MPP environment given the fault tolerance inherent to the hardware redundancy of the architecture. Also, because CPU resources are not shared in this environment (memory and disk) and operational transactions are relatively predictive, the database design can generally be tuned to optimize performance by minimizing or eliminating resource contention.

Another technique to ensure the best overall performance of the ODS is to frequently purge or move to the data warehouse from the ODS environment. Data that sits around the ODS and has a low probability of access is an anathema to the efficient running of the environment.

Ongoing Management—The Data Warehouse

The primary issue of ongoing data warehouse success is the management of the data volume that arises in it. Truly enormous amounts of data tend to accumulate in the data warehouse. In response, the DWA needs to make sure that the volumes of data that reside in the data warehouse belong there.

The way that the DWA ensures that no dormant data creeps into the data warehouse is to employ a data warehouse usage monitor. This monitor tracks very closely who uses what data in the data warehouse. By understanding what data has been used, the DWA is able to understand what data has not been used so that steps can be taken to archive or delete it. In addition, the DWA can employ this usage information to tune the data warehouse through indexing, partitioning, or summarizing of data.

The second aspect of data warehousing that needs to be managed over time is that of the quality of data within the data warehouse in terms of completeness and accuracy. As time passes, it is inevitable that data of inferior quality creeps into the data warehouse. The DWA has the task of identifying and correcting the data that is incorrect in the data warehouse.

Ongoing Management—The Data Mart

In many ways, the data mart is the easiest of the environments to manage over time because:

- It is a relatively small environment, in terms of data.
- It is a self-contained environment.

- It is relevant to only one department.
- Data is already scrubbed and integrated upon arriving at the data mart.
- The hardware and software found in the data mart environment are amenable to change.

The challenges related to the administration of the data mart environment over time are as follows:

- Metadata infrastructure
  - The building of the infrastructure
  - The maintenance of the infrastructure
  - The compatibility of the infrastructure with the tools found in the environment
- Capacity planning as data volumes and the end-user community grows
- Performance tuning as end-user demands grow

Ongoing Management—Internet and Intranet

The two most pressing issues of network management for the CIF over time are those of network capacity and the capability to handle a mixed transmission workload. As time passes, the data volume passed into the CIF and throughout the CIF grows. The configuration that is adequate one year will most likely be inadequate the next.

Another problem is that of an ever-increasing mixed workload. As long as the workload is small, predictable, and homogeneous, the line used to handle the transmissions is not a big issue. In contrast, as the demands on volume grow and as the workload passed over the line grows in diversity, the selection of the line becomes a major issue.

Monitoring the Corporate Information Factory

Because of the diversity of processing and the wide disparity in the parameters of success found in the CIF, it should come as no surprise that different kinds of monitors are required for the management of the CIF (see Figure 16.2).

The figure shows the following monitors:

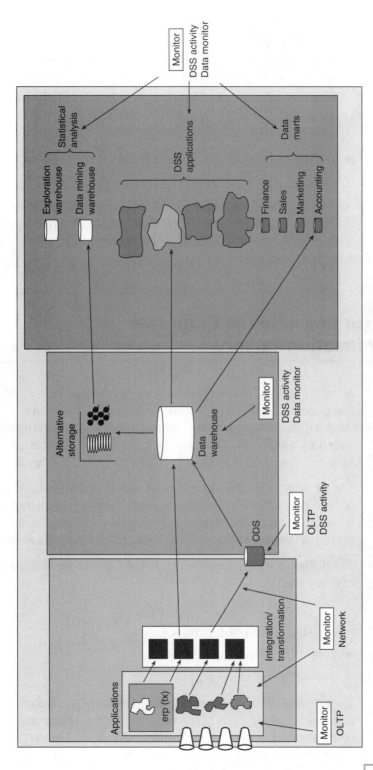

Figure 16.2 The different kinds of monitors that are needed for the management of the CIF.

- **OLTP monitors.** OLTP monitors are designed to manage transaction response times.

- **DSS monitors.** DSS activity monitors look at system activity from the standpoint of DSS activity, not OLTP activity. Among other things, a DSS monitor can help identify dormant data inside a data warehouse.

- **Network monitors.** Similar to OLTP monitors, network monitors keep track of general network activity.

- **Data monitors.** A data monitor looks at such things as growth and quality of data.

All monitors are related, but when the particulars of one monitor are compared with the particulars of another, very real differences start to emerge in the technology used to capture information and the means by which the information is used.

Security within the Corporate Information Factory

An important requirement is the need to manage security between the different components of the CIF. Figure 16.3 shows that there needs to be security among different applications; among applications and the ODS; among the data warehouse and the data marts, ODS, and applications; and among data marts. In short, every component of the CIF can end up having its own security.

The security levels that are required vary for each component and each instance of each component. For example, some data marts may not require any security, while other data marts require great security. Some applications may require simple logon/logoff security, while other applications require DBMS-based security.

The different security needs across the CIF can be divided into different levels of classifications:

- 1%—very high levels of security
- 2%—high levels of security
- 25%—some levels of security
- 74%—little or no security

These levels show that only a small fraction of the data in the CIF needs a truly high degree of security. At the other end of the spectrum, most data needs little or no security. The way that different levels of security are implemented is

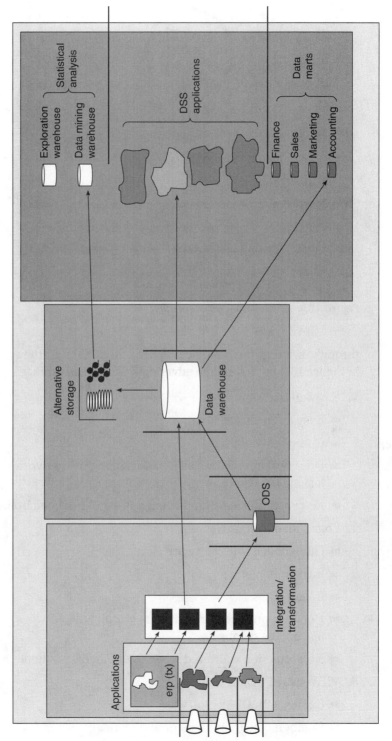

Figure 16.3 Security in the CIF is first sectioned off by component.

261

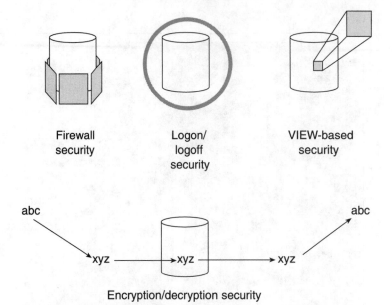

Firewall security

Logon/ logoff security

VIEW-based security

Encryption/decryption security

Figure 16.4 Different levels of security.

through different technological approaches. Each of the approaches depicted in Figure 16.4 has its unique advantages and disadvantages:

1. Firewall security:
   - Easy to construct
   - Cheap
   - Does not protect data as it passes along the network, either entering or leaving the database
   - No protection is offered when a firewall has been breached

2. Logon/logoff security:
   - Often comes with software
   - Easy to implement
   - Cheap
   - Does not protect data as it passes along the network, either entering or leaving the database
   - No protection is offered when logon/logoff has been breached

3. VIEW-based DBMS security:
   - Comes with DBMS software
   - Cumbersome to implement and manage
   - Cheap

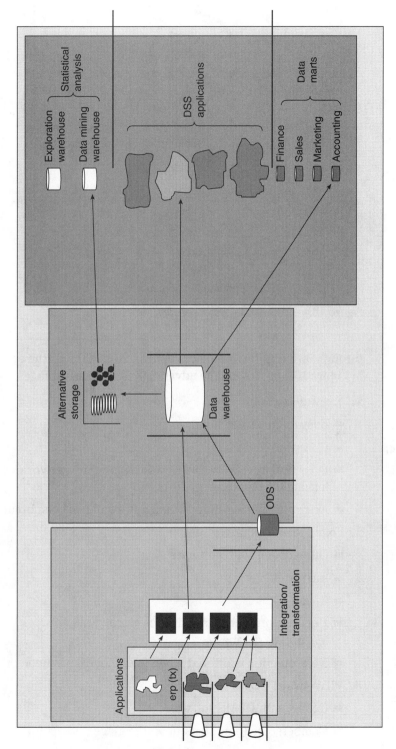

Figure 16.3 Security in the CIF is first sectioned off by component.

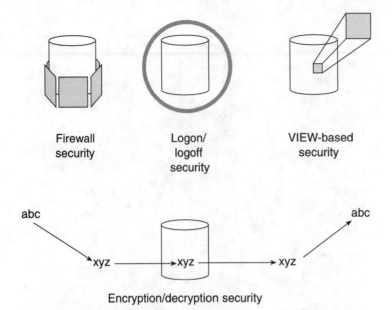

Firewall security

Logon/ logoff security

VIEW-based security

Encryption/decryption security

Figure 16.4 Different levels of security.

through different technological approaches. Each of the approaches depicted in Figure 16.4 has its unique advantages and disadvantages:

1. Firewall security:
   - Easy to construct
   - Cheap
   - Does not protect data as it passes along the network, either entering or leaving the database
   - No protection is offered when a firewall has been breached

2. Logon/logoff security:
   - Often comes with software
   - Easy to implement
   - Cheap
   - Does not protect data as it passes along the network, either entering or leaving the database
   - No protection is offered when logon/logoff has been breached

3. VIEW-based DBMS security:
   - Comes with DBMS software
   - Cumbersome to implement and manage
   - Cheap

- Does not protect data as it passes along the network, either entering or leaving the database
- No protection is offered when VIEW has been breached

4. Encryption/decryption:
   - Relatively expensive
   - Not necessarily difficult to implement
   - Does not allow data to be accessed for general-purpose processing
   - Protects data as it passes along the network, either entering or leaving the database
   - Protection is offered when firewall, logon/logoff, and/or VIEW have been breached

The different types of security have different levels of effectiveness and costs. In general, the less effective the type of security, the less it costs and the fewer the restrictions that accompany the technique. Conversely, the greater the level of security, the greater the cost and the more restrictions that accompany the technique. The different approaches to security can be used alone or in combination with each other.

Archival Processing

This is a key aspect of systems management in a maturing information ecosystem. Although a steady and predictable data flow exists throughout the CIF and although data resides in the data warehouse for lengthy periods of time, nevertheless archival processing is needed to ensure the optimal use of resources and recoverability of the CIF. Figure 16.5 shows that data is archived from the different components of the CIF. Each instance of archival has its own unique set of considerations.

Application Archiving

One reason for an application archival processing is transaction-recovery backup. Periodically—typically daily—data is removed from the applications log or journal tape and is placed onto an archive log. The transaction archive log is used for recovery of an online database in the case of a failure where full backup and recovery must be done.

The second case for an application archival is to provide a location and vehicle for detailed transaction adjustments. When accounting activity is done in the applications environment, it may be necessary to keep a long-standing record of the activities that occurred there. If such a record is necessary, then an

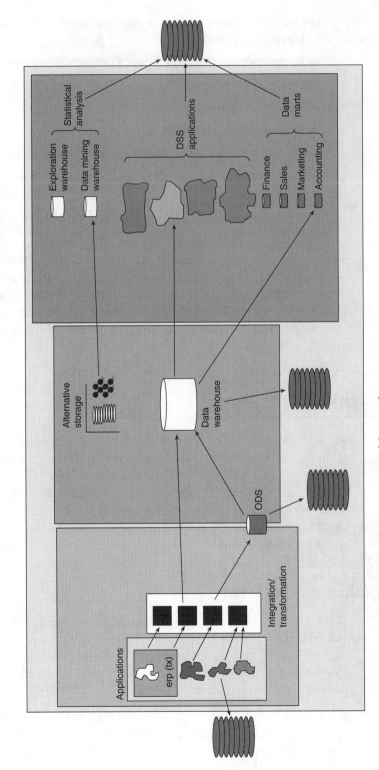

Figure 16.5 Data is periodically archived onto sequential forms of storage.

archival log must be kept. In any case, when the archival log is kept at the applications level, the age of the data is minimal. The data is rarely more than a month old inside the archives themselves.

Operational Data Store Archiving

Nearly all data that ages in the ODS passes to the data warehouse. Therefore, it is unusual to have an archiving facility in the ODS environment. On those rare occasions where an archiving facility is in the ODS environment, it is because some summary data has been created. Since the ODS contains dynamic summary data only, it may make sense to keep an archival log of what the dynamic summary values were as created. Such a log can serve many purposes. One such purpose is as a backup to the information that was available to a crucial decision.

Data Warehouse Archiving

The very essence of the data warehouse is archival data. For this reason, it may seem strange that the data warehouse itself should occasionally have its own data archived. However, as the data volume in the data warehouse grows and as the probability of the usage of that data decreases, the data in the data warehouse needs to be archived. Of course, if the probability of data usage truly goes to zero, then the data should be removed, not archived. However, once data has gone through the process of systemization and integration, the cost of reconstructing the data if it should ever be needed again is such that nearly all data in the data warehouse should be archived, not purged.

Data Mart Archiving

The data marts, like the data warehouse, need to be archived occasionally. In the case of the data marts, data that is the most granular is purged the quickest. The higher the degree of summarization, the less likely a unit of data is to be purged from the data mart environment.

Another important factor relating to the archiving of information from the data mart environment is that this environment does not grow to the size of the data warehouse. Because of this difference in size, the archiving of data from the data mart is done much less frequently and much less rigorously than the archiving that is done in the data warehouse environment.

Archiving Medium

The archiving here is done to a medium that can hold bulk amounts of data, but where the electronic image and record substance can be maintained. The usual case is for the retrieval of the first archival record to take as much as a minute and the access of subsequent records to occur at regular electronic speeds.

A standard storage medium for archival storage is siloed storage. It can store electronic images very inexpensively and provide quick access once the first record is retrieved.

Another consideration of archival processing is that of the reliability and longevity of the medium itself. It goes without saying that any medium used for archiving must be able to physically store the data for long periods of time with a very low rate of corruption.

Summary

Because of the very large differences in content, operation, and processing among the components of the CIF, the ongoing issues of maintenance and operation are likewise very different.

Different kinds of monitors are used to capture key content information within each component of the CIF. This information is used to support such management activities as capacity planning, performance tuning, and quality control.

Managing security is an important aspect of the CIF; in general, security is accomplished on a component-by-component basis. Different levels of security can be applied in different places. The greater the degree of security, the more the cost and the restrictions of the security. Different types of security can be used in conjunction with each other.

One of the essential systems management activities within the CIF is the occasional archiving of the data.

Wow! You have come a long way on your journey. You started this journey by understanding what components comprise the corporate information factory and how these components can be combined to enable decision support capabilities. You continued your journey and discovered variations to the architecture and the cost of pursuing these variations. Additionally, you were provided insight into how to build and manage the corporate information factory. So what's left? Well . . . what if you had multiple corporate information factories with multiple data warehouses? This is the focus of the next chapter.

CHAPTER 17

Multiple Data Warehouses across a Large Enterprise

When people set out to build a data warehouse and a corporate information factory, they usually have a limited scope in mind. What happens when more than one data warehouse and more than one corporate information factory are built across the enterprise? Integrating data cross an entire enterprise makes problems even more complex. Large, complex, and diverse enterprises that contain multiple data warehouses and corporate information factories are found in many places, including

- State and national governments
- Multinational organizations
- Organizations with multiple vertical lines of business

Multiple data warehouses and data marts can grow up in large complex enterprise environments in which multiple corporate information factories coexist. Trying to apply the principles of data warehousing across such a grand vista is a challenging task. Although it appears to offer the promise of true enterprise integration, integrating data warehousing and the corporate information factories across the enterprise is difficult to implement given the complexity of these environments. This chapter will address these difficulties and show how data warehouses and the corporate information factory can be

Agree on the Value of Integration

The first enterprise wide issue we will address is that of internal politics. To what extent does the corporation recognize a need for a comprehensive, integrated enterprise framework?

If there is no organizational momentum toward a common goal, then the best architecture or the best framework in the world is bound to fail. The organizational consensus (or at least a majority opinion) must be that there is an enterprise problem. If no organizational agreement can be reached as to what the larger enterprise problem is, then there is little point in proceeding toward the building of a data warehouse and a corporate information factory framework across the enterprise.

With internal cooperation, the data warehouse and a corporate information factory can lead to an architecture that meaningfully stretches across the enterprise.

applied across the entire enterprise environment to achieve enterprise-wide integration.

Define the Need for Integration

The first step toward achieving an enterprise architecture is the determination of whether a need for or the existence of business integration exists across different parts of the enterprise. In some cases business integration already exists. In some cases, undoubtedly, a need for business integration must be met. It makes no sense to build (or attempt to build) integration into the systems of the enterprise framework across multiple data warehouses and corporate information factories when no business justification can be made for such integration.

Suppose that a bank has a data warehouse for retail customers, a data warehouse for trust customers, and another data warehouse for home loans. The bank decides to build an integrated data warehouse and a corporate information factory for all lines of business, based on the business need, to integrate customers and process across different lines of business. Does this type of enterprise data warehouse make sense? Absolutely!

Suppose that the bank has foreclosed on a steel mill. Does it make sense to try to integrate the customers of the steel mill with bank loan customers? Only if the bank is trying to get into the steel-making business does such business integration make sense. When business integration across the enterprise does not make sense, a data warehouse reflecting that integration correspondingly does not make sense.

Define the Enterprise Framework

In order to create the larger enterprise framework consisting of multiple data warehouse and corporate information factories, it is necessary to introduce new definitions and conventions for portraying the corporate enterprise framework. These definitions and conventions provide a common language by which to communicate the framework.

Business Domain

Every data warehouse has a *business domain*. A business domain for a data warehouse consists of the systems, procedures, transactions, and activities in support of the data warehouse in which data is captured, edited, adjusted, audited, and created. The business domain includes both systems and transactional activities conducted by the corporation. It includes the operational users, the analytical users, and their activities. Figure 17.1 depicts the business domain of a data warehouse.

The business domain of a data warehouse includes the places where data is created and managed. For example, in a manufacturing data warehouse, the business domain might start where an assembly line creates a product, or the manufacturing business domain could include the loading dock of the manufacturing corporation where raw and unfinished goods are received. Or the manufacturing business domain could include the systems that manage the shipment of products out of the manufacturing plant. In short, everywhere detailed data is created and then shipped to the data warehouse is part of the business domain of a data warehouse.

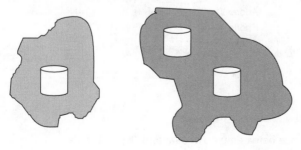

Figure 17.1   Each data warehouse serves a business domain.

The business domain of a data warehouse also includes systems that create and use secondary, nondetailed data. These secondary systems are typically analytical systems, which take detailed data and sub type or super type the detailed data to aid analysis. The result is aggregated or summarized data—in other words, nondetailed data whose basis is detailed data belonging to the business domain of the data warehouse. This nondetailed, analysis-oriented data also belongs to the business domain of the data warehouse.

As an example of nondetailed data belonging to the business domain of a manufacturer, consider an accounting system that groups together shipments of products of finished goods that go out the door. The data—monthly total product—is a type of nondetailed data belonging to the business domain of the manufacturing data warehouse.

Occurrences and Types of Data

A "type of" data refers to a generic classification of business domain data and is the specification that the data warehouse designer produces. Collectively, the different "type of" data form a template describing the content and structure of data that is of interest within the business domain. For example, the data warehouse designer may specify that one type of data might be an "employee."

Occurrences of data are fundamentally different from "type of" data. The occurrences of data refer to the actual rows of data that populate the systems. Figure 17.2 shows the difference between an occurrence of data and a type of data. For example, if the type of data is employee, the occurrences of the type might include:

- "Bill Inmon"
- "Claudia Imhoff"
- "Joyce Montanari"

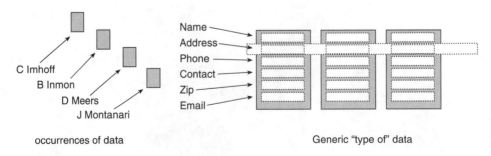

C Imhoff
B Inmon
D Meers
J Montanari

occurrences of data

Name
Address
Phone
Contact
Zip
Email

Generic "type of" data

Figure 17.2 The difference between type of data and "type of" data.

- "Dan Meers"
- "Bob Terdeman"
- "Jon Geiger"

Owned Data

Every unit of data in a data warehouse is owned by only one owner. When data is owned in a data warehouse, the ownership can occur in several ways. Either data occurrences can be owned, or data elements within a data type can be owned. Every data occurrence within a data type can be owned. Every data occurrence is owned and every "type of" data is owned by one owner. Figure 17.3 illustrates this concept.

For example, a data warehouse may own the right to create or delete records for:

- "Bill Inmon"
- "Claudia Imhoff"
- "Joyce Montanari"
- "Dan Meers"

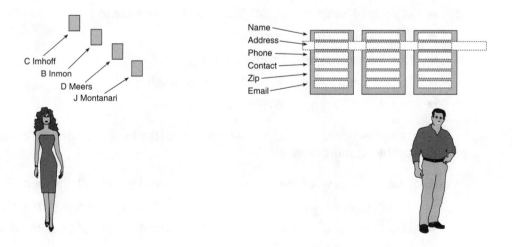

Figure 17.3 Different end-user communities "own" the right to update and manage data.

- "Bob Terdeman"
- "Jon Geiger"

from the data warehouse. The owner of the data warehouse would then have the ability to throw away the entire record for Joyce Montanari, or any other record.

The other type of ownership is by the element within type. It is possible for data warehouse ABC to own the occurrence for these people and for data warehouse BCD to own an data element within the record for the occurrences. For example, the state-wide data warehouse owns the records for:

- "Bill Inmon"
- "Claudia Imhoff"
- "Joyce Montanari"
- "Dan Meers"
- "Bob Terdeman"
- "Jon Geiger"

The Department of Motor Vehicles, however, owns the data for drivers licensing inside each record:

- "Bill Inmon," license 2278665, no tickets
- "Claudia Imhoff," license 3376229, one moving violation
- "Joyce Montanari," license 3398117, no tickets
- "Dan Meers," license 1187227, three parking tickets
- "Bob Terdeman," license 2289917, expired Jan. 15
- "Jon Geiger," license 2287655, no tickets

Where the owner of the data resides outside of the business domain, coordination problems must be worked out:

- What happens when there is a residency record but no driving record?
- What happens when there is a driving record and no residency record?
- What happens when the residency of an individual drops? Does the driving record also get dropped?

Ownership can also be classified as *physical* or *content*. A database administrator typically owns the physical data. When recovery needs to be done, the database administrator is called upon, but content of data is owned as well.

When accounting finds that an error has occurred in the data warehouse, it is accounting's responsibility to repair the data content.

Shared Data

There is only one owner of data at any moment in time. As such, data that is owned can exist in only one place in the enterprise. However, data can be shared innumerable times across the enterprise; data may not be shared at all; or data can be shared one place, two places, and so forth.

The data owner holds the right to create, delete, and modify the data in the warehouse. No one else has these rights. When data is created and ownership is established, it can be moved to another data warehouse. When owned data is moved to a separate warehouse, the data that is moved is called "shared data." Shared data carries the actual owner with it. By attaching the actual owner, data can be reshared with no loss of integrity. Additionally, data that is shared across data warehouses carries with it the date of sharing. This date is important because the data owner may decide to alter the data at a later point in time. When the data that has been shared is used, it is assumed that the data is accurate only as of the moment in time of the date of sharing.

In order to keep shared data up to date, the organization doing the sharing must periodically return to the owner to make sure that the shared data is in synch with the owned data. Figure 17.4 illustrates shared data and owned data.

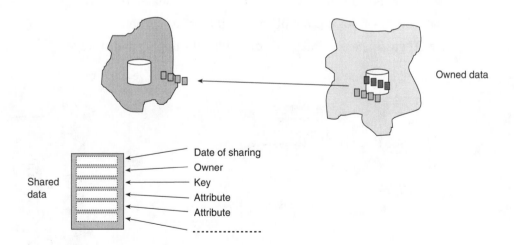

Figure 17.4 Owned versus shared data.

Sharing Data across Multiple Data Warehouses

The essence of the multiple related data warehouse environment is ability to share data across the environments while maintaining integrity of data ownership. Many forms of data sharing occur across the multiple data warehouse environments. Some of the more common ways that data can be shared are presented here.

Simple Sharing

The simplest way that data can be shared across multiple data warehouse environments is when one data warehouse sends a simple, single unit of data to another warehouse. Packaged with the single data unit is the sharing date and owner specification. Figure 17.5 shows this simple form of sharing.

In Figure 17.5, one data warehouse—the owning data warehouse—has simply packaged up a unit of data and passed it to another warehouse. When the data arrives at the receiving warehouse, it is incorporated wherever it makes sense.

As an example of the simple data passage from one data warehouse to another, consider a single manufacturer of vehicles. One division manufactures cars, and the other division manufactures motorcycles. The manufacturer decides that having each division have its own separate relationships with external vendors might not be a good idea. A single relationship to external vendors might make sense for several reasons:

- There might be a discount given for consolidated orders.
- There is a single point of contact if there are problems.
- There is the possibility of consolidated shipping and storage.

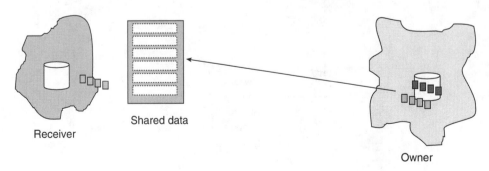

Receiver

Shared data

Owner

Figure 17.5 Simple sharing.

Obviously, there is a real case for business integration across the different car and motorcycle manufacturing divisions. To try and consolidate relations with outside suppliers, the motorcycle division sends some basic information to the car manufacturing division where the corporate wide consolidation will be done, including:

- The part that is received from an external manufacturer
- The amount of parts that have been received
- Where the parts have been received and where they are stored

Related Occurrences of Data

Sharing multiple related occurrences of data increases the number of records that are passed. Figure 17.6 shows this type of sharing.

As an example of the sharing of multiple related occurrences of data, suppose that a car distributorship sends a monthly record of the automobiles that have been delivered to the automobile manufacturer. This is the same as the simple passage of data except that it occurs on a monthly basis, and over time, multiple shared records are passed.

Or consider the case of both a motorcycle manufacturer and an automobile manufacturer. In this case, the motorcycle manufacturer sends information every time a shipment is received from an external supplier. A historical record is made of the shipments.

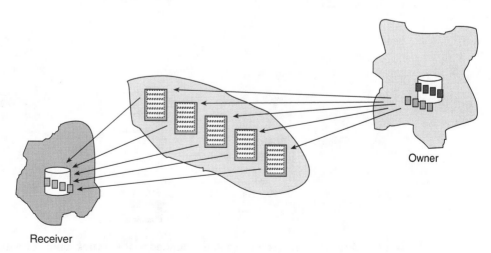

Figure 17.6 Multiple related occurrences of data that are shared.

Other Relationships

In these two types of shared data, a simple passage of multiple data occurrences occurs from one data warehouse environment to the next. On some occasions, however, a tighter relationship between the data that is passed and one or the other environments is referenced. This type of sharing is very similar to the OLTP notion of referential integrity. There is a substantial difference between *grounded* data warehouse sharing and referential integrity—in the data warehouse the relationships that are referenced are all referenced in relation to some moment in time. In OLTP referential integrity, the relationship is understood to be active and ongoing.

Grounded Relationships–The Sender Is Grounded

As an example of a grounded relationship in which the sending data warehouse environment is grounded, look at Figure 17.7.

In a grounded relationship, a direct relationship exists between the record of shared data and some single record in the data warehouse being referenced. Grounding can reference the owning data warehouse (the normal case) or the sharing warehouse (the not-so-normal case).

In Figure 17.7, the automobile distributor sends information about shipments to the manufacturer. In this case, the information sent to the manufacturer includes the actual distributorship that received an allotment of cars. In other words, the distributor has added specific instruction information to the data before shipping it to the manufacturer.

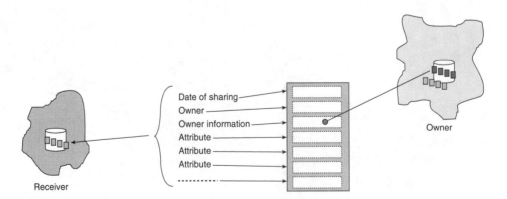

Figure 17.7 A record that is shared can be grounded to the owner, forming a simple relationship.

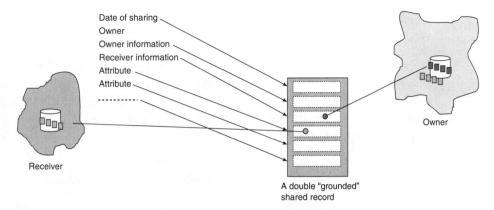

Figure 17.8 Once the shared data is received, it can have further grounding added to it.

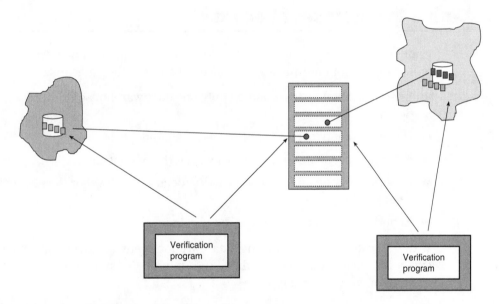

Figure 17.9 Verification programs ensure that specified relationships are valid.

Grounded Relationship—The Receiver Is Grounded

After the data is sent by the owning data warehouse, data can have further grounding attached to it. Figure 17.8 shows a case in which after receiving data from an external data warehouse, the information is further processed.

In Figure 17.8, data passed to the manufacturer is further processed to attach the plant where the car was originally manufactured to the distributors data.

Verifying the Integrity of the Grounded Relationship

In order to make sure that the integrity of the grounded relationships remains intact, it is often wise to create and execute programs that verify the integrity of the grounded relationship. Figure 17.9 shows the programs that read the shared data and that make sure the data that is referenced in the data warehouse is indeed valid.

Figure 17.9 shows that a program reads the distributors shared data and makes sure that a distributorship that is referenced in the shared data actually exists.

Define the System of Record

Applying the foregoing data conventions creates what can be termed the system of record for enterprise warehouse data across the enterprise:

- Ensuring that data is owned by only one data warehouse or business domain
- Ensuring that data that is not owned is shared
- Ensuring that shared data carries with it the date of sharing
- Ensuring that ownership can be at the occurrence level or the element level within type of data
- Ensuring the integrity of a grounded relationship

With the system of record for the data warehouse environment, only one owner exists for each occurrence of data, and only one owner exists for each data element of within a data type.

Establishing and maintaining a system of record for the data warehouse environment across the enterprise then is the key to being able to create and manage data in an enterprise-wide integrated environment.

The concept of the system of record is not new. In the beginning of the data warehouse experience there was the system of record for the data source going into the data warehouse. Figure 17.10 shows the system of record for source data.

In Figure 17.10, the data source flowing into the data warehouse is carefully identified and outlined. Some legacy data goes into the data warehouse, and

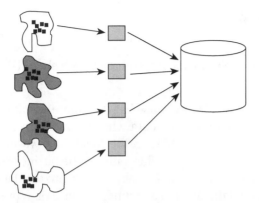

Figure 17.10 The system of record as it applies to the source of data feeding the warehouse.

other legacy data does not. Some legacy data goes into the data warehouse only under certain conditions. Other legacy data goes into the data warehouse and needs to be converted, and so forth. The system of record for source data is a carefully documented and conceived statement of how legacy detailed data will flow into and support the data needed in the data warehouse.

The same sort of concept holds for the system of record data in the data warehouse. The discipline required by the system of record for the data warehouse environment creates an environment in which different data warehouses can operate in a cohesive manner with other warehouses in order to create a truly enterprise architecture of data.

Local Data Warehouses

Another important convention is that of the designation of a local data warehouse. A local data warehouse is one in which the business domain for the data warehouse is entirely self-contained. In other words, there is a single, well-defined business domain that is supported by a single data warehouse. In a pure local data warehouse, no data is in the data warehouse that is owned by another warehouse.

As an example of a local data warehouse, consider a retailer whose warehouse contains detailed information about all of the sales made for the past two years. The warehouse is self contained with no references to external systems or data warehouses.

A Variation of a "Pure" Local Data Warehouse

A variation of the local warehouse is the local warehouse with shared data. Figure 17.11 shows such a warehouse.

In Figure 17.11, most data in the local warehouse has its source as data coming from the business domain, but there is some data whose ownership is outside the business domain. This data that is placed in the local data warehouse is shared data. The ownership of the shared data lies outside the business domain of the local data warehouse. The acquisition date or passage into the data warehouse is stored with the shared data. In such a manner the less than pure local data warehouse is populated with shared data whose source and ownership is outside the local warehouse.

As an example of an impure local data warehouse, suppose that the retailer with the pure data warehouse decides to allow data into the warehouse whose origin is outside the business domain. The retailer decides to allow shipment information into the retailing data warehouse. The shipment information includes:

- Who the shipper was
- The date of shipment
- The date of receipt
- Who signed off for the shipment
- The status of the shipment upon receipt

The external data is collected by an agency other than one inside the business domain of the retailer. The information is then given to the retailer for further consideration. If the information given to the retailer about shipment is incorrect, it is not in the province of the retailer to check to see if the information is valid.

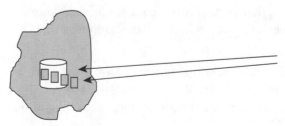

Figure 17.11 A local warehouse with shared data.

Global Data Warehouses

A global data warehouse occurs where the business domains of two or more local business domains and/or local warehouses intersect. Unlike a local warehouse where there is a single business domain, a global warehouse reflects an intersection of multiple business domains. There may or may not be a local data warehouse for the local business domain that is intersected. The global warehouse has the complex task of representing more than one business domain. Figure 17.12 illustrates a global data warehouse.

As an example of a global data warehouse, suppose that a corporation sells to multinational organizations such as IBM, HP, Ford, DuPont, Dow, and others. There is a desire to set up a global data warehouse for sales across the world. Some information in the global warehouse will represent sales across the world, but other information pools contain local sales information that is unique to or peculiar to one locale. There will be a Latin American set of databases for unique Latin American business, a set of databases for China, and another set of databases for the business in France. At the center of these separate worldwide systems will be the global warehouse.

Note that these separate worldwide systems may or may not have a separate local data warehouse. The global data warehouse may function as the intersection of different business domains. with no data warehouse for the business domain, or the global data warehouse may function where the business domains have a local data warehouse. Both forms of the global data warehouse are valid.

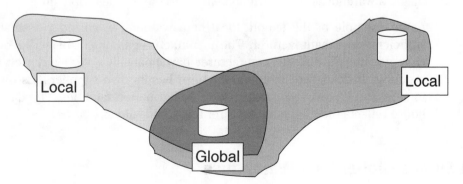

Figure 17.12   An example of a global data warehouse.

Types of Warehouses in the Enterprise

There are then (at least!) six distinct possibilities for the different kinds of warehouses found in the enterprise environment:

1. A simple local data warehouse in which there is no sharing of business domain

2. A simple global data warehouse in which there is a sharing of multiple local business domains but no local data warehouses

3. Multiple local data warehouse in which there is no sharing of data

4. Multiple local data warehouse in which there is sharing of data

5. Multiple local data warehouses in which there is intersection of business domain and a global data warehouse

6. Multiple local data warehouses in which there is intersection of business domain and a global data warehouse and a separate business domain for the global data warehouse

Figure 17.13 shows the six normal possibilities for the states of data warehouses as they exist inside the enterprise.

A Simple Local Data Warehouse

The most basic structuring of a data warehouse is that of the simple local data warehouse, as seen in Figure 17.14.

Figure 17.14 shows that there are basic systems that feed data to the single data warehouse. The legacy application systems move detailed data to the data warehouse through a layer of integration and transformation. The only data found in the data warehouse is that which belongs to the business domain.

As an example of the simple local data warehouse, consider a small, self-sufficient steel manufacturer. The manufacturer is not dispersed geographically nor does the steel manufacturer participate in a vertically rich line of products. Instead, the steel manufacturer has its own suppliers, its own customers, and its own manufacturing and distribution facilities. The data warehouse reflects the steel manufacturer and stands alone.

A Simple Global Data Warehouse

Suppose that a state government wanted to have a nonredundant warehouse environment. The state government recognized that:

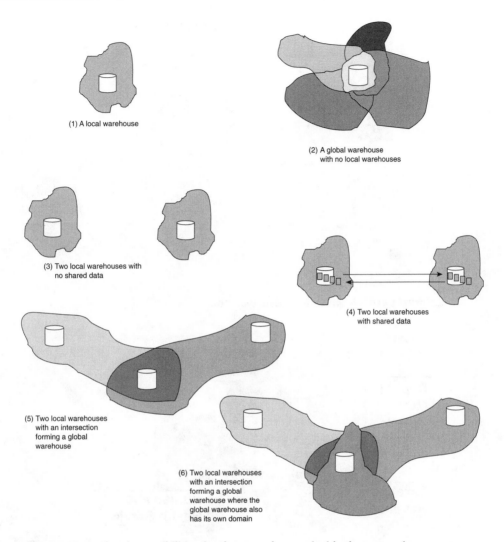

(1) A local warehouse

(2) A global warehouse
with no local warehouses

(3) Two local warehouses with
no shared data

(4) Two local warehouses
with shared data

(5) Two local warehouses
with an intersection
forming a global
warehouse

(6) Two local warehouses
with an intersection
forming a global
warehouse where the
global warehouse also
has its own domain

Figure 17.13 The six possibilities for data warehouses inside the enterprise.

- Some data was common across nearly all state agencies. The data that was common across all state agencies was not very complicated. It consisted of such basic entities as:
  - Resident
  - Tax payer
  - Property
- Much of the other data was peculiar to the different state agencies. The Department of Motor Vehicles had traffic data that was unique to and useful only to its department; the Department of Justice had data that was

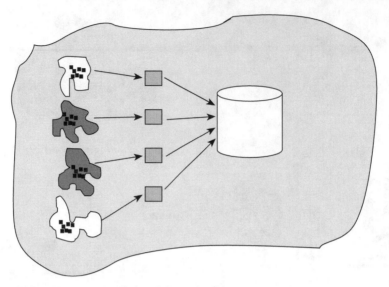

Figure 17.14 A simple local data warehouse.

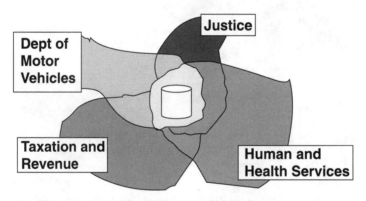

Figure 17.15 A simple global data warehouse.

of interest only to its department; the Health and Human Services department had data that was peculiar to its department's needs; and so forth.

A global warehouse was constructed in order to reflect the common data across different state agencies, as seen in Figure 17.15.

The different components of the global data warehouse were owned by different agencies. Some agencies owned certain classes of data occurrences. Other agencies owned certain elements of data types. In the end, each occurrence of data was owned by only one agency, and each data element was owned by only

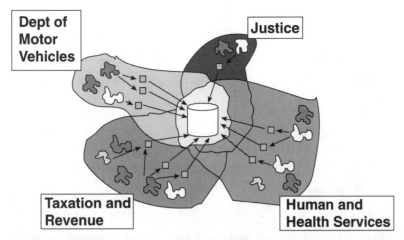

Figure 17.16 The global warehouse is supported by local operational systems.

one agency. But, all agencies could access and analyze data across the global data warehouse.

In addition, each agency had its own supporting systems that were not directly tied into the global data warehouse. Figure 17.16 shows the departmental supporting systems.

The non-data warehouse supporting systems support the data that is peculiar to the business of the department, which is not part of the global data warehouse.

From an analytical perspective, analysis can be done on both global and nonglobal data warehouse data at the same time. An analyst in the Department of Motor Vehicles can look at and report on data from both the global data warehouse and its own nondata warehouse environment. By the same token, an analyst from the Health and Human Services Department can look at and report from the global data warehouse and its own nonglobal data warehouse at the same time.

Figure 17.17 shows the ability of the analytical component of each department to integrate the different sources of data into the environment, all in the same analysis.

Multiple Unrelated Local Data Warehouses

Consider the Army and the Navy. For all practical purposes, these entities consider themselves to be very separate entities, at least when it comes to their information systems. From a larger perspective—that of the enterprise—these different arms of the services have business domains that do not intersect. Because there is no common business interest, there is no intersection.

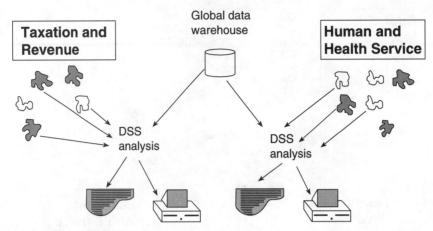

Figure 17.17 DSS at the departmental level is supported by both local systems and the global data warehouse.

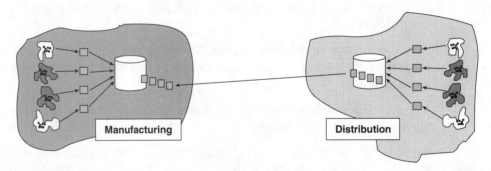

Figure 17.18 Sharing data where there are no strong intersections.

Relationship between Business Domains

Now suppose that the enterprise approach is taken in a corporation that recognizes that there is an interest in sharing data between different business domains even where there is no common intersection between those domains.

Imagine a large manufacturer who has a manufacturing group and a distribution group. Although the two organizations do not recognize any formal relationship or intersection between them, they do recognize the need to share data. Figure 17.18 depicts the sharing of data across the two groups.

As data is shared, the data ownership is kept intact, as well as the sharing date. If the analyst using the shared data desires to have very current data, then the organization containing the shared data must go back to the owner and make sure that the data contents are as fresh as the analyst desires.

In such a manner can two very different groups share data without losing the integrity of the data.

Intersecting Interests

Now suppose that a company has two groups whose interests intersect. For example, suppose that a company has a European and an American corporation. Some systems and services serve both the European and the American interests. Of course, there will be some systems and some services that serve only European or only American interests. In this case, the global interests were numerous enough to warrant their own warehouse. Figure 17.19 shows this occurrence.

A global warehouse is constructed based on data from the intersecting business domains. Data arrives in the global warehouse from:

- The local data warehouse
- Local systems

If data arrives in the global data warehouse from a local data warehouse, it is treated as shared data. The data ownership does not change even though the data exists in both the global and the local data warehouse. And, when the data source is a local system, then the global data warehouse becomes the data owner.

Note that ownership can be by occurrence or type in the global data warehouse.

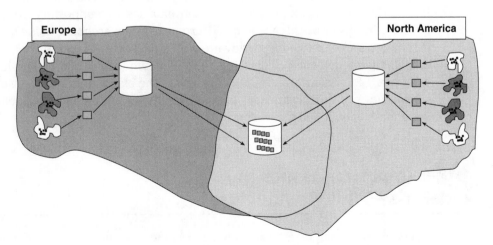

Figure 17.19 A global warehouse that represents the intersection of different local warehouses using shared data.

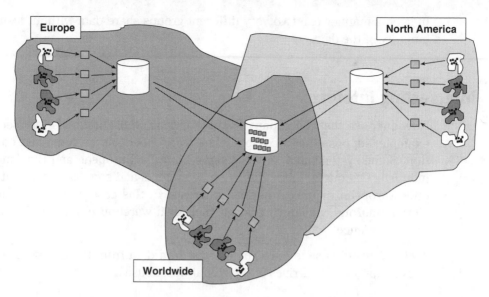

Figure 17.20 A separate worldwide function.

An Extended Global Warehouse

The global data warehouse previously described assumes that all of the data in the global data warehouse will come from one or the other local warehouse. In many cases that will be correct. What about the case in which the global data warehouse has its own directly supporting source systems that are independent of a local data warehouse? Figure 17.20 shows such a case.

In Figure 17.20, there is a global warehouse in which data can come from a local data warehouse, a local system, or from a system supporting global data by itself. In this case, there is a local European data warehouse, a local American data warehouse, and a worldwide global data warehouse. Any given data unit—either occurrence or data type—has its own unique source and its own ownership. Stated differently, any data unit in the global data warehouse has a single data source and a single data owner. In such a manner, a global data warehouse is built and maintained.

Other Important Issues in Enterprise-Wide Architecture

There are other important issues when it comes to considering an enterprise-wide architecture. One issue is data marts. Most normal data marts reside entirely inside a local business domain, but it is possible to have a global data mart. A global data mart is one in which the data is pulled from more than one enterprise data mart. The data warehouse feeding the global data mart could be a local or a global data mart. And, there could be any number of data warehouses feeding the data mart. A global data mart can create and analyze a truly global perspective of data.

Another issue is that of the programs that pass data from an owner to a sharer (or multiple sharers). These programs operate on a push basis, not a pull basis.

Summary

This chapter has addressed the issues of an enterprise-wide approach to data warehousing. We began by defining the following conventions:

- Business domain
- Ownership of data
- Sharing of data
- Local data warehouse
- Global data warehouse

These conventions and definitions all lead to a system of record for enterprise-data warehousing. After the system of record for enterprise data warehousing is created, a meaningful framework and architecture for building and establishing an enterprise framework is possible. Figure 17.21 depicts what the enterprise multiple data warehouse environment would look like.

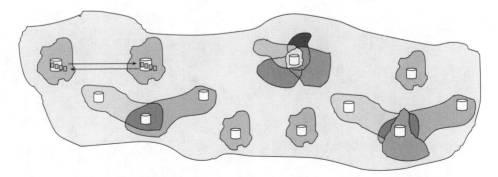

Figure 17.21 What the enterprise multiple data warehouse environment looks like. The enterprise system of record surrounds all of the data warehouses and other systems in the enterprise.

Well, it is time to set sail on the sea of information and the destination is clear. Today's business is quickly redefining itself from one in which products are targeted to the masses to one in which products are tailored to the customer. Unfortunately, today's information systems were not designed for targeting products to the masses. What is needed is a comprehensive and adaptive information solution that can leverage these systems to quickly deliver on the evolving needs of the business. This solution must be able to quickly exploit best-of-breed technologies as they become available. Additionally, this solution must promote an iterative delivery strategy that evolves the information ecosystem while demonstrating incremental value to the business. The CIF presented in these pages is such a solution that has proven itself over time.

We hope that this book has helped you understand the potential promise of the CIF in supporting the evolving information needs of your business. Additionally, we hope this book will help you charter your course in its use and evolution.

Bon voyage!

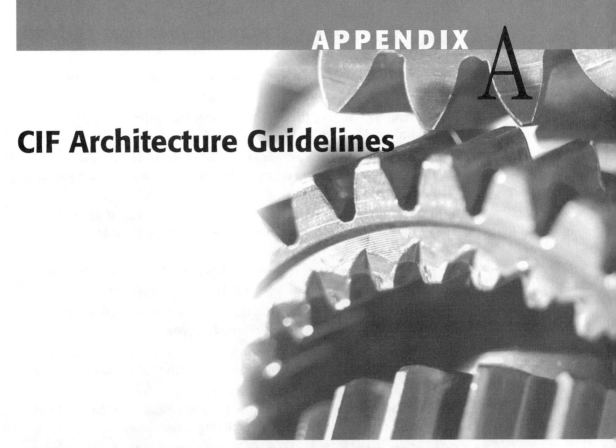

CIF Architecture Guidelines

These guidelines review **all** aspects of corporate information factory architecture. Upon finding a discrepancy or omission, the reviewer can choose to go into a topic much more deeply than that suggested by the guidelines, or a topic can be omitted if it is optional.

Throughout this review, reference will be made to the corporate information factory. You can download a copy of the corporate information factory at www.billinmon.com. Also, a CIF foldout apeared in the January 2000 issue of DM Review.

The review of the corporate information factory concentrates on the following areas:

1. **Standard CIF components.** This part of the review assesses which CIF components are currently in existence or should exist.

2. **Other CIF components.** This part of the review assesses integrating optional components to the CIF. These components include ERP, CRM, and other analytical applications.

3. **CIF variations.** This part of the review assesses variations to the CIF. These variations include the distributed data warehouse and global data warehouse.

4. **Standard operations.** This part of the review determines whether the operations of the CIF components are proper.

5. **Monitoring.** This part of the review assesses how effectively the CIF is being monitored.

6. **Data mart and end-user access.** This part of the review assesses whether the data mart is operating under the guidelines mandated by the CIF architecture.

7. **Data warehouse reconciliation/adjustment.** This part of the review ensures that, if the reconciliation is happening, the appropriate infrastructure exists.

8. **Data warehouse error corrections.** This part of the review discusses the need for and approaches to error detection and correction.

9. **CIF privacy/security.** This part of the review ensures that the CIF architects have not forgotten security and privacy.

10. **Volumes of data.** This part of the review ensures that architectural measures have been taken in order to minimize the data amount found in the CIF.

11. **Exploration warehouse.** This part of the review assesses the need and consideration for implementing an exploration warehouse.

12. **Technology overlay.** This part of the review assesses the inventory and completeness of the technical architecture.

13. **Design overlay.** This part of the review assesses the database design being employed for the various components of the CIF.

14. **Web interface.** This part of the review assesses the implications of integrating Web data into the CIF.

15. **Development methodology.** This part of the review assesses the different methodologies and where they are best employed in the CIF.

16. **Metadata.** This part of the review examines the metadata infrastructure.

17. **CIF organizational management.** This part of the review examines the people behind the CIF.

18. **Data warehouse performance.** This part of the review examines how technology, technique, and components of the CIF architecture can be used to optimize the effectiveness of the data warehouse.

19. **Budgeting.** This part of the review examines some of the considerations when budgeting.

20. **End-to-end speed of flow.** This part of the review examines the importance of the timeliness of data flow in the CIF.

21. **CIF management.** This part of the review examines considerations for managing the CIF.

22. **History of CIF.** This part of the review examines the importance of tracking the evolution of the CIF.

1. Standard CIF Components

Purpose

The purpose of this section is to determine which components of the corporate information factory are currently in existence and which components will exist shortly. Some components are optional—the ODS, the exploration warehouse, and alternate storage. Other components are not—data warehouse, data marts, I & T layer, and metadata.

Points to Be Raised

1. Describe the current architecture:
   - What corporate information factory components exist today?
   - What corporate information factory components are being built today?
   - What corporate information factory components are being planned for tomorrow?
   - Has a data warehouse been built, or is one going to be built?
   - What is the order in which the components of the corporate information factory are being built?
   - If there is an overall architectural plan, how does the plan differ/coincide with the corporate information factory?

2. Describe the architecture in terms of technological foundations (hardware, software, etc.) for each architectural component.

3. Describe the architecture in terms of the groups supporting/owning each component.

4. Describe the architecture from the standpoint of the business function being supported at each component.

I & T Layer

The Issues

One way to do the transformations between the legacy environment and the data warehouse is to create the transformations manually, using COBOL, Perl, or some other language. For very small warehouses, such an approach may be acceptable. For anything other than the smallest of warehouses, however, a manual approach is a colossal waste of time and money. The next approach is to create the interface automatically. Two automatic approaches can be taken—code-driven or engine driven. The code-driven approach is the most flexible, covering the most territory. The engine-approach, in which data is entered and converted into a parameter driven engine, is simpler. There are advantages and disadvantages to both the code-driven and engine-driven approaches to the automation of the interface creation to the data warehouse environment.

Specific Questions

1. Which Extract, Transform, and Load (ETL) tool has been chosen?
   - Will it support the volume of data that must pass through it?
   - Will it support the different transformations that have to be made?
   - Will it automatically produce the documentation and metadata needed?
   - Will it require a difficult learning curve?
   - Will the transformation, once made, be able to be maintained easily?
   - What is the cost of the ETL tool?
   - Will the ETL tool support the different DBMs needed in a native access made?
   - Will the ETL support changed data capture?
   - How much custom coding will be needed with the ETL?

ODS (optional)

The Issues

An ODS is a hybrid between an operational environment and a DSS environment. The ODS most often appears when a significant amount of transaction processing occurs, such as at a bank, retailer, airline reservation, and so forth. The ODS can also be used for direct customer interface, in which data is gathered, analyzed, and assimilated in the data warehouse environment and passed to the ODS. The ODS is then used for the purpose of direct interface with the consumer. The ODS is always the most complex component to build. If an ODS is to be built, then it is advisable to build it *after* the data warehouse is built. Trying to build the ODS before the data warehouse is built merely delays the creation of the corporate information factory.

The ODS is an optional structure. Where there is a lot of OLTP processing, there usually is a need for the ODS.

Specific Questions

1. Has the transaction processing rate for the ODS been determined?

2. Is the ODS class I, II, III, or IV?

3. What transport mechanism will be used to move data from the operational environment to the ODS environment?

4. What number of users will be supported?

5. What DSS processing will be done from the ODS?

6. What portion of the ODS database design will be star join or snowflake schema, and what portion will be normalized?

7. What data model has been built for the ODS?

8. What processing model has been built for the ODS?

9. What supporting technology is there for the ODS . . .

   - Hardware?
   - Software?
   - End-user access and analysis?
   - Monitoring?

10. Was the ODS built before the data warehouse or vice versa?

Data Warehouse

The Issues

The data warehouse is the heart of the corporate information factory. The data warehouse contains the granular, historical, integrated, corporate data that feeds all the other components of the corporate information factory. There is an argument that you do not need to build the data warehouse. This is pure baloney. The data warehouse contains a huge amount of data. Different design techniques are required for the management of the data found in the data warehouse. The data warehouse is an essentially normalized structure. If a star join is used here, inevitably the data warehouse serves one community effectively at the expense of everyone else. The data warehouse is not optional. However, the data warehouse is built in iterations. It is patently a mistake to build the data warehouse using what can be termed as the "big bang" approach.

Specific Questions

1. What is the technological foundation of the data warehouse?
2. How big is the data warehouse today?
3. At what rate is the data warehouse growing?
4. How much dormant data is in the data warehouse?
5. What data model was used for the data warehouse?
6. Is the data structure for the data warehouse normalized?
7. If the data model for the data warehouse is a star join or snowflake schema, which users will have their access optimized? Which users will have their access to the data in the warehouse deoptimized?
8. Describe the level of granularity found in the data warehouse.
9. Is the data found in the data warehouse truly integrated?
10. Describe the sources of data for the data found in the data warehouse.
11. Is the data warehouse scalable?
12. How much history is found in the data warehouse?
13. What happens to data that is removed from the data warehouse?
14. How many architectural components does the data warehouse support?
15. Is the data warehouse being used directly for analysis today?
16. Is the data warehouse being used to support exploration processing today?
17. What indexes are found in the data warehouse?

Data Mart

The Issues

No corporate information factory is complete without data marts. Data marts are where different departments store their own departmental data. Data marts are fed from the data warehouse. Data marts use highly denormalized data structures called star joins or snowflake structures. Data marts contain significantly less data than data warehouses. The data found in data marts is significantly more denormalized, summarized, and aggregated than the data found in the data warehouse environment. The departments that have data marts typically are the accounting, marketing, sales, finance, and human resources departments. The technology found in the data mart environment is typically HOLAP, MOLAP, and ROLAP technology. The data mart environment is typically owned by the department, not the central IT function. The data mart environment *never* passes data to another data mart directly. Instead, the data is passed indirectly through the data warehouse.

Specific Questions

1. Is the source of data for the data mart the data warehouse and the data warehouse alone?
2. Describe how many data marts there are.
3. For each data mart, describe who the owner is.
4. For each data mart, describe the technological foundation of:

   Hardware?

   Software?
5. What is the rate of data movement into the data mart?
6. How much data manipulation must be done to prepare the data coming from the data warehouse?
7. How large is the data mart?
8. How can the data mart be described?
   - HOLAP?
   - ROLAP?
   - MOLAP?
   - Other?
9. Is there a significant overlap of detailed data from the data mart environment to the data warehouse environment?
10. Are the users of the data mart primarily farmers? Middle management?
11. Is there a passage of data directly from one data mart to another?

Exploration Warehouse (optional)

The Issues

The exploration warehouse is not for everyone. Usually only older, more mature corporations with large amounts of data have exploration warehouse.

For many companies, exploration, needs can be met from the data warehouse itself. It is only when there starts to be a significant amount of exploration processing that there is a need for a separate processing facility for exploration.

The exploration warehouse is not just a copy of the data warehouse, although the data warehouse usually serves as a source for the exploration warehouse. The exploration warehouse also incorporates external data as a source. When data is contributed by the data warehouse, it is contributed as a subset of data. Finally, as data passes into the exploration warehouse, convenience fields are created, and data elements not needed for exploration processing are dropped. For these reasons, the exploration warehouse is not merely a copy of the data warehouse.

Usually the exploration warehouse is a temporary database that lives as long as the exploration analysis occurs. Occasionally, the analysis results are such that the exploration warehouse turns into a data mart.

Specific Questions

1. How many explorers are being supported?
2. How many queries are being submitted?
3. What is the business nature of the exploration processing?
4. What subject areas are being included?
5. Are there multiple explorations occurring?
6. What is the length of the average exploration project?
7. How much data is being added to the exploration warehouse?
8. Is external data being added to the exploration warehouse?
9. What is the underlying technology for the exploration warehouse?
10. How much is the data compacted as the data is moved from the data warehouse to the exploration warehouse?
11. What convenience fields are being created as data passes into the exploration warehouse?

Alternate Storage (optional)

The Issues

Alternate storage takes two forms—fat storage and near-line storage. Fat storage is storage that is disk based but is slower and cheaper than high-performance disk storage. Near-line storage is tape based but is still accessible by online queries.

Alternate storage becomes appropriate only when the data warehouse exceeds 500 GB or so. Note that today's data warehouse may only be 100 GB. But, if the rate of growth is large enough, alternate storage may still be appropriate.

The data that is placed in alternate storage is inactively used data. In a large warehouse, *most* of the data in the warehouse will be inactively used. Alternate storage greatly reduces the costs of the data warehouse environment. In addition alternate storage can set the stage for exploration processing.

Alternate storage normally works in conjunction with standard DBMS, extending the DBMS seamlessly and transparently.

Specific Questions

1. How much dormant data is in actively used storage now?
2. What is the ratio of data in actively used storage and data in alternate storage?
3. What form of alternate storage is being used?
4. What cross media storage manager is being used?
5. What data monitor is being used?
6. How much data passes from actively used storage to alternate storage each day?
7. How much data passes from alternate storage to actively used storage each day?
8. Is alternate storage used to directly satisfy requests from the exploration warehouse?
9. Is alternate storage able to be accessed and manipulated independently?

2. Other Components of the CIF

Purpose

Although the standard components of the corporate information factory have been discussed, there are other components as well. These components include the ERP environment, the CRM environment, the analytical applications environment, etc. Each of these environments have their own peculiar considerations.

Points to Be Raised

The ERP and CRM environments can become complicating factors when it comes to the corporate information factory. At some point, these environments cease to be self-contained and become a part of a larger architecture. Great care must be taken to ensure that this point does not slide under the covers.

ERP

The Issues

The ERP considerations must be reviewed on a case-by-case basis. For example, the considerations of SAP are very different than the considerations of Oracle Financials or J D Edwards.

SAP

The Issues

Many issues are associated with data warehouses and SAP:

- Does the corporation have only SAP and no data warehouse?
- Does the corporation have SAP and an early release of BW?
- Does the corporation have SAP and the latest release of BW?
- Does the corporation have SAP, BW, and other ERP software?
- Does the corporation have SAP, BW, and external data in a data warehouse?

In addition to these major architectural issues, another whole set of issues relate to SAP, such as:

- The barrier imposed by using German terminology
- The fact that SAP calls their data warehouse an ODS
- The fact that SAP has no real ODS

BAAN

The Issues

BAAN has not recognized the need for a data warehouse, which in a way makes the choices simpler. There is, of course, a need for a data warehouse whether BAAN recognizes it or not. The question is how to realize that data warehouse from BAAN data. The usual alternatives are:

- Create an alternative data warehouse using standard extraction tools and a standard DBMS.
- Build the data warehouse using PeopleSoft as an infrastructure and simply move operational data from BAAN to PeopleSoft.

PeopleSoft

The Issues

Fortunately a very solid infrastructure for a data warehouse is built in People-Soft. Of the ERP vendors, PeopleSoft stands out as the best example of ERP and data warehousing. Anyone with PeopleSoft not using EPM is making a mistake.

J D Edwards

The Issues

J D Edwards has not recognized the need for a data warehouse, which in a way makes the choices simpler. There is, of course, a need for a data warehouse whether J D Edwards recognizes it or not. The question is how to realize that data warehouse from J D Edwards data.

The usual alternatives are:

- Create an alternative data warehouse using standard extraction tools and a standard DBMS.
- Build the data warehouse using Rodin as part of the infrastructure and simply move operational data from J D Edwards to PeopleSoft.

Oracle Financials

The Issues

Because of the limited functional scope of Oracle Financials, there may or may not be a need for a data warehouse associated with Oracle Financials.

e-Business

The Issues

The e-Business web site throws off data faster than any other component of the architecture. Typically, click stream data is thrown off at an amazing rate. In addition the Web site needs access to integrated corporate data. Usually the Web site is serviced with an ODS. The data warehouse collects the Web site generated data after the data has passed through a granularity manager.

CRM

The Issues

CRM is a data warehouse application, although the CRM vendors do not recognize it as such. CRM requires integrated and historical data, most of which surround the customer. CRM often comes in packages. Do not create the CRM environment as a separate or satellite data warehouse environment. Instead, have the CRM environment as integrated into the data warehouse/corporate information factory environment as possible.

Other Analytical Applications

The Issues

Many other types of analytical applications exist. Most analytical applications are a form of data warehouse applications, although the vendors of analytical applications do not recognize them as such. Analytical applications require integrated and historical data. Analytical applications often come in packages. Do not create the analytical applications environment as a separate or satellite data warehouse environment. Instead, have the analytical applications environment as integrated into the data warehouse/corporate information factory environment as possible.

3. Corporate Information Factory Variations

Purpose

Although the corporate information factory often takes the classical form (hub and spoke), the CIF sometimes has variations. These variant forms have special architectural considerations.

Distributed Data Warehouse

The Issues

One mutant form of the corporate information factory occurs when there is a distributed data warehouse. In this case, the detailed data making up the data warehouse is scattered over more than one physical database, creating a need to see that:

- No redundancy exists among the physical databases.
- Data can be accessed across the physical databases.
- Processing can be synchronized across physical databases, and so forth.

Specific Questions

1. Why is the data warehouse to be distributed?
2. Does the distribution of the data warehouse fit with the business model?
3. Have the complications of the logistics of operation been considered?
4. How will the mutual data exclusivity within any given distributed component be maintained?
5. How will the common tables and reference tables be shared?

Global Data Warehouse

The Issues

Occasionally, a global data warehouse exists. The global data warehouse has the same issues as a distributed warehouse in addition to the fact that a global data warehouse has a centralized warehouse (usually called a headquarters data warehouse). The headquarters data warehouse is at a higher level of granularity than the local data warehouses that feed data into it.

Specific Questions

1. Has the headquarters site been identified?
2. Have all the local sites been identified?
3. Will the development be managed centrally?
4. What will be the role of local development?
5. Have language issues been considered?
6. What length of time will be allocated for the development of the data warehouse?
7. What does the centrally developed data model look like?
8. How will the local sites conform to the data model if local business practices vary widely from the data model?

9. Will there be local buy in?

10. How will the differences in technology across the local sites and the headquarters site be accounted for?

11. Are there legal issues with the passage of data across international boundaries?

12. What data volume will flow from the local sites to the headquarters database?

13. Will the local staging area be used as a local data warehouse?

14. If the local staging area will not be used as a data warehouse, is there going to be another local data warehouse?

4. Standard Operations

Purpose

The purpose of this section is to determine whether the components operation of the corporate information factory are proper. If there is a discrepancy here, there should be a very thorough and detailed review because a discrepancy here usually indicates a serious structural flaw.

Points to Be Raised

1. Describe the flow of data throughout the CIF.

2. The data flow (at least 99 percent of the volume of data) flows in a predictable and regular manner as indicated by the architectural diagram. If a different flow is indicated, there is cause for alarm.

3. There is a backflow of very small amounts of data. Usually the data is parametrically sensitive. If the backflow is anything other than a physically small amount of data, there is cause for concern.

4. There is a standard data flow from the operational world into the data warehouse, and then from the data warehouse elsewhere. If this standard pattern has been altered, there is cause for serious concern.

Normal

The Issues

The normal data flow of the corporate information factory is from left to right. This means that 99 percent of the data flows this direction. The exceptions are the data flow to and from near-line storage/alternative storage and the data warehouse. In addition data flows in bulk to the data mart/analytical application environment.

The data flow can be either regular or sporadic. For example, the data flow from the legacy/operational environment is almost always regular and scheduled, but the data flow to the exploration warehouse is almost always irregular, on a project-driven basis.

Reverse

The Issues

There is a reverse data flow throughout the corporate information factory. For example, it is possible to flow data from the data warehouse to the ODS or to the legacy/operational environment. However, this flow is *very* small compared to the normal flow of data. In addition there is *never* a flow of data in reverse to anywhere where there has not been a normal flow of data. For example, there is never a direct data flow from one data mart to another, nor is there a flow from alternative storage to the legacy/application environment.

Update versus Snapshots

The Issues

Data is inserted into the data warehouse environment in terms of snapshots. Each snapshot has a time stamp on it. If an update is made to the data warehouse, it is made in terms of creating another snapshot of data. It is *never* acceptable to go into the data warehouse, find a record, and alter its value. There are many consequences of doing a direct update into the data warehouse; *all* of which are negative.

Specific Questions

1. Is data being updated in the data warehouse? Why?

5. Monitoring

Purpose

The corporate information factory environment in general and the data warehouse environment in particular need to be monitored. The activity, the data volume, and the rate of change are all important characteristics that the company *must* have a handle on.

Points to Be Raised

1. Describe where the monitors have been placed.
2. Describe what is being monitored.
3. Is the output of the monitoring being analyzed on an exception bases?
4. What is the overhead of monitoring?
5. Can the monitoring be done in a single place? By a single organizational unit?
6. Is there a creation of baselines for the purpose of comparisons?

Data Warehouse

The Issues

The data warehouse needs to have several things periodically examined. Some of those things are:

- The growth of the volume of data
- The specific places where growth is occurring by tables and by rows
- The growth of system activity
- The growth of activity by user
- The growth of activity by transaction type
- The growth of activity by unit of time

Network

The Issues

The network, like the data warehouse, needs to have several things periodically examined. Some of those things are:

- The flow of data from one component to another
- The growth of the volume of data
- The specific places where growth is occurring by tables and by rows
- The growth of system activity
- The growth of activity by user
- The growth of activity by transaction time
- The growth of activity by unit of time

Alternate Storage

The Issues

Alternate storage needs to be monitored to see that the data inside alternate storage is not being frequently accessed.

Specific Points

1. What is the hit rate internal to alternate storage?

6. Data Mart and End-User Access

Purpose

Data marts are where most end users—farmers in particular—access their data. Data marts are where people with a like set of requirements—usually departments—have their own data mart. The data mart is optimized to meet the needs of a given department. Typical departments that have data marts include finance, marketing, sales, accounting, and so forth. The data in the data mart is denormalized according to the access needs of the department. The structure most often found in data marts is the star join. The star join consists of a fact table and several dimension tables. Typically, multidimensional technology is found housing the data marts. Data marts support a wide variety of access.

The data found in the data mart should have as a source the data warehouse. Data being loaded into the data mart directly from an operational source is a mistake in every case.

Data in the data mart is much more denormalized, summarized and aggregated than the data found in the data warehouse.

The purpose of this review portion is to ensure that the data mart operates under the architectural guidelines mandated by the corporate information factory architecture.

Points to Be Raised

1. Is data being passed directly from one data mart to another data mart?
2. Does the data mart have a foundation of star join data?
3. How large is each data mart?
4. At what rate is each data mart growing?

7. Data Warehouse Reconciliation/Adjustment

Purpose

One of the most difficult aspects of the corporate information factory is that of the need for reconciliation across the different components. In particular reconciliation becomes an issue for financial systems. Several issues must be considered:

- The data being reconciled must be at the same level of granularity.
- The transactions that cause a change in values must be stored in both the operational system and the data warehouse environment.
- Tight time synchronization must exist between the operational environment and the data warehouse environment.
- An independent audit needs to be available for both the operational and the data warehouse environment.
- Record control processing needs to be at the ETL level of the architecture.

Reconciliation can be done, but it requires a large effort and is never done casually.

The purpose of this review portion is to ensure that if reconciliation is going to be done the infrastructure exists for it to be done.

Points to Be Raised

1. Is reconciliation between the data mart and the data warehouse being done?
- How often?
- By whom?
- How are discrepancies resolved?

8. Data Warehouse Error Correction

Purpose

Error correction is done in several places throughout the corporate information factory. In theory, error correction can be done back in the operational systems, but it is seldom done there because of the reluctance of management and developers to go back into older code. In addition, even if error correction is done in the operational environment, correction there does not mitigate the problems of errors that arise as two or more applications are being integrated. The most likely place for errors to be corrected is at the point of integration and transformation. It is here that the data is exposed and that integration and conversion is being done. A great opportunity for data correction exists at this point. Even if data is perfectly cleaned as it enters the data warehouse, there is need for another level of error correction. As data enters the data warehouse, the data is accurate, but as time passes and the business changes, the data becomes corrupted. Periodically, the data needs audited and corrected, even if it has been loaded perfectly.

Specific Points

1. Describe how error correction is done.

9. Corporate Information Factory Privacy/Security

Purpose

Security and privacy data are two of the more important issues of the corporate information factory, even though these issues are often forgotten. Although there are typically security features on many of the pieces of technology that house the different components of the corporate information factory, a systematic security architecture should be placed over the corporate information factory.

The purpose of this review portion is to ensure that security and privacy have not been forgotten by the corporate information factory architects.

Points to Be Raised

1. Describe the strategy for security/privacy.
2. Describe the needs for privacy/security from a business perspective.
3. What exposures are there?
4. What is the cost of the security infrastructure?
5. Who is in a position to administer a security/privacy program?

10. Volumes of Data

Purpose

The single largest issue facing the corporate information factory architect is that of the data volumes that wind up in the corporate information factory. The data warehouse attracts lots of data, and the Web site can generate huge amounts of data. The historical nature of the data warehouse is one reason why data finds its way there. Many techniques can be used to manage the data volumes found in the corporate information factory:

- Use alternative storage to hold inactive data
- Edit and filter out unneeded data
- Adjust the granularity of data
- Ensure that there is a minimum of redundancy of data throughout the corporate information factory
- Pass data as quickly as possible through the corporate information factory

The purpose of this section is to ensure that architectural measures have been taken in order to minimize the amount of data found in the corporate information factory.

Points to Be Raised

1. How much data is in the CIF environment today?
2. What is the rate of growth?
3. How much history is being kept?
4. What are the dormancy ratios in the different components of the CIF?
5. To what extent does data overlap from one component to another in the CIF?
6. How is the growth of data being measured?
7. Where is the budget for new acquisition of data coming from?

Projections

The Issues

The corporate information factory architect can periodically do projections to try to predict what growth will be like. Lots of factors that go into these projections:

- What business factors will affect growth?
- How long is historical data to be kept?

- What new subject areas are to be added?
- What level of granularity is to be kept?
- How much summary data is being created?
- Is the summary data being monitored to determine what data will be used and not be used in the long term?

Rate of Growth

The Issues

The volume of data found in the corporate information factory is not just a function of how much data is in the CIF now but also what is the rate of growth.

Current Status

The Issues

Although the growth rate is certainly an important factor, how much data there is in the corporate information factory today is also very important.

Going over the Line

The Issues

There comes a day when conventional storage is not a long-term option. Usually that day comes when the company reaches around 500 GBS of storage. Analysis needs to be done to determine when a company has outgrown conventional storage and how prepared it is for the next step.

Preparing for the Future

The Issues

When a company "goes over the line," how prepared are they for a change in architecture? What will the impact of alternative storage be when the move needs to be made?

Alternative Storage

The Issues

The single most effective step the company can take to prepare for the volumes of data that will inhabit the corporate information factory is to move data to alternative storage. After data is moved to alternative storage, a cross media storage manager and an activity monitor are needed. The activity monitor determines what data needs to be moved to alternative storage, and the cross media storage manager moves the data to and from high-performance disk storage and alternative storage.

Data Placement Rules

The Issues

Data needs to be placed judiciously across the different storage media. Highly active data needs to be placed in high-performance disk storage. Inactively used data needs to be placed in alternative storage. There is a constant shuffling of data back and forth from high-performance disk storage to alternative storage.

In addition if any amount of exploration processing is going on, data is moved from alternative storage to the exploration warehouse as exploration processing needs dictate.

11. Exploration Warehouse

Purpose

The exploration warehouse is designed to accommodate unstructured exploration queries. Under most normal circumstances a company does not need an exploration warehouse until it is doing exploration processing on a regular basis. Stated differently, as long as the company is doing only a modicum of exploration queries, those queries can be done from the data warehouse.

The exploration warehouse is not merely a copy the data warehouse; Many differences are evident between the data warehouse and the exploration warehouse.

Points to Be Raised

1. What is the business purpose of the exploration warehouse?
2. How long is the exploration project expected to take?
3. Who is leading the exploration effort?
4. On what platform is the exploration warehouse to be placed?
5. What is the budget for the exploration warehouse?
6. What source of data will be used?

From the data warehouse?

From external sources?

7. What are the response time requirements for queries?

8. How frequently will the exploration warehouse be refreshed?

9. What subject areas will be found in the exploration warehouse?

10. How much historical data will be found in the exploration warehouse?

Queries

The Issues

Exploration queries are typically very long because they access detailed and historical data. It is not unusual for an exploration query to run for 24 hours or more. In many cases the data beneath the exploration query cannot change from one iteration of analysis to another.

Specific Questions

Many issues relate to the exploration warehouse:

- How many queries are running in the exploration mode?
- Do the queries require that the exploration warehouse be frozen from one query to the next?
- Are there different groups of people submitting the same or nearly the same queries?
- Is the data the queries run on at the right level of granularity?
- As the queries are being run, is the analyst making note of what convenience fields would be useful?

Volumes of Data

The Issues

As a rule, the exploration warehouse takes up a lot of space because the data needed for exploration needs to be at a detailed level and the exploration analyst needs a lot of history. The good news is that most exploration warehouses are of a temporary nature. When the analysis has concluded, the infrastructure used to house the exploration warehouse can be reclaimed.

The bad news is that data enters the exploration warehouse at a very granular state. In addition, the exploration data usually is very historical.

Some exploration technologies condense the data greatly, such as Sand Technology's Nucleus product.

Specific Questions

1. Can the exploration data be loaded quickly?

2. Is there documentation as to what data is in the exploration warehouse?

3. Can the contents of the exploration warehouse be altered easily?

4. Is the data in the exploration warehouse able to process Boolean analysis efficiently?

5. Can the results of an analysis be saved and reinterpreted at a later point in time?

External Data

The Issues

External data plays a very important role in the exploration warehouse. With external data, a sharp contrast can be made between internal and external data. This contrast is the source of many important insights.

There are several issues with external data:

- The acquisition of the external data
- The cost of external data
- The frequency with which external data needs to be refreshed
- The alignment and integration of external data with internal data
- The cleansing of external data
- The aging of external data
- The coordination with other groups of people who might have a use for the external data

Specific Questions

1. What is the source of external data?

2. What is the cost of external data?

3. Will more than one iteration of external data be acquired?

4. How much editing of the external data will be needed?

5. How much external data integration will be needed?

6. Can the external data be used elsewhere in the corporation?

7. How quickly will the external data age?

8. How much external data will be acquired?

9. Where will the external data be stored?

10. What technology will be used to house the external data?

12. Technology Overlay

Purpose

The architecture of the corporate information factory needs to be made practical by embodying the components in one or more technologies. The corporate information factory is sufficiently complex that not one technology will be optimal everywhere. The specialty processing that is done in one part of the corporate information factory is different enough from other parts that an advantage in one place may be a disadvantage elsewhere.

The corporate information factory architect must piece the CIF together with different technologies, each of which are optimal for where within the corporate information factory they reside.

The technology found in the corporate information factory needs to be measured by in many ways:

- Cost
- Capacity
- Scalability
- Performance
- Ability to be integrated
- Functionality
- Long-term viability of the vendor
- Ease of vendor relationships
- Compatibility with other technologies
- Ease of installation
- Ease of operation

Points to Be Raised

1. Describe the technology to be used for each of the components that have already been built and that will be built in the future.

2. How will data be passed from one technology to another?

   - In terms of volumes of data

   - In terms of compatibility of technology

3. How will meaning and definition of data be passed from one technology to the next?

4. What happens when large volumes of data are passed from one component of the architecture to another?

System

The Issues

The operating systems houses and manages all other software. The common operating systems are:

- UNIX
- MVS
- NT
- LINUX

Hardware

The Issues

Hardware is a commodity for the most part throughout the corporate information factory.

Typical hardware units include:

- The central processor
- Storage
- Communication devices
- Monitors
- Printers

DBMs

The Issues

Many kinds of DBMs types are found throughout the corporate information factory.

Some of the types and examples include:

- General Purpose
  - Oracle
  - DB2
  - SQL Server
  - Informix
  - Teradata
  - Hyperion
  - ESS Base
  - CA

End-User Tool

The Issues

There are many kinds of end-user tools. Some of the end-user tools include:

- SAS Institute
- Business Objects
- Epiphany
- Cognos
- IBI
- Brio
- CA
- Lotus
- Excel
- WordPerfect
- FirstChoice

- Seagate
- MicroStrategy

Each of the different end-user tools have their own advantages and disadvantages.

Middleware

The Issues

Middleware takes many forms in the corporate information factory.

Some of the forms of middleware include:

- ETL processing
- Replication
- Change data capture
- Metadata movement
- Cube preparation
- Cross media storage management

Some of the issues of middleware include:

- Does the middleware offer sufficient bandwidth?
- Does the middleware perform the functionality needed?
- Does the middleware operate efficiently?
- What is the cost of the middleware?
- Is the middleware compatible with the technologies with which it must interface, etc.?

TX Management

The Issues

Depending on the context of transaction management there are many facets. If the context is online transaction management, some of the issues are:

- What throughput (measured in transactions per second) are a possibility?
- What locking overhead is there?
- How is deadly embrace handled?
- What tuning capabilities are there?

If the context is DSS transaction management, some of the issues are:

- What data is being touched by the transaction?
- Are update and nonupdate transactions being separated?
- Are exploration transactions being separated from farmer transactions?
- Is output data being staged?

If the context is exploration transactions, some of the issues are:

- Are the transactions being run on condensed data?
- Are the transactions being run on main memory only data?
- Is the data frozen from one transaction to the next?
- Are the results of the transaction being stored for analysis as a part of a heuristic analysis?

13. Design Overlay

Purpose

Many different ways exist to do database and transaction design throughout the corporate information factory. The following guidelines are suggested:

Operational environment	Denormalized design optimized for transaction performance
Data warehouse environment	Slightly denormalized design to accommodate many types of usage
ODS environment	Mixed design—some star join; some normalized design
Data mart environment	Star join/snowflake design
Exploration environment	Normalized, detailed data
Alternative storage environment	Normalized, flat file

Normalization

The Issues

A normalized design is inefficient in that normalization forces the system to gather data every time a query is run. However given the totality of the transactions and the different types of transactions that have to be run, the normalized approach is efficient in that it favors no one type of access over any other type.

As a rule, the normalized approach is good for detailed, granular data, such as that found in the data warehouse.

Star Join/Snowflake

The Issues

The star join structure is good for optimizing performance where requirements are known, but the problem with the star join approach is that it optimizes performance for one group of people at the expense of everyone else. Therefore, the star join is good for data mart design, where people of a like mind access data along the same path.

A snowflake structure is nothing more than multiple star joins aggregated together.

14. Web Interface

Purpose

The Web interface is one of the critical points of the corporate information factory. When the organization starts to engage in eCommerce, the Web becomes the center point of the contact with the end user on the Internet. Some of the issues that relate to the Web interface are:

The volume of data being generated on the Web

The granularity of the data being generated on the Web

The response time in getting data from the corporate information factory to the Web

The integration of the data from the Web to the corporate information factory

The technology compatibility between the technology found on the Web and the technology found on the corporate information factory

Granularity Management

The Issues

Unlike almost anywhere else in the corporate information factory, the data generated on the Web is at too *low* a level of granularity. This means that there is *too* much data to be useful. The challenge on the Web designer and the corporate information factory manager is to weed out the data that is not necessary. In some cases, data is discarded. In other cases, data is stored in a summary or aggregated from.

ODS Support

The Issues

There are (at least) two types of ODS found in the Web/corporate information factory environment. One type of IDS is internal to the Web site itself. The other type of ODS is external to the Web site, residing in the corporate information factory. Both types of ODS are critical to the operation.

Web Internal ODS

The web internal ODS sits inside the Web site and interacts directly with the HTML manager.

Corporate Information Factory ODS

The corporate information factory ODS sits outside of the Web site and services the many different requests from the Web site. The ODS interfaces directly with the data warehouse and stores the many different corporate pieces of aggregated, integrated information.

Clickstream Management

The Issues

One of the most important aspects of the Web environment is that of the collection and management of the click stream. The click stream is where the end user leaves a path as to where the user has gone and what activities the end user has engaged in. Many issues are related to the clickstream:

- How to deal with the volumes of data created by the clickstream
- How to separate out meaningful data from the nonmeaningful data
- How to interface the clickstream data with the corporate information factory data

15. Development Methodology

Purpose

There are three general approaches to developing a corporate information factory environment:

- A classical *structured* approach, in which requirements are gathered into a general design on an all-at-once basis
- A *circular* approach, in which only a few requirements are gathered, the system developed, changes made, and more requirements are gathered again
- An *iterative* approach, in which the next development cycle is determined after the results of the current iteration of development are completed

The different approaches apply to different places in the corporate information factory environment:

Operational environment	Structured
Data warehouse environment	Circular
ODS	Combination of structured and circular
Data mart environment	Structured
Exploration environment	Iterative
Alternative storage environment	Combination of structured and circular

NOTE

There are *dire consequences* if the wrong development approach is used for a component of the corporate information factory. Either the implementation will be needlessly delayed or the product of the implementation will fail to meet user expectations in terms of performance, completeness, and quality. It is a mistake to use a structured approach on the data warehouse.

Points to Be Raised

1. Is the right methodology being used in the right place?

16. Metadata

Purpose

Metadata is the glue that holds together the corporate information factory. Metadata is any data form other than the actual data content itself. For the corporate information factory to function, there must be communication and coordination from one component to the next. Without metadata, the corporate information factory is merely a bunch of technologies operating in an independent and uncoordinated manner.

The problem with metadata across the CIF is that there are many different forms of metadata for each component, but no metadata that can bind one component to another component. For example, the data warehouse may have its metadata, and the data marts may have their metadata, but meaningful exchange of metadata from one component to the next is not a possibility.

The metadata found in the technology of each component can be called locally contained metadata. For example, if the data warehouse were in Oracle, Oracle would locally contain all the metadata about the data warehouse.

Points to Be Raised

1. Describe the strategy for collecting and managing metadata across the corporate information factory.

Locally Gathered and Contained

The Issues

For each component of the corporate information factory, what metadata is locally contained? Is there a need to capture some metadata that is not currently being captured?

Shared

The Issues

After the metadata is gathered locally, it needs to be shared. The sharing of metadata is a complex subject. Some of the facets of sharing include:

- The physical transport of the metadata
- The physical structure and format of the metadata
- The interpretation of the metadata upon arriving at the destination
- The establishment and maintenance of the system of record for the metadata

System of Record

The Issues

There can be only one owner of metadata definition throughout the corporate information factory. If there is ever a case in which there are multiple owners of the same metadata unit or no owner of a metadata unit, the integrity of the metadata is destroyed. However, when metadata is shared across the corporate information factory, there needs to be a formal system of record.

Central Repository

The Issues

The notion of the central repository dates back to the days of the mainframe. In the mainframe environment, everything was centralized. However, in the data warehouse environment, the components of the corporate information factory are very much decentralized. For this reason, the centralized repository approach to metadata management is very circumspect.

17. CIF Organizational Management

Purpose

Behind the corporate information factory is a team of people. The skills of the people typically include:

- Data modeling
- Programming
- Data base administration
- Design
- Project management
- End-user liaison
- Management communication

The number and the organization of the people executing these skills varies widely. The purpose of this section is to examine the people behind the corporate information factory.

Points to Be Raised

1. For the different components of the corporate information factory describe the:

- Management organization
- Development organization
- Operations management
- End-user organization

Organizationally Managed

The Issues

The shape of the organization determines the priorities of development and maintenance of the organization, which go a long way toward explaining the success or failure of the data warehouse and the corporate information factory. As a rule, multiple organizations have a hand in managing and owning different parts of the corporate information factory. Centralized IT management is responsible for:

- Operational component
- I & T component
- ODS
- Data warehouse
- Alternative storage

Different departments are responsible for the various data marts. The various data marts include:

- Marketing
- Sales
- Finance
- Accounting
- Human resources
- Engineering
- Actuary

Separate project groups are responsible for the exploration warehouse, and different applications are responsible for analytical applications.

18. Data Warehouse Performance

Purpose

Performance across the corporate information factory is important, but it varies widely. For example, good performance in the exploration component would hardly be considered good performance elsewhere. For another example, OLTP performance is not to be found outside of the operational environment and the ODS. At the center of the corporate information factory is the data warehouse. Performance here is most critical because poor performance here has an impact on all other environments.

There are many facets to data warehouse performance. Some will be applicable in one case, and others will not be applicable at all, depending on the data warehouse being examined.

Indexing

The Issues

The classical way to get better performance is to add indexes. This works to a limited extent in the world of the data warehouse. If all the other alternatives have been exhausted, adding indexes can enhance performance. If other factors, such as the amount of dormant data have not been considered, however, then adding indexes may actually harm performance.

A good way to tell what indexes should be added is to use a monitor to see what data is being accessed, how it is being accessed, and what queries are being run.

ODS

The Issues

One of the primary attractions of an ODS is that of supporting OLTP performance. You should be able to get very high performance out of a properly built ODS. If there is a demand for true OLTP performance in the corporate information factory, then the ODS is the place to fulfill those requirements.

Data Marts

The Issues

Data marts enhance performance in the corporate information factory in a host of ways—some obvious and some not so obvious. When an organization builds a data mart:

- Cycles are removed from the data warehouse processing workload.
- The data can be customized for the users of the data mart.
- The granularity of data can be altered to optimize the performance of the data mart users.
- The specific requirements of the data mart users can be accommodated.

Near-Line Storage

The Issues

Near-line storage is the biggest enhancement for performance in the data warehouse/corporate information factory environment. The performance boost comes when inactive/dormant data is moved to near-line storage. The emancipation of the actively used storage enhances performance in a very fundamental way. *No other single approach to performance is as effective as the movement of inactive storage to near-line storage in the data warehouse environment.*

Denormalization

The Issues

Denormalization is effective when there is a known, regularly occurring pattern of access to data. After that pattern is determined, the data can be arranged to accommodate the efficient access of the data.

Some of the many forms of denormalization are:

- The creation of arrays of data
- The deliberate introduction of redundancy
- The physical placement of data in the same block
- The merging of tables

Exploration Warehouse

The Issues

The exploration warehouse enhances performance by removing untoward and very long queries from the high-performance job stream. After the large queries are removed, the workload is free to execute in an unfettered manner.

Summarization

The Issues

When a company regularly looks at detailed data by summarizing the detailed data, it simply makes sense to summarize data once and then let everyone access it. It is much more efficient to access one unit of summarized data than it is to access many detailed data units, which in turn have to be summarized.

Aggregation

The Issues

When a company regularly looks at detailed data by aggregating the data, it makes sense to aggregate data once and then let everyone access it. It is much more efficient to access one unit of aggregated data than it is to access many detailed data units, which in turn have to be aggregated.

Redundancy

The Issues

When the same unit of data is used repeatedly in conjunction with other data units on a regular and frequent basis, it makes sense to store the data unit redundantly. Care must be taken because the redundant data takes up more space, thereby increasing the size of the data warehouse.

Physical Colocation

The Issues

When different data units are used together in a regular and frequent basis, performance can be enhanced by causing the different data units to be physically placed in the same physical data block.

Optimal Loading

The Issues

When dealing with large data amounts, the time needed to load must be factored into the performance equation. There are lots of ways to mitigate the time requirements for the loading of data:

- Parallelize the load stream
- Delay the load stream until the system is lightly burdened
- Load indexes separately

Monitoring

The Issues

There is one operational key to the long-term management of performance. Monitoring the activity that passes through the data warehouse environment allows the administrator to see:

- When the workload peaks and valleys are
- What queries are consuming the most time and resources
- What users are the most active
- Whether explorers are using the system
- What data is used the most
- Where the hot spots are

Service-Level Agreements

The Issues

Service-level agreements are most effective in the OLTP environment but have some applicability to the data warehouse/corporate information factory environment. In order to be effective, service-level agreements must factor in both farmer transactions and explorer transactions.

19. Budgeting

Purpose

Budgeting is one of the most important aspects of the ongoing development of the corporate information factory because it is through budgeting that different parts of the corporate information factory grow or do not grow. Budgeting is usually done on a component-by-component basis. Different departments budget for the data marts; statisticians and research personnel budget for exploration warehouse facilities; applications budget for analytical applications and ODS; and so forth. Usually centralized operations pays for the data warehouse and the ETL facilities.

20. End-to-End Speed of Flow

Purpose

The rate at which data flows through the corporate information factory is of great importance. If it takes a long time for an occurrence of data to pass from the operational environment to the data mart or the exploration environment, then the business usefulness of the corporate information factory is limited. In order for there to be maximum usefulness of the CIF, data must be able to pass very rapidly through the corporate information factory as business circumstances warrant.

21. CIF Management

Purpose

The focus of most organizations is on the building of the corporate information factory. After the corporate information factory or parts of the corporate information factory are built, it must be maintained. Some of the many issues to the ongoing maintenance of the corporate information factory are:

- Managing performance
- Managing the volumes of data that appear
- Managing the emergence of new corporate information factory componentry
- Managing users expectations
- Managing the growth of the corporate information factory in light of the available budget
- Keeping track of new technologies

How Monitored

The Issues

The first step toward proactive management of the corporate information factory is to monitor the environment. The monitoring needs to keep track of:

- The growth of data
  - The raw rate of growth
  - The demographics of the growth
  - The probability of access of the growth of data
- The growth of queries
  - The types of queries
  - The demographics of queries
  - The average response time and how it is changing
- The types of data usage
  - Farmer usage
  - Explorer usage
  - Data-mining usage
  - Tourist usage

Capacity Planning

The Issues

Capacity planning in the corporate information factory environment is usually done on an *ad hoc*, informal basis.

Doing classical capacity planning in which the workload is modeled is almost an impossibility in the corporate information factory environment because:

- The workload is so variable.
- The workload arrival rate is so unpredictable.
- There is a mixture of farmers, explorers, and miners in the same workload.

Management on an Exception Basis

The Issues

In the initial days of the corporate information factory it is possible for the administrator to devote individual attention to the monitoring of each component. As time passes, however, and as the different corporate information factory components grow and as new components are built, it becomes a nightmare to try to manage the day-to-day activities of each of the components on an individual basis. To this end, the corporate information factory administrator determines certain baseline criteria for the management of each of the CIF components and then monitors the component in relation to those parameters. Only when the administrator is alerted that one or more of the parameters have been violated does the administrator pay individual attention to the component.

Monitor Overhead

The Issues

Every monitor has overhead. There is no way to create a monitor that does not have its own unique overhead. However, every monitor's overhead differs from every other monitor's overhead. The administrator must be aware of the overhead and must be aware that over time the overhead may change. The cost of a monitor is not in just the license cost but also in the cost of the overhead.

Monitor Complexity

The Issues

Every monitor has complexity. There is no way to create a monitor that does not have its own unique complexity. However, every monitor's complexity differs from every other monitor's complexity. The administrator must be aware of the complexity and that over time the complexity may change. The cost of a monitor is not in just the license cost but also in the cost of the complexity.

22. History of the CIF

Purpose

Every corporate information factory development effort has a history. Some corporate information factories grow naturally. Others grow with a great deal of pain—the same component (usually the data warehouse is built and rebuilt several times). The politics of the corporate information factory change as well as the budgets. The history of the corporate information factory explains much of what is going on with the CIF right now.

How Long

The Issues

How long has the corporate information factory been under construction?

How Big

The Issues

How large is the corporate information factory today?

At What Rate

The Issues

At what rate is the corporate information factory growing?

The Order of Components

The Issues

What order have the components of the corporate information factory been built?

Glossary

access The operation of seeking, reading, or writing data on a storage unit.

access method A technique used to transfer a physical record from or to a mass storage device.

access mode A technique in which a specific logical record is obtained from or placed onto a file assigned to a mass storage device.

access pattern The general sequence by which the data structure is accessed (such as from tuple to tuple, from record to record, from segment to segment, and so on).

access Plan the control structure produced during program preparation and used by a database manager to process SQL statements during application execution.

access time The time interval between the instant an instruction initiates a request for data and the instant the first of the data satisfying the request is delivered. Note that there is a difference—sometimes large—between the time data is first delivered and the time when *all* the data is delivered.

accuracy A qualitative assessment of freedom from error or a quantitative measure of the magnitude of error, expressed as a function of relative error.

active data dictionary A data dictionary that is the sole source for an application program insofar as metadata is concerned.

activity   (1) The lowest-level function on an activity chart (sometimes called the "atomic level"); (2) a logical description of a function performed by an enterprise; (3) a procedure (automated or not) designed for the fulfillment of an activity.

activity ratio   The fraction of records in a database that have activity or are otherwise accessed in a given period of time or in a given batch run.

address   An identification (a number, name, storage location, byte offset, and so on) for a location where data is stored.

addressing   The means of assigning data to storage locations and locating the data upon subsequent retrieval on the basis of the key of the data.

ad hoc processing   One-time-only, casual access and manipulation of data on parameters never before used.

after image   The snapshot of data placed on a log upon the completion of a transaction.

agent of change   A motivating force large enough not to be denied—usually the aging of systems, changes in technology, radical changes in requirements, and so on.

AIX (Advanced Interactive eXecutive)   IBM's version of the UNIX operating system.

algorithm   A set of statements organized to solve a problem in a finite number of steps.

alias   An alternative label used to refer to a data element.

alphabetic   A representation of data using letters—upper- and/or lowercase-only.

alphanumeric   A representation of data using numbers and/or letters and punctuation.

alternative storage   An extension to the data warehouse that enables vast amounts of infrequently used, dormant data to be stored and accessed economically. There are two forms of alternative storage, secondary storage and near-line storage.

analytical processing   The usage of the computer to produce an analysis for management decisions, usually involving trend analysis, drill-down analysis, demographic analysis, profiling, and so on.

ANSI   American National Standards Institute.

anticipatory staging   The technique of moving blocks of data from one storage device to another with a shorter access time, in anticipation of their being needed by a program in execution or a program soon to go into execution.

API (Application Program Interface)   The common set of parameters needed to connect the communications between programs.

application   A group of algorithms and data interlinked to support an organizational requirement.

application blocking of data   The grouping into the same physical unit of storage multiple occurrences of data controlled at the application level.

application database   A collection of data organized to support a specific application.

archival database   A collection of data of a historical nature. As a rule, archival data cannot be updated. Each unit of archival data is related to a moment in time now passed.

area   In network databases, a named collection of records that can contain occurrences of one or more record types. A record type can occur in more than one area.

artifact   A design technique used to represent referential integrity in the DSS environment.

artificial intelligence   The capability of a system to perform functions typically associated with human intelligence and reasoning.

association   A relationship between two entities that is represented in a data model.

associative storage   (1) A storage device whose records are identified by a specific part of their contents rather than their name or physical position in the database; (2) content-addressable memory. *See also* parallel search storage.

atomic   (1) Data stored in a data warehouse; (2) the lowest level of process analysis.

atomic database   A database made up of primarily atomic data; a data warehouse; a DSS foundation database.

atomicity   The property where a group of actions is invisible to other actions executing concurrently, yielding the effect of serial execution. It is recoverable with successful completion (commit) or total backout (rollback) of previous changes associated with that group.

atomic level data   Data with the lowest level of granularity. Atomic level data sits in a data warehouse and is time-variant (accurate as of some moment in time now passed).

attribute   A property that can assume values for entities or relationships. Entities can be assigned several attributes (such as a tuple in a relationship consists of values). Some systems also allow relationships to have attributes as well.

audit trail   Data that is available to trace activity, usually update activity.

authorization identifier   A character string that designates a set of privilege descriptors.

availability   A measure of the reliability of a system, indicating the fraction of time the system is up and available divided by the amount of time the system should be up and available. Note that there is a difference between a piece of hardware being available and the systems running on that hardware also being available.

backend processor   A database machine or an intelligent disk controller.

back up   To restore the database to its state at some previous moment in time.

backup A file serving as a basis for backing up a database. Usually a snapshot of a database at some previous moment in time.

Backus-Naur Form (BNF) A metalanguage used to specify or describe the syntax of a language. In BNF, each symbol on the left side of the forms can be replaced by the symbol strings on the right side of the forms to develop sentences in the grammar of the defined language. Synonymous with Backus-Normal Form.

backward recovery A recovery technique that restores a database to an earlier state by applying previous images.

base relation A relation that is not derivable from other relations in the database.

batch Computer environment in which programs (usually long-running, sequentially oriented) access data exclusively, and user interaction is not allowed while the activity is occurring.

batch environment A sequentially dominated mode of processing; in batch, input is collected and stored for later processing. Once collected, the batch input is transacted sequentially against one or more databases.

batch window The time at which the online system is available for batch or sequential processing. The batch window occurs during nonpeak processing hours.

before image A snapshot of a record prior to an update, usually placed on an activity log.

bill of materials A listing of the parts used in a manufacturing process along with the relation of one part to another insofar as assembly of the final product is concerned. The bill of materials is a classical recursive structure.

binary element A constituent element of data that exists as either of two values or states—either true or false, or one or zero.

binary search A dichotomizing search with steps where the sets of remaining items are partitioned into two equal parts.

bind (1) To assign a value to a data element, variable, or parameter; (2) the attachment of a data definition to a program prior to the execution of the program.

binding time The moment when the data description known to the dictionary is assigned to or bound to the procedural code.

bit-(b)inary digi(t) The lowest level of storage. A bit can be in a 1 state or a 0 state.

bit map A specialized form of an index indicating the existence or nonexistence of a condition for a group of blocks or records. Bit maps are expensive to build and maintain, but provide very fast comparison and access facilities.

block (1) A basic unit of structuring storage; (2) the physical unit of transport and storage. A block usually contains one or more records (or contains the space for one or more records). In some DBMS, a block is called a page.

blocking   Combining of two or more physical records so that they are physically colocated together. The result of their physical colocation is that the records can be accessed and fetched by execution of a single machine instruction.

block splitting   The data management activity where data in a filled block is written into two unfilled blocks, leaving space for future insertions and updates in the two partially filled blocks.

B-tree   A binary storage structure and access method that maintains order in a database by continually dividing possible choices into two equal parts and reestablishing pointers to the respective sets, while not allowing more than two levels of difference to exist concurrently.

buffer   An storage area that holds data temporarily in main memory while data is being transmitted, received, read, or written. A buffer is often used to compensate for the differences in the timing of the transmission and execution of devices. Buffers are used in terminals, peripheral devices, storage units, and CPUs.

bus   The hardware connection that allows data to flow from one component to another (such as from the CPU to the line printer).

business intelligence   Represents those systems that help companies understand what makes the wheels of the corporation turn and to help predict the future impact of current decisions. These systems place a key role in strategic planning process of the corporation. Systems that exemplify business intelligence include medical research, customer profiling, market basket analysis, customer contact analysis, market segmentation, scoring, product profitability, and inventory movement.

business management   Those systems needed to effectively manage actions resulting from the business intelligence gained. If business intelligence helps companies understand *what* makes the wheels of the corporation turn, business management helps *direct* the wheels as the business landscape changes. To a large extent, these systems augment, extend, and eventually displace capabilities provided by business operations. Systems that exemplify business management include product management, campaign management, inventory management, resource management, and customer information management.

business operations   Represents those systems that run the day-to-day business. These systems have traditionally made up the legacy environment and provided a competitive advantage by automating manual business processes to gain economies of scale and speed to market. Systems that exemplify business operations include accounts payable, accounts receivable, billing, order processing, compensation, and lead list generation.

byte   A basic unit of storage-made up of eight bits.

C   A programming language.

cache A buffer usually built and maintained at the device level. Retrieving data out of a cache is much quicker than retrieving data out of a cylinder.

call To invoke the execution of a module.

canonical model A data model that represents the inherent structure of data without regard to its individual use or hardware or software implementation.

cardinality (of a relation) The number of tuples (rows) in a relation. *See also* degree (of a relation).

CASE Computer Aided Software Engineering.

catalog A directory of all files available to the computer.

chain An organization where records or other items of data are strung together.

chain list A list where the items cannot be located in sequence, but where each item contains an identifier (pointer) for finding the next item.

channel A subsystem for input to and output from the computer. Data from storage units, for example, flows into the computer by way of a channel.

character A member of the standard set of elements used to represent data in the database.

character type The characters that can represent the value of an attribute.

checkpoint An identified snapshot of the database, or a point at which the transactions against the database have been frozen or have been quiesced.

checkpoint/restart A means of restarting a program at some point other than the beginning-for example, when a failure or interruption has occurred. *N* checkpoints may be used at intervals throughout an application program. At each of these points, sufficient information is stored to permit the program to be restored to the moment when the checkpoint was established.

child A unit of data existing in a 1:*n* relationship with another unit of data called a parent, where the parent must exist before the child can exist, but the parent can exist even when no child unit of data exists.

CICS (Customer Information Control System) An IBM teleprocessing monitor.

CIO (chief information officer) The manager of all the information processing functions in an organization.

circular file (queue) An organization of data where a finite number of units of data are allocated. Data is then loaded into those units. Upon reaching the end of the allocated units, new data is written over older data at the beginning of the queue. Sometimes called a *wrap-around* queue.

claimed block A second or subsequent physical block of data designated to store table data, after the originally allocated block has run out of space.

class (of entities) All possible entities held by a given proposition.

CLDS The facetious name of the system development lifecycle of analytical, DSS systems. CLDS is so named because it is the reverse of the name of the classical systems development life cycle—SDLC.

cluster (1) In Teradata, a group of physical devices controlled by the same AMP; (2) in DB2 and Oracle, the practice of physically colocating data in the same block based on its content.

cluster key The key around which data is clustered in a block (DB2/Oracle).

coalesce To combine two or more sets of items into a single set.

COBOL (Common Business Oriented Language) Computer language for the business world. A very common language.

CODASYL model A network database model that was originally defined by the Database Task Group (DBTG) of the COnference on DAta SYstem Language (CODASYL) organization.

code (1) To represent data or a computer program in a form that can be accepted by a data processor; (2) to transform data so that it cannot be understood by anyone who does not have the algorithm necessary to decode the data prior to presentation (sometimes called *encode*).

collision The event that occurs when two or more records of data are assigned to the same physical location. Collisions are associated with randomizers or hashers.

column A vertical table where values are selected from the same domain. A row is made up of one or more columns.

command (1) The specification of an activity by the programmer; (2) the actual execution of the specification.

commit A condition raised by the programmer signalling to the DBMS that all update activity done by the program should be executed against a database. Prior to the commit, all update activity can be rolled back or cancelled with no adverse effects on the contents of the database.

commit protocol An algorithm to ensure that a transaction is successfully completed.

commonality of data Similar or identical data that occurs in different applications or systems. The recognition and management of data commonality is one of the foundations of conceptual and physical database design.

communication network The collection of transmission facilities, network processors, and so on, which provides for data movement among terminals and information processors.

compaction   A technique for reducing the number of bits required to represent data without losing the contents of the data. With compaction, repetitive data is represented very concisely.

component   A data item or array of data items whose component type defines a collection of occurrences with the same data type.

compound index   An index spanning multiple columns.

concatenate   To link or connect two strings of characters, generally for the purpose of using them as a single value.

conceptual schema   A consistent collection of data structures expressing the data needs of the organization. This schema is a comprehensive, base-level, and logical description of the environment where an organization exists, free of physical structure and application system considerations.

concurrent operations   Activities executed simultaneously or during the same time interval.

condensation   The process of reducing the volume of data managed without reducing the logical consistency of the data. Condensation is essentially different than compaction.

connect   To forge a relationship between two entities, particularly in a network system.

connector   A symbol used to indicate that one occurrence of data has a relationship to another occurrence of data. Connectors are used in conceptual database design and can be implemented hierarchically, relationally, in an inverted fashion, or by a network.

content addressable memory   A main storage area that can be addressed by the contents of the data in the memory, as opposed to conventional location addressable memory.

contention   The condition that occurs when two or more programs try to access the same data simultaneously.

continuous time span data   Data organized so that a continuous definition of data over a period of time is represented by one or more records.

control character   A character whose occurrence in a particular context initiates, modifies, or stops an operation.

control database   A utilitarian database containing data not directly related to the application being built. Typical control databases are audit databases, terminal databases, security databases, and so on.

cooperative processing   The capability to distribute resources (programs, files, and databases) across the network.

coordinator The two-phase commit protocol defines one database management system as coordinator for the commit process. The coordinator is responsible for communicating with the other database manager involved in a unit of work.

corporate information factory (CIF) The physical embodiment of the information ecosystem. The CIF was first introduced by W. H. Inmon in the early '80s.

CPU Central processing unit.

CPU-bound The state of processing where the computer cannot produce more output, because the CPU portion of the processor is being used at 100 percent capacity. When the computer is CPU-bound, typically the memory and storage processing units are less than 100 percent utilized. With modern DBMS, it is much more likely that the computer is I/O-bound, rather than CPU-bound.

CSP (Cross System Product) An IBM application generator.

CUA (Common User Access) Specifies the ways in which the user interface to systems will be constructed.

current value data Data whose accuracy is valid as of the moment of execution, as opposed to time-variant data.

cursor (1) An indicator that designates a current position on a screen; (2) a system facility that allows the programmer to thumb from one record to the next after the system has retrieved a set of records.

cursor stability An option that enables data to move under the cursor. Once the program has used the data examined by the cursor, it is released. As opposed to repeatable read.

cylinder The storage area of DASD that can be read without movement of the arm. The term originated with disk files, in which a cylinder consisted of one track on each disk surface so that each of these tracks could have a read/write head positioned over it simultaneously.

DASD *See* direct access storage device.

data A recording of facts, concepts, or instructions on a storage medium for communication, retrieval, and processing by automatic means and presentation as information that is understandable by human beings.

data administrator (DA) The individual or organization responsible for the specification, acquisition, and maintenance of data management software and the design, validation, and security of files or databases. The data model and the data dictionary are usually the responsibility of the DA.

data aggregate A collection of data items.

database   A collection of interrelated data stored (often with controlled, limited redundancy) according to a schema. A database can serve single or multiple applications.

database administrator (DBA)   The organizational function charged with the day-to-day monitoring and care of the databases. The DBA is more closely associated with physical database design than the DA is.

database key   A unique value that exists for each record in a database. The value is often indexed, although it can be randomized or hashed.

database machine   A dedicated-purpose computer that provides data access and management through total control of the access method, physical storage, and data organization. Often called a *backend processor*. Data is usually managed in parallel by a database machine.

database management system (DBMS)   A computer-based software system used to establish and manage data.

database record   A physical root and all of its dependents (in IMS).

DatacomDB   A database management system created by CA.

data definition   The specification of the data entities, their attributes, and their relationships in a coherent database structure to create a schema.

data definition language (DDL) the language used to define the database schema and additional data features that allows the DBMS to generate and manage the internal tables, indexes, buffers, and storage necessary for database processing. Also called a *data description language*.

data description language   *See* data definition language.

data dictionary   A software tool for recording the definition of data, the relationship of one category of data to another, the attributes and keys of groups of data, and so forth.

data division (COBOL)   The section of a COBOL program that consists of entries used to define the nature and characteristics of the data to be processed by the program.

data-driven development   The approach to development that centers around identifying the commonality of data through a data model and building programs that have a broader scope than the immediate application. Data-driven development differs from traditional application-oriented development, which is generally process-driven.

data-driven process   A process whose resource consumption depends on the data by which it operates. For example, a hierarchical root has a dependent. For one occurrence, there are two dependents for the root. For another occurrence of the root, there may be 1,000 occurrences of the dependent. The same program that accesses the root and all its dependents will use very different amounts of resources when operating against the two roots, although the code will be exactly the same.

data element   (1) An attribute of an entity; (2) a uniquely named and well-defined category of data that consists of data items, and that is included in the record of an activity.

data engineering   The planning and building of data structures according to accepted mathematical models on the basis of the inherent characteristics of the data itself, and independent of hardware and software systems. *See also* information engineering.

data independence   The property of being able to modify the overall logical and physical structure of data without changing any of the application code supporting the data.

data item   A discrete representation having the properties that define the data element to which it belongs. *See also* data element.

data item set (dis)   A grouping of data items, each of which directly relates to the key of the grouping of data in which the data items reside. The data item set is found in the mid-level model.

data manipulation language (DML)   (1) A programming language that is supported by a DBMS and used to access a database; (2) language constructs added to a higher-order language (such as COBOL) for the purpose of database manipulation.

data mart   Contains data from the data warehouse tailored to support the specific analytical requirements of a given business unit. This business unit could be defined to be as broad as a division or as narrow as a department.

data mining warehouse   A sister component to the exploration warehouse. In early stages, a single exploration warehouse is sufficient to support the needs of explorers and miners. As time goes on, the miners need their own environment—the data mining warehouse. The exploration warehouse helps explorers find and interpret patterns and make assertions and hypotheses, whereas the data mining warehouse helps miners validate assertions and hypotheses.

data model   (1) The logical data structures, including operations and constraints provided by a DBMS for effective database processing; (2) the system used for the representation of data (such as the ERD or relational model).

data record   An identifiable set of data values treated as a unit, an occurrence of a schema in a database, or a collection of atomic data items describing a specific object, event, or tuple.

data security   The protection of the data in a database against unauthorized disclosure, alteration, or destruction. There are different levels of security.

data set   A named collection of logically related data items, arranged in a prescribed manner, and described by control information, to which the programming systems has access.

data storage description language (DSDL)   A language to define the organization of stored data in terms of an operating system and device-independent storage environment. *See also* device media control language.

data structure   A logical relationship among data elements that is designed to support specific data manipulation functions (such as trees, lists, and tables).

data type   The definition of a set of representable values that is primitive and without meaningful logical subdivisions.

data view   *See* user view.

data volatility   The rate of change of the contents of data.

data warehouse   A collection of integrated subject-oriented databases designed to support the DSS function, where each unit of data is relevant to some moment in time. The data warehouse contains atomic data and lightly summarized data.

data warehouse administrator (DWA)   Represents the organization responsible for managing the data warehouse environment.

DB2   A database management system created by IBM.

DB/DC   Database/data communications.

DBMS language interface (DB I/O module)   Software that applications invoke in order to access a database. The module in turn has direct access with the DBMS. Standard enforcement and standard error checking are often features of an I/O module.

deadlock   *See* deadly embrace.

deadly embrace   The event that occurs when transaction A desires to access data currently protected by transaction B, while at the same time transaction B desires to access data that is currently being protected by transaction A. The deadly embrace condition is a serious impediment to performance.

decision support system (DSS)   A system used to support managerial decisions. Usually, DSS involves the analysis of many units of data in a heuristic fashion. As a rule, DSS processing does not involve the update of data.

decompaction   The opposite of compaction. Once data is stored in a compacted form, it must be decompacted to be used.

decryption   The opposite of encryption. Once data is stored in an encrypted fashion, it must be decrypted to be used.

degree (of a relation)   The number of attributes or columns of a relation. *See also* cardinality of a relation.

delimiter   A flag, symbol, or convention used to mark the boundaries of a record, field, or other unit of storage.

demand staging   The movement of blocks of data from one storage device to another device with a shorter access time, when programs request the blocks and the blocks are not already in the faster access storage.

denormalization   The technique of placing normalized data in a physical location that optimizes the performance of the system.

derived data   Data whose existence depends on two or more occurrences of a major subject of the enterprise.

derived data element   A data element that is not necessarily stored, but that can be generated when needed (such as age as of the current date and date of birth).

derived relation   A relation that can be obtained from previously defined relations by applying some sequence of retrieval and derivation operations (such as a table that is the combination of others and some projections). *See also* a virtual relation.

design review   The quality assurance process where all aspects of a system are reviewed publicly prior to the striking of code.

device media control language (DMCL)   A language used to define the mapping of the data onto the physical storage media. *See also* data storage description language.

direct access   Retrieval or storage of data by reference to its location on a volume. The access mechanism goes directly to the data in question, as is generally required with online use of data. Also called *random access* or *hashed access*.

direct access storage device (DASD)   A data storage unit where data can be accessed directly without having to progress through a serial file such as a magnetic tape file. A disk unit is a direct access storage device.

directory   A table specifying the relationships between items of data. Sometimes it is a table or index giving the addresses of data.

distributed catalog   A distributed catalog is needed to achieve site autonomy. The catalog at each site maintains information about objects in the local databases. The distributed catalog keeps information on replicated and distributed tables stored at that site and on remote tables located at another site that cannot be accessed locally.

distributed database   A database controlled by a central DBMS, but where the storage devices are geographically dispersed or not attached to the same processor. *See also* parallel I/O.

distributed environment A set of related data processing systems, where each system has the capacity to operate autonomously, but where applications can execute at multiple sites. Some of the systems may be connected with teleprocessing links into a network in which each system is a node.

distributed free space Space left empty at intervals in a data layout, to permit the insertion of new data.

distributed request A transaction across multiple nodes.

distributed unit of work The work done by a transaction that operates against multiple nodes.

division An operation that partitions a relation on the basis of the contents of data found in the relation.

DL/1 IBM's Data Language One, used for describing logical and physical data structures.

domain The set of legal values from which actual values are derived for an attribute or a data element.

download The stripping of data from one database to another, based on the content of data found in the first database.

drill-down analysis The type of analysis where examination of a summary number leads to the exploration of the components of the sum.

DSS application data mart Similar to a departmental data mart in form but different in terms of breadth of user community. Whereas the departmental data mart supports only a department/division within a company, the DSS application data mart supports all users of a particular analytic application. As a result, the user community can span many departments/divisions. Business domains where these analytic applications are common include customer relationship management (CRM) and enterprise resource planning (ERP).

dual database The practice of separating high-performance, transaction-oriented data from decision support data.

dual database management systems The practice of using multiple database management systems to control different aspects of the database environment.

dumb terminal A device used to interact directly with the end user, where all processing is done on a remote computer. A dumb terminal acts as a device that gathers data and displays data only.

dynamic SQL SQL statements that are prepared and executed within a program, while the program is executing. In dynamic SQL, the SQL source is contained in host language variables rather than being coded into the application program.

dynamic storage allocation A technique where the storage areas assigned to computer programs are determined during processing.

dynamic subset of data A subset of data selected by a program and operated on only by the program, and released by the program once it ceases execution.

EDI Electronic Data Interchange.

EIS (Executive Information Systems) Systems designed for the top executives, featuring drill-down analysis and trend analysis.

embedded pointer A record pointer (that is, a means of internally linking related records) that is not available to an external index or directory. Embedded pointers are used to reduce search times, but also require maintenance overhead.

encoding A shortening or abbreviation of the physical representation of a data value (such as male = "M", female = "F").

encryption The transformation of data from a recognizable form to a form unrecognizable without the algorithm used for the encryption. Encryption is usually done for the purpose of security.

enterprise The generic term for the company, corporation, agency, or business unit. Usually associated with data modelling.

entity A person, place, or thing of interest to the data modeller at the highest level of abstraction.

entity-relationship attribute (ERA) model A data model that defines entities, the relationship between the entities, and the attributes that have values to describe the properties of entities and/or relationships.

entity-relationship diagram (ERD) A high-level data model-the schematic showing all the entities within the scope of integration and the direct relationship between those entities.

event A signal that an activity of significance has occurred. An event is noted by the information system.

event discrete data Data relating to the measurement or description of an event.

expert system A system that captures and automates the usage of human experience and intelligence.

exploration warehouse an ad hoc environment intended to off-load complex and unpredictable query activity from the data warehouse. Unlike the data mart, which supports a user community that asks relatively simple and predictable types of questions (the farmer), questions asked by the user community of the exploration warehouse (the explorer and miner) can be characterized as complex and unpredictable. The type of analysis performed is statistical in nature and used to do such things as forecast inventory and create models to segment customers and detect fraud.

extent   (1) A list of unsigned integers that specifies an array; (2) a physical unit of disk storage attached to a data set after the initial allocation of data has been made.

external data   (1) Data originating from other than the operational systems of a corporation; (2) data residing outside the central processing complex.

external schema   A logical description of a user's method of organizing and structuring data. Some attributes or relationships can be omitted from the corresponding conceptual schema or can be renamed or otherwise transformed. *See also* view.

external world   Where business and commerce take place. The external world consists of transaction producers and information consumers. Without the external world, there would be no need for the corporate information factory.

extract   The process of selecting data from one environment and transporting it to another environment.

field   *See* data item.

file   A set of related records treated as a unit and stored under a single logical file name.

first in first out (FIFO)   A fundamental ordering of processing in a queue.

first in last out (FILO)   A standard order of processing in a stack.

flag   An indicator or character that signals the occurrence of some condition.

flat file   A collection of records containing no data aggregates, nested repeated data items, or groups of data items.

floppy disk   A device for storing data on a personal computer.

foreign key   An attribute that is not a primary key in a relational system, but whose values are the values of the primary key of another relation.

format   The arrangement or layout of data in or on a data medium or in a program definition.

forward recovery   A recovery technique that restores a database by reapplying all transactions using a before image from a specified point in time to a copy of the database taken at that moment in time.

fourth-generation language   Language or technology designed to allow the end user unfettered access to data.

functional decomposition   The division of operations into hierarchical functions (that is, activities) that form the basis for procedures.

granularity The level of detail contained in a unit of data. The more detail there is, the lower the level of granularity. The less detail there is, the higher the level of granularity.

graphic A symbol produced on a screen representing an object or a process in the real world.

hash To convert the value of the key of a record into a location on disk.

hash total A total of the values of one or more fields, used for the purposes of auditability and control.

header record or header table A record containing common, constant, or identifying information for a group of records that follow.

heuristic The mode of analysis in which the next step is determined by the results of the current step of analysis. Used for decision support processing.

hierarchical model A data model providing a tree structure for relating data elements or groups of data elements. Each node in the structure represents a group of data elements or a record type. There can be only one root node at the start of the hierarchical structure.

hit An occurrence of data that satisfies some search criteria.

hit ratio A measure of the number of records in a file expected to be accessed in a given run. Usually expressed as a percentage-the number of input transactions/ number of records in the file x100 = hit ratio.

homonyms Identical names that refer to different attributes.

horizontal distribution The splitting of a table across different sites by rows. With horizontal distribution, rows of a single table reside at different sites in a distributed database network.

host The processor receiving and processing a transaction.

Huffman code A code for data compaction in which frequently used characters are encoded with fewer bits than infrequently used characters.

IDMS A network DBMS from CA.

IEEE Institute of Electrical and Electronics Engineers.

image copy A procedure in which a database is physically copied to another medium for the purposes of backup.

IMS (Information Management System) An operational DBMS by IBM.

index The portion of the storage structure maintained to provide efficient access to a record when its index key item is known.

index chains Chains of data within an index.

indexed sequential access method (ISAM) A file structure and access method in which records can be processed sequentially (such as in order or by key) or by directly looking up their locations on a table, thus making it unnecessary to process previously inserted records.

index point A hardware reference mark on a disk or drum used for timing purposes.

indirect addressing Any method of specifying or locating a record through calculation (such as by locating a record through the scan of an index).

information Data that human beings assimilate and evaluate to solve problems or make decisions.

information center The organizational unit charged with identifying and accessing information needed in DSS processing.

information ecosystem A comprehensive information solution that complements traditional business intelligence (i.e., analytics) with capabilities to deliver business management (customer care, account consolidation, and so on). This will allow companies to capitalize on a changing business landscape characterized by customer relationships and customized product delivery.

information engineering (IE) The discipline of creating a data-driven development environment.

input/output (I/O) The means by which data is stored and/or retrieved on DASD. I/O is measured in milliseconds (mechanical speeds) whereas computer processing is measured in nanoseconds (electronic speeds).

instances A set of values representing a specific entity belonging to a particular entity type. A single value is also the instance of a data item.

integration and transformation (I & T) layer A software component of the corporate information factory, which is responsible for collecting, integrating, transforming, and moving data from the applications to the data warehouse and ODS, and from the data warehouse to the data marts, exploration warehouse, and data mining warehouse.

integrity The property of a database that ensures that the data contained in the database is as accurate and consistent as possible.

intelligent database A database that contains shared logic as well as shared data and automatically invokes that logic when the data is accessed. Logic, constraints, and controls relating to the use of the data are represented in an intelligent data model.

interactive A mode of processing that combines some of the characteristics of online transaction processing and batch processing. In interactive processing, the end user interacts with data over which he or she has exclusive control. In addition, the end user can initiate background activity to be run against the data.

interleaved data   Data from different tables mixed into a simple table space, where there is commonality of physical colocation based on a common key value.

internal schema   The schema that describes logical structures of the data and the physical media over which physical storage is mapped.

interpretive   A mode of data manipulation in which the commands to the DBMS are translated as the user enters them (as opposed to the programmed mode of process manipulation).

intersection data   Data that is associated with the junction of two or more record types or entities, but which has no meaning when disassociated with any records or entities forming the junction.

inverted file   A file structure that uses an inverted index, where entries are grouped according to the content of the key being referenced. Inverted files provide for the fast spontaneous searching of files.

inverted index   An index structure organized by means of a nonunique key to speed the search for data by content.

inverted list   A list organized around a secondary index instead of around a primary key.

I/O (Input/Output Operation)   Input/output operations are the key to performance because they operate at mechanical speeds, not at electronic speeds.

I/O bound   The point after which no more processing can be done because the I/O subsystem is saturated.

ISAM   *See* indexed sequential access method.

"is a type of"   An analytical tool used in abstracting data during the process of conceptual database design (for example, a cocker spaniel is a type of dog).

ISDN (Integrated Services Digital Network)   A telecommunications technology that enables companies to transfer data and voice through the same phone lines.

ISO   International Standards Organization.

item   *See* data item.

item type   A classification of an item according to its domain, generally in a gross sense.

iterative analysis   The mode of processing in which the next step of processing depends on the results obtained by the existing step in execution; also known as heuristic processing.

JAD (Joint Application Design) An organization of people—usually end users—to create and refine application system requirements.

join An operation that takes two relations as operands and produces a new relation by concatenating the tuples and matching the corresponding columns when a stated condition holds between the two.

judgement sample A sample of data where it is accepted or rejected for the sample based on one or more parameters.

junction From the network environment, an occurrence of data that has two or more parent segments. For example, an order for supplies must have a supplier parent and a part parent.

justify To adjust the value representation in a character field to the right or to the left, ignoring blanks encountered.

keeplist A sequence of database keys maintained by the DBMS for the duration of the session.

key A data item or combination of data items used to identify or locate a record instance (or other similar data groupings).

key compression A technique for reducing the number of bits in keys; used in making indexes occupy less space.

key, primary A unique attribute used to identify a single record in a database.

key, secondary A nonunique attribute used to identify a class of records in a database.

label A set of symbols used to identify or describe an item, record, message, or file. Occasionally, a label may be the same as the address of the record in storage.

language A set of characters, conventions, and rules used to convey information, and consisting of syntax and semantics.

latency The time taken by a DASD device to position the read arm over the physical storage medium. For general purposes, average latency time is used.

least frequently used (LFU) A replacement strategy in which new data must replace existing data in an area of storage; the least frequently used items are replaced.

least recently used (LRU) A replacement strategy in which new data must replace existing data in an area of storage; the least recently used items are replaced.

level of abstraction The level of abstraction appropriate to a dimension. The level of abstraction that is appropriate is entirely dependent on the ultimate user of the system.

line The hardware by which data flows to or from the processor. Lines typically go to terminals, printers, and other processors.

line polling The activity of the teleprocessing monitor in which different lines are queried to determine whether they have data and/or transactions that need to be transmitted.

line time The length of time required for a transaction to go either from the terminal to the processor or the processor to the terminal. Typically, line time is the single largest component of online response time.

linkage The ability to relate one unit of data to another.

linked list The set of records in which each record contains a pointer to the next record on the list. *See also* chain.

list An ordered set of data items.

living sample A representative database typically used for heuristic statistical analytical processing in place of a large database. Periodically the very large database is selectively stripped of data so that the resulting living sample database represents a cross section of the very large database at some moment in time.

load To insert data values into a database that was previously empty.

locality of processing In a distributed database, the design of processing so that the remote access of data is eliminated or reduced substantively.

local site support Within a distributed unit of work, a local site update allows a process to perform SQL update statements referring to the local site.

local transaction In a distributed DBMS, a transaction that requires reference only to data that is stored at the site where the transaction originated.

lockup The event that occurs when an update is done to a database record, and the transaction has not yet reached a commit point. The online transaction needs to prevent other transactions from accessing the data while the update is occurring.

log A journal of activity.

logging The automatic recording of data with regard to the access of the data, the updates to the data, and so on.

logical representation A data view or description that does not depend on a physical storage device or a computer program.

loss of identity When data is brought in from an external source and the identity of the external source is discarded, a loss of identity occurs. It is common practice with microprocessor data.

LU6.2 (Logical Unit Type 6.2) A peer-to-peer data stream with a network operating system for program-to-program communication. LU6.2 allows mid-range machines to talk to one another without the involvement of the mainframe.

machine learning   The capability of a machine to improve its performance automatically, based on past performance.

magnetic tape   (1) The storage medium most closely associated with sequential processing; (2) a large ribbon on which magnetic images are stored and retrieved.

main storage database (MSDB)   A database that resides entirely in main storage. Such databases are very fast to access but require special handling at the time of update. Another limitation of MSDBs are that they can only manage small amounts of data.

master file   A file that holds the system of records for a given set of data (usually bound by an application).

maximum transaction arrival rate (MTAR)   The rate of arrival of transactions at the moment of peak period processing.

message   (1) The data input by the user in the online environment that is used to drive a transaction; (2) the output of a transaction.

metadata   (1) Data about data; (2) the description of the structure, content, keys, and indexes of data.

metalanguage   A language used to specify other languages.

metaprocess   Descriptive information about the code or process(es) that act against data.

microprocessor   A small processor serving the needs of a single user.

migration   The process by which frequently used items of data are moved to more readily accessible areas of storage and infrequently used items of data are moved to less readily accessible areas of storage.

mips (million instructions per second)   The standard measurement of processor speed for minicomputers and mainframe computers.

mode of operation   A classification for systems that execute in a similar fashion and share distinctive operational characteristics. Some modes of operation are operational, DSS, online, interactive.

modulo   An arithmetic term describing the remainder of a division process. 10 modulo 7 is 3. Modulo is usually associated with the randomization process.

MOLAP   Multidimensional online analytical processing supports OLAP using specialized, proprietary multidimensional database technology.

multilist organization   A chained file organization in which the chains are divided into fragments and each fragment is indexed. This organization of data permits faster access to the data.

multiple key retrieval This requires data searches on the basis of the values of several key fields (some or all of which are secondary keys).

MVS (Multiple Virtual Storage) IBM's mainline operating system for mainframe processors. There are several extensions of MVS.

Named Pipes Program-to-program protocol with Microsoft's LAN Manager. The Named Pipes API supports intra- and inter-machine process-to-process communications.

natural forms First normal form-data that has been organized into two-dimensional flat files without repeating groups. Second normal form-data that functionally depends on the entire candidate key. Third normal form-data that has had all transitive dependencies on data items other than the candidate key removed. Fourth normal form-data whose candidate key is related to all data items in the record, and that contains no more than one nontrivial multivalued dependency on the candidate key.

natural join A join in which the redundant logic components generated by the join are removed.

natural language A language generally spoken, whose rules are based on current usage and not explicitly defined by grammar.

navigate To steer a course through a database, from record to record, by means of an algorithm that examines the content of data.

network This consists of a collection of circuits, data-switching elements, and computing systems. The switching devices in the network are called communication processors. A network provides a configuration for computer systems and communication facilities within which data can be stored and accessed, and within which DBMS can operate.

network model A data model that provides data relationships on the basis of records and groups of records (that is, sets) in which one record is designated as the set owner and a single member record can belong to one or more sets.

nine's complement The transformation of a numeric field calculated by subtracting the initial value from a field consisting of all nines.

node A point in the network at which data is switched.

nonprocedural language Syntax that directs the computer as to what to do, not how to do it. Typical nonprocedural languages include RAMIS, FOCUS, NOMAD, and SQL.

normalize To decompose complex data structures into natural structures.

null An item or record for which no value currently exists or possibly may ever exist.

numeric A representation using only numbers and the decimal point.

occurrence *See* instances.

offset pointer An indirect pointer. An offset pointer exists inside a block and the index points to the offset. If data must be moved, only the offset pointer in the block must be altered; the index entry remains untouched.

OLAP Online analytical processing is a category of software technology that enables analysts, managers and executives to perform ad hoc data access and analysis based on its dimensionality. This form of multidimensional analysis provides business insight through fast, consistent, interactive access to a wide variety of possible views of information.

online storage Storage devices and storage mediums where data can be accessed in a direct fashion.

operating system Software that enables a computer to supervise its own operations and automatically call in programs, routines, languages, and data as needed for continuous operation throughout the execution of different types of jobs.

operational data Data used to support the daily processing a company does.

operations The department charged with the running of the computer.

oper-mart A component of the corporate information factory used to support tactical decision-making. Similar in form to the data mart, it differs in that its source of data is the operational data store, *not* the data warehouse.

optical disk A storage medium using lasers as opposed to magnetic devices. Optical disk is typically write-only, is much less expensive per byte than magnetic storage, and is highly reliable.

ORACLE A DBMS by ORACLE Corp.

order To place items in an arrangement specified by rules such as numeric or alphabetic order. *See* sort.

OS/2 The operating system for IBM's Personal System.

OSF Open Software Foundation.

OSI (Open Systems Interconnection) overflow (1) The condition in which a record or a segment cannot be stored in its home address because the address is already occupied. In this case, the data is placed in another location referred to as overflow; (2) the area of DASD where data is sent when the overflow condition is triggered.

ownership The responsibility of updating operational data.

padding A technique used to fill a field, record, or block with default data (such as blanks or zeros).

page (1) A basic unit of data on DASD; (2) a basic unit of storage in main memory.

page fault A program interruption that occurs when a page that is referred to is not in main memory and must be read in from external storage.

page fixed The state in which programs or data cannot be removed from main storage. Only a limited amount of storage can be page fixed.

paging In virtual storage systems, the technique of making memory appear to be larger than it really is by transferring blocks (pages) of data or programs into external memory.

parallel data organization An arrangement of data in which the data is spread over independent storage devices and is managed independently.

parallel I/O The process of accessing or storing data on multiple physical data devices.

parallel search storage A storage device in which one or more parts of all storage locations are queried simultaneously for a certain condition or under certain parameters. *See also* associative storage.

parameter An elementary data value used as a criteria for qualification, usually of searches of data or in the control of modules.

parent A unit of data in a 1:n relationship with another unit of data called a child, where the parent can exist independently, but the child cannot exist unless there is a parent.

parsing The algorithm that translates syntax into meaningful machine instructions. Parsing determines the meaning of statements issued in the data manipulation language.

partition A segmentation technique in which data is divided into physically different units. Partitioning can be done at the application or the system level.

path length The number of instructions executed for a given program or instruction.

peak period The time when the most transactions arrive at the computer with the expectation of execution.

performance The length of time from the moment a request is issued until the first of the results of the request are received.

periodic discrete data A measurement or description of data taken at a regular time interval.

physical representation (1) The representation and storage of data on a medium such as magnetic storage; (2) the description of data that depends on such physical factors as the length of elements, records, pointers, and so on.

pipes Vehicles for passing data from one application to another.

plex or network structure   A relationship between records or other groupings of data in which a child record can have more than one parent record.

plug compatible manufacturer (PCM)   A manufacturer of equipment that functionally is identical to that of another manufacturer (usually IBM).

pointer   The address of a record, or other groupings of data contained in another record, so that a program may access the former record when it has retrieved the latter record. The address can be absolute, relative, or symbolic, and hence the pointer is referred to as absolute, relative, or symbolic.

pools   The buffers made available to the online controller.

populate   To place occurrences of data values in a previously empty database. *See also* load.

precision   The degree of discrimination with which a quantity is stated. For example, a three-digit numeral discriminates among 1,000 possibilities, from 000 to 999.

precompilation   The processing of source text prior to compilation. In an SQL environment, SQL statements are replaced with statements that will be recognized by the host language compiler.

prefix data   Data in a segment or a record used exclusively for system control; usually unavailable to the user.

primary key   *See* key, primary.

primitive data   Data whose existence depends on only a single occurrence of a major subject area of the enterprise.

privacy   The prevention of unauthorized access and manipulation of data.

privilege descriptor   A persistent object used by a DBMS to enforce constraints on operations.

problems database   The component of a DSS application where previously defined decision parameters are stored. A problems database is consulted to review characteristics of past decisions and to determine ways to meet current decision-making needs.

processor   The hardware at the center of the execution of computer programs. Generally speaking, processors are divided into three categories-mainframes, minicomputers, and microcomputers.

processor cycles   The hardware's internal cycles that drive the computer (such as initiate I/O, perform logic, move data, perform arithmetic functions, and so on).

production environment   The environment where operational, high-performance processing is run.

program   A set of instructions that tells the computer what to do. Programs are sometimes referred to as applications and/or software.

program area   The portion of main memory in which application programs are executed.

progressive overflow   A method of handling overflow in a randomly organized file that does not require the use of pointers. An overflow record is stored in the first available space and is retrieved by a forward serial search from the home address.

projection   An operation that takes one relation as an operand and returns a second relation that consists of only the selected attributes or columns, with duplicate rows eliminated.

proposition   A statement about entities that asserts or denies that some condition holds for those entities.

protocol   The call format used by a teleprocessing monitor.

punched cards   An early storage medium on which data and input were stored. Today punched cards are rare.

purge data   The data on or after which a storage area may be overwritten. Used in conjunction with a file label, it is a means of protecting file data until an agreed-upon release date is reached.

query language   A language that enables an end user to interact directly with a DBMS to retrieve and possibly modify data managed under the DBMS.

record   An aggregation of values of data organized by their relation to a common key.

record-at-a-time processing   The access of data a record at a time, a tuple at a time, and so on.

recovery   The restoration of the database to an original position or condition, often after major damage to the physical medium.

redundancy   The practice of storing more than one occurrence of data. In the case where data can be updated, redundancy poses serious problems. In the case where data is not updated, redundancy is often a valuable and necessary design tool.

referential integrity   The facility of a DBMS to ensure the validity of a predefined relationship.

reorganization   The process of unloading data in a poorly organized state and reloading the data in a well-organized state. Reorganization in some DBMSs is used to restructure data. Reorganization is often called *reorg* or an *unload/reload* process.

repeating groups   A collection of data that can occur several times within a given record occurrence.

ROLAP   Relational online analytical processing supports OLAP using techniques that allow multidimensionality to be implemented in a two-dimensional RDBMS. Star join schema is a common database design technique used in this environment.

rolling summary   A form of storing archival data where the most recent data has the lowest level of detail stored and the older data has higher levels of detail stored.

scope of integration   The formal definition of the boundaries of the system being modelled.

SDLC (System Development Life Cycle)   The classical operational system development lifecycle that typically includes requirements gathering, analysis, design, programming, testing, integration, and implementation. Sometimes called a *waterfall* development lifecycle.

sequential file   A file in which records are ordered according to the values of one or more key fields. The records can be processed in this sequence starting from the first record in the file, and continuing to the last record in the file.

serial file   A sequential file in which the records are physically adjacent, in sequential order.

set-at-a-time processing   Accessing data by groups, each member of which satisfies some selection criteria.

snapshot   A database dump or the archiving of data as of one moment in time.

star join schema   A relational database design technique that organizes data around its multidimensionality in terms of business dimensions and measurements (a.k.a., facts).

storage hierarchy   Storage units linked to form a storage subsystem, in which some units are fast to access and consume small amounts of storage, but which are expensive, and other units are slow to access and are large, but are inexpensive to store.

subject database   A database organized around a major subject of the corporation. Classical subject databases are for customer, transaction, product, part, vendor, and so on.

system log   An audit trail of relevant system events (for example, transaction entries, database changes, and so on).

system of record   The definitive and singular source of operational data. If data element abc has a value of 25 in a database record, but a value of 45 in the system of record, by definition the first value must be incorrect. The system of record is useful for the management of data redundancy.

table   A relation that consists of a set of columns with a heading and a set of rows (i.e., tuples).

time stamping   The practice of tagging each record with some moment in time, usually when the record was created or when the record was passed from one environment to another.

time-variant data   Data whose accuracy is relevant to some moment in time. The three common forms of time-variant data are continuous time span data, event discrete data, and periodic discrete data. *See also* current value data.

transition data   Data possessing both primitive and derived characteristics; usually very sensitive to the running of the business. Typical transition data includes interest rates for a bank, policy rates for an insurance company, retail sale prices for a manufacturer/distributor, and so on.

trend analysis   The process of looking at homogeneous data over a spectrum of time.

true archival data   Data at the lowest level of granularity in the current level detail database.

update   To change, add, delete, or replace values in all or selected entries, groups, or attributes stored in a database.

user   A person or process issuing commands or messages and receiving stimuli from the information system.

Recommended Reading

Articles

Adelman, Sid. "The Data Warehouse Database Explosion." *DMR* (December 1996). A very good discussion of why volumes of data are growing as fast as they are in the data warehouse environment and what can be done about it.

"An Architecture for a Business and Information System." *IBM Systems Journal* 17, no. 1 (1988). A description of IBM's understanding of the data warehouse.

Ashbrook, Jim. "Information Preservation." *CIO Magazine* (July 1993). An executive's view of the data warehouse.

Bair, John. "It's about Time! Supporting Temporal Data in a Warehouse." *INFODB* 10, no. 1 (February 1996). A good discussion of some of the aspects of time-variant data in the DSS/data warehouse environment.

Ballinger, Carrie. "TPC's Emerging Benchmark for Decision Support." *DBMS* (December 1993). A description of the extension of the TPC benchmark to include DSS.

Discount Store News. "Retail Technology Charges Up at KMart." (February 17, 1992). A description of the technology employed by KMart for its data warehouse, ODS environment.

"The Doctor of DSS." DBMS Interview. *DBMS magazine* (July 1994). An interview with Ralph Kimball.

Geiger, Jon. "Data Element Definition." *DMR* (December 1996). A good description of the definitions required in the system of records.

————. "Information Management for Competitive Advantage." *Strategic Systems Journal* (June 1993). A discussion of how the data warehouse and the Zachman framework have advanced the state of the art.

————. "What's in a Name." *Data Management Review* (June 1996). A discussion of the implications of naming structures in the data warehouse environment.

Gilbreath, Roy. "Health Care Data Repositories: Components and a Model." *Journal of the Healthcare Information and Management Systems Society* 9, no. 1 (Spring 1995). An excellent description of information architecture as it relates to health care.

————. "Informational Processing Architecture for Outcomes Management." A description of the data warehouse as it applies to health care and outcomes analysis. Under review.

Gilbreah, Roy, Jill Schilp, and Robert Rickton. "Towards an Outcomes Management Informational Processing Architecture." *HealthCare Information Management* 10, no. 1 (Spring 1996). A discussion of the architected environment as it relates to health care.

Goldberg, Paula, Robert Lambert, and Katherine Powell. "Guidelines for Defining Requirements for Decision Support Systems." *Data Resource Management Journal* (October 1991). A good description of how to define end-user requirements before building the data warehouse.

Graham, Stephen, analyst. "The Foundations of Wisdom." IDC Special Report (April 1996). International Data Corp. (Toronto, Canada). The definitive study on the return on investment for the data warehouse as well as the measurement of cost-effectiveness.

————. "The Financial Impact of Data Warehousing." *Data Management Review* (June 1996). A description of the cost-benefit analysis report done by IDC.

Hackney, Doug. "Vendors Are Our Friends." *Data Management Review* (June 1996). Doug Hackney talks about beneficial relationships with vendors.

Hufford, Duane. "A Conceptual Model for Documenting Data Synchronization Requirements." American Management Systems Data synchronization and the data warehouse.

———. "Data Administration Support for Business Process Improvement." American Management Systems' data warehouse and data administration.

———. "Data Warehouse Quality, Part I." *Data Management Review* (January 1996). A description of data warehouse quality.

———. "Data Warehouse Quality—Part II." *Data Management Review* (March 1996). The second part of the discussion on data quality.

Imhoff, Claudia. "Data Steward." *ComputerWorld* (September 4, 1995). Provides an overview of the data steward's role in the data warehouse environment. Additionally, this role is contrasted to the traditional role of a data analyst.

———. "End Users: Use 'em or Lose 'em." *DMR* (November 1996). An excellent discussion of the ways to manage the end-user data warehouse effort.

Imhoff, Claudia, and Jon Geiger. "Data Quality in the Data Warehouse." *Data Management Review* (April 1996). Provides insights and guidelines for defining and measuring quality in the data warehouse environment.

Imhoff, Claudia, and Ryan Sousa. "Information Ecosystem—Administration." *Data Management Review* (March 1997). Details the components and techniques used in administering the information ecosystem.

———. "Information Ecosystem—Corporate Information Factory." *Data Management Review* (February 1997). Details the parts and pieces of the Corporate Information Factory as defined by Bill Inmon. In addition, reviews the business relevance of the capabilities produced.

———. "Information Ecosystem—Information Services." *Data Management Review* (May 1997). Discusses how Information Services is used to provide a common navigation interface to the information ecosystem (metadata, data delivery, DSS tools), how this interface facilitates the coordination of people and process and how it ultimately provides a common knowledge fabric.

————. "Information Ecosystem—Introduction." *Data Management Review* (January 1997). Introduction to the information ecosystem.

————. "Information Ecosystem—People and Process." *Data Management Review* (April 1997). Details suggested organizational structures and roles. Additionally reviews processes for building, using, and managing the information ecosystem.

Inmon, W. H. "The Anatomy of a Data Warehouse Record." *Data Management Review* (July 1995). A description of the internal structure of a data warehouse record.

————. "At the Heart of the Matter." *Data Base Programming/ Design* (July 1988). Primitive and derived data and what the differences are.

————. "Building the Data Bridge." *Data Base Programming/ Design* (April 1992). Ten critical success factors in building the data warehouse.

————. "The Cabinet Effect." *Data Base Programming/Design* (May 1991). A description of why the data warehouse-centered architecture does not degenerate into the spider web environment.

————. "Chargeback in the Information Warehouse." *Data Management Review* (March 1993). Chargeback in the data warehouse can be both a blessing and a curse. This article addresses both sides of the issue.

————. "Choosing the Correct Approach to Data Warehousing: 'Big Bang' vs Iterative." *Data Management Review* (March 1996). A discussion of the proper strategic approach to data warehousing.

————. "Commentary: The Migration Path." *ComputerWorld* (July 29, 1996). A brief description of some of the issues of migrating to the data warehouse.

————. "Cost Justification in the Data Warehouse." *Data Management Review* (June 1996). A discussion of how to justify DSS and the data warehouse on the cost of reporting.

————. "Data Structures in the Information Warehouse." *Enterprise Systems Journal* (January 1992). A description of the common data structures found in the data warehouse.

————. "The Data Warehouse—All Your Data at Your Fingertips." *Communications Week* (August 29, 1994). An overview of the data warehouse.

————. "The Data Warehouse: Managing the Infrastructure." *Data Management Review* (December 1994). A description of the data warehouse infrastructure and the budget associated with it.

———. "Data Warehouse—A Perspective of Data over Time." *370/390 Data Base Management* (February 1992). A description of the relationship of the data warehouse and the management of data over time.

———. "Data Warehouse and Contextual Data: Pioneering a New Dimension." *Data Base Newsletter* 23, no. 4 (July/August 1995). A description of the need for contextual data over time, as found in the data warehouse.

———. "The Data Warehouse and Data Mining." *CACM* 39, no. 11 (November 1996). A description of the relationship between data mining and data warehouse.

———. "Data Warehouse Lays Foundation for Bringing Data Investment Forward." *Application Development Trends* (January 1994). A description of the data warehouse and the relation to legacy systems.

———. "Data Warehouse Security: Encrypting Data." *Data Management Review* (November 1996). A description of some of the challenges of data warehouse security and industrial strength security.

———. "EIS and the Data Warehouse." *Data Base Programming/Design* (November 1992). The relationship between EIS and the data warehouse.

———. "EIS and Detail." *Data Management Review* (January 1995). A description of how much detail is needed to support EIS and the role of summarized data in the data warehouse environment.

———. "From Transactions to the Operational Data Store." *INFO DB* (December 1995). A discussion about how quickly transactions in the operational environment go into the operational data store.

———. "The Future in History." *DMR* (September 1996). A discussion of the value of historical information.

———. "Going against the Grain." *Data Base Programming/Design* (July 1990). A description of the granularity issue and how it relates to the data warehouse.

———. "Growth in the Data Warehouse." *Data Management Review* (December 1995). A description of why the data warehouse grows so fast and the phenomenon of increasing growth of data and decreasing data used.

———. "Knowing Your DSS End-User: Tourists, Explorers, Farmers." *DMR* (October 1996). A description of the different categories of end users.

———. "The Ladder of Success." *Data Management Review* (November 1995). Building and managing the data warehouse environment entails more than selecting a platform. This article outlines the many necessary steps required to achieve a successful data warehouse environment.

————. "Managing the Data Warehouse: The Data Content Card Catalog." *DMR* (December 1996). An introduction to the notion of a data content card catalog, that is, stratification of data content.

————. "Managing the Data Warehouse Environment." *Data Management Review* (February 1996). Defining who the data warehouse administrator is.

————. "Measuring Capacity in the Data Warehouse." *Enterprise Systems Journal* (August 1996). A discussion of how capacity should be measured in the data warehouse and DSS environment.

————. "Metadata: A Checkered Past, a Bright Future." *370/390 Data Base Management* (July 1992). A conversation about metadata and how metadata relates to the data warehouse.

————. "Monitoring the Data Warehouse Environment." *Data Management Review* (January 1996). What is a data monitor for the data warehouse environment and why would you need it?

————. "Multidimensional Data Bases and Data Warehousing." *Data Management Review* (February 1995). A description of how current detailed data in the data warehouse fits with multidimensional DBMS.

————. "Neat Little Packages." *Data Base Programming/Design* (August 1992). A description of how data relationships are treated in the data warehouse.

————. "The Need for Reporting." *Data Base Programming/Design* (July 1992). The different kinds of reports found throughout the different parts of the architecture.

————. "Now Which Is Data, Which Is Information?" *Data Base Programming/Design* (May 1993). The difference between data and information.

————. "The Operational Data Store." *INFODB* 9, no. 1 (February 1995). A description of the ODS.

————. "Performance in the Data Warehouse Environment." *Data Warehouse Report* Issue 3 (Autumn 1995). A description of the different aspects of performance in the data warehouse environment.

————. "Performance in the Data Warehouse Environment—Part 2." *Data Warehouse Report* (Winter 1995). A continuation of the prior article on data warehouse performance.

———. "Profile/Aggregate Records in the Data Warehouse." *Data management Review* (July 1995). A description of how profile/aggregate records are created and used in the data warehouse environment.

———. "Profiling the DSS Analyst." *Data Management Review* (March 1995). A description of DSS analysts as farmers and explorers.

———. "Rethinking Data Relationships for Warehouse Design." *Sybase Server* 5, no. 1 (Spring 1996). A discussion of the issues of data warehouse data relationships.

———. "SAP and the Data Warehouse." *DMR* (July/Aug 1996). A description of why data warehouse is still needed in the face of SAP.

———. "Security in the Data Warehouse: Data Privatization." *Enterprise Systems Journal* (March 1996). Data warehouse requires a very different approach to security than the traditional VIEW-based approach offered by DBMS vendors.

———. "The Structure of the Data Warehouse." *Data Management Review* (August 1993). This article addresses the different levels of data found in the data warehouse.

———. "Summary Data: The New Frontier." *Data Management Review* (May 1996). A description of the different types of summary data including dynamic summary data and static summary data, lightly summarized data and highly summarized data, and so on.

———. "Transformation Complexity." *Data Management Review* (September 1995). Why automating the transformation process is a superior idea to manually programming the transformations that are required in order to build the data warehouse.

———. "Untangling the Web." *Data Base Programming Design* (May 1993). Exploring the factors that turn data into information.

———. "User Reaction to the Data Warehouse." *DMR* (December 1996). A description of the different user types in data warehousing.

———. "Virtual Data Warehouse: The Snake Oil of the 90's." *Data Management Review* (April 1996). A discussion of the virtual data warehouse and how the concept tries to attach itself to the legitimacy of the data warehouse.

———. "Winds of Change." *Data Base Programming/Design* (January 1992). Data administration and the data warehouse—

a description of how data administration evolved to where it is today.

Inmon, W. H., and Chuck Kelley. "The 12 Rules of Data Warehouses." *Data Management Review* (May 1994). A description of the defining characteristics of the data warehouse.

Inmon, W. H., and Michael Loper. "The Unified Data Architecture: A Systems Integration Solution." Auerbach Publications (1992). The original paper (republished in a revised state) suggesting that a data architecture was in order for future systems development.

Inmon, W. H., and Phyliss Koslow. "Commandeering Mainframe Database for Data Warehouse Use." *Application Development Trends* (August 1994). A discussion of optimal data warehouse use inside the mainframe.

Inmon, W. H., and Sue Osterfelt. "Data Patterns Say the Darndest Things." *Computerworld* (February 3, 1992). A description of the usage of the data warehouse in the DSS community and how informational processing can be derived from a warehouse.

"In the Words of Father Inmon." *MIS* (February 1996). An interview with Bill Inmon in November of 1995 in Australia.

Jordan, Arthur. "Data Warehouse Integrity: How Long and Bumpy the Road?" *Data Management Review* (March 1996). A discussion of the issues of data quality inside the data warehouse.

Kador, John. "One on One." Interview with Bill Inmon, Midrange Systems (October 27, 1995). A discussion about data warehouse with Bill, including some of the history of how data warehouse came to be.

Kimball, Ralph. "Is ER Modelling Hazardous to DSS?" *Data Warehouse Report* (Winter 1995). A dialogue on dimensional modelling versus ER modelling.

Kimball, Ralph, and Kevin Strehlo. "Why Decision Support Fails and How To Fix It." *Datamation* (June 1994). A good description of fact tables and star joins, with a lengthy discussion about Ralph's approach to data warehouse and decision support.

Konrad, Walecia. "Smoking Out the Elusive Smoker." *BusinessWeek* (March 16, 1992). A description of database marketing in the advertising restricted marketing environment.

Lambert, Bob. "Break Old Habits to Define Data Warehousing Requirements." *Data Management Review*. A description of how the end user should be approached to determine DSS requirements.

Lambert, Bob. "Data Warehousing Fundamentals: What You Need to Know to Succeed." *Data Management Review* (March 1996). Several significant strategies for data warehousing to guide you through a successful implementation.

Laney, Doug. "Are OLAP and OLTP Like Twins?" *DMR* (December 1996). A comparison of the two environments.

"Liberate Your Data." *Forbes* (March 7, 1994). An interesting but naive article about the data warehouse as viewed from the uninformed businessperson.

Myer, Andrea. "An Interview with Bill Inmon." *Inside Decisions* (March 1996). An interview discussing the start of data warehousing, the use of data warehousing for competitive advantages, the origins of Prism Solutions, and building the first data warehouse.

O'Mahoney, Michael. "Revolutionary Breakthrough in Client/Server Data Warehouse Development." *Data Management Review* (July 1995). A description of older legacy development methodologies versus modern iterative methodologies.

Rudin, Ken. "Parallelism in the Database Layer." *DMR* (December 1996). An excellent discussion of the differences between DSS parallelism and OLTP parallelism.

Rudin, Ken. "Who Needs Scalable Systems." *DMR* (November 1996). A good discussion of the issues of scalability in the data warehouse environment.

Sloan, Robert, and Hal Green. "An Information Architecture for the Global Manufacturing Enterprise." Auerbach Publications (1993). A description of information architecture in the large-scale manufacturing environment.

Swift, Ron. "Creating Value Through a Scalable Data Warehouse Framework." *DMR* (November 1996). A very nice discussion of the data warehousing issues scale.

Tanler, Richard. "Data Warehouses and Data Marts: Choose Your Weapon." *Data Management Review* (February 1996). A description of the differences between data marts and the current-level detail of the data warehouse.

Tanler Richard. "Taking Your Data Warehouse to a New Dimension on the Intranet." *Data Management Review* (May 1996). A discussion of the different components of the data warehouse as they relate to the intranet.

Thiessen, Mark. "Proving the Data Warehouse to Management and Customers: Where Are the Savings?" A presentation given at the 1994 Data Warehouse Conference; for foils and handouts.

Verity, John W. and Russell Mitchell. "A Trillion Byte Weapon." *BusinessWeek* (July 31, 1995). A description of some of the larger data warehouses that have been built and how they play a role in business competition.

Wahl, Dan, and Duane Hufford. "A Case Study: Implementing and Operating an Atomic Database." *Data Resource Management Journal* (April 1992). A description of the U.S. Army DSS data architecture.

Welch, J. D. "Providing Customized Decision Support Capabilities: Defining Architectures." Auerbach Publications (1990). Discusses decision support systems and architecture (based on the PacTel Cellular DSS architecture).

Winsberg, Paul. "Modeling the Data Warehouse and the Data Mart." *INFODB* (June 1996). A description of architecture and modelling as it relates to different types of data warehouses.

Wright, George. "Developing a Data Warehouse." *DMR* (October 1996). A very good discussion of snapshots and the basic structures of data warehouses.

Ambeo Tech Topics

1. **Monitoring Data Warehouse Activity.** Activity in the data warehouse needs to be monitored for a variety of reasons. This tech topic describes monitoring techniques and considerations, as well as a description of why activity monitoring needs to be done.

2. **Chargeback in the Data Warehouse DSS Environment.** Chargeback is an extremely useful way to get the end user to take responsibility for the resources that are being consumed. This tech topic addresses the issues of chargeback.

3. **Iterative Development Using a Data Model.** Data modeling is an essential part of the data warehouse design process. This tech topic explains how iterative development can be done and at the same time how the data model is incorporated into the development process.

4. **What is a Data Mart?** Data marts are a natural emanation from the data warehouse. This tech topic outlines the salient characteristics of the data mart.

5. **Data Mining—An Architecture.** Using the data warehouse is an art. This tech topic relates the underlying architecture of the data warehouse to the sophisticated way in which the data warehouse can be used.

6. **Data Mining—Exploring the Data.** Once the data is gathered and organized, and the architecture for exploitation has been built, the task remains to use the data. This tech topic addresses how data can be mined, once the architecture is built.

7. **Building the Data Mart or the Data Warehouse First?** Although the data mart is a companion to the data warehouse, data mart vendors try to encourage people to build the data mart without building the data warehouse. This tech topic addresses the issues relevant to this important design decision.

8. **Monitoring Data Warehouse Data.** Although activity monitoring is very important, so is monitoring the data itself in the data warehouse. The growth of the data, the quality of the data, and the actual content of the data are all at stake in this issue.

9. **Data Warehouse Administration.** With DSS and a data warehouse comes the need to manage the environment. A new organizational function has arisen—data warehouse administration. This tech topic addresses the charter of data warehouse administration and other important data management issues.

10. **Metadata in the Data Warehouse: A Statement of Vision.** Metadata is an important part of the data warehouse environment. Metadata has a dual, conflicting role. In some cases, metadata must be shared; in other cases, it needs to be managed autonomously. This tech topic addresses the distributed metadata architecture that enables metadata to simultaneously be distributed and to be managed autonomously.

11. **Data Warehouse Administration in the Organization.** Once the need for data warehouse administration is recognized, the question arises—where should the DWA function be placed in the organization? This tech topic addresses the issues of the organization placement of the DWA function.

12. **Managing the Refreshment Process.** Data periodically needs to be refreshed from the legacy environment into the data warehouse. The refreshment process is much more complex than one would ever imagine. This tech topic addresses the issues of data warehouse refreshment.

13. **Data Stratification in the Data Warehouse.** How do you tell someone what is inside a 1 terabyte data warehouse? How many customers? Of what type? Of what age? Living where? Buying how much per year? This tech topic addresses the technique of stratifying data in order to create a library "table of contents" that describes the actual content of data inside a data warehouse.

Ambeo can be reached at 303-221-4000; Fax: 303-221-4010.

Books

Brackett, Mike. *The Data Warehouse Challenge* (1996). New York: John Wiley & Sons.

Devlin, Barry. *Data Warehouse: From Architecture to Implementation* (1997). Reading, Massachusetts: Addison Wesley.

Inmon, W. H. *Building the Data Warehouse*, 2d ed. (1996). New York: John Wiley & Sons.

———. *Information Systems Architecture: Development in the '90s* (1992). New York: John Wiley & Sons.

———. *Rdb/VMS: Developing the Data Warehouse* (1993). New York: John Wiley & Sons.

———. *Third Wave Processing: Database Machines and Decision Support Systems* (1990). New York: John Wiley & Sons.

Inmon, W. H., Claudia Imhoff, and Greg Battas. *Building the Operational Data Store*, 2nd ed. (1999). New York: John Wiley & Sons.

Inmon, W. H., Claudia Imhoff, and R.H. Terdeman. *Exploration Warehousing: Turning Business Information into Business Opportunity* (2000). New York: John Wiley & Sons.

Inmon, W. H., and R.D. Hackathorn. *Using the Data Warehouse* (1994). New York: John Wiley & Sons.

Inmon, W. H., John A. Zachman, and Jonathan G. Geiger. *Data Stores, Data Warehousing, and the Zachman Framework* (1997). New York: McGraw-Hill.

Inmon, W.H., J. D. Welch, and Katherine L. Glassey. *Managing the Data Warehouse* (1997). New York: John Wiley & Sons.

Kelly, Sean. *Data Warehousing—The Key to Mass Customization* (1994). New York: John Wiley & Sons.

Kimball, Ralph. *The Data Warehouse Toolkit* (1996). New York: John Wiley Sons.

Love, Bruce. *Enterprise Information Technologies* (1993). New York: John Wiley & Sons.

Parsaye, Kamran, and Marc Chignell. *Intelligent Database Tools and Applications* (1989). New York: John Wiley & Sons.

Index